School Choice

SCHOOL CHOICE

A Balanced Approach

William H. Jeynes

 PRAEGER

AN IMPRINT OF ABC-CLIO, LLC
Santa Barbara, California • Denver, Colorado • Oxford, England

Library of Congress Cataloging-in-Publication Data

Jeynes, William.
  School choice : a balanced approach / William H. Jeynes.
    pages cm
  Includes bibliographical references and index.
  ISBN 978–1–4408–2835–5 (hardback) — ISBN 978–1–4408–2836–2 (ebook) 1. School choice—United States. 2. Alternative education—United States. I. Title.
  LB1027.9.J49 2014
  379.1′11—dc23   2013046859

ISBN: 978–1–4408–2835–5
EISBN: 978–1–4408–2836–2

18 17 16 15 14   1 2 3 4 5

This book is also available on the World Wide Web as an eBook.
Visit www.abc-clio.com for details.

Praeger
An Imprint of ABC-CLIO, LLC

ABC-CLIO, LLC
130 Cremona Drive, P.O. Box 1911
Santa Barbara, California 93116-1911

This book is printed on acid-free paper ∞

Manufactured in the United States of America

Contents

Contents

Acknowledgments

I am very thankful to many individuals who played a large role in making this work possible. I want to thank numerous people in the academic world at Harvard University and the University of Chicago for helping me give birth to this project and in guiding me through the early stages of writing many of these chapters. I especially want to thank the late Bob Jewell for his encouragement in writing on school choice topics. I also want to thank Larry Hedges for teaching me how to conduct a meta-analysis, when I was his graduate student. I also want to thank three people whose input into this project helped shape the direction of the book. These individuals are Wendy Naylor, Jack Klenk, and Dick Carpenter. I also want to thank several dear friends whose encouragement with respect to this project touched me deeply. Among these dear friends are Wayne Ruhland, Jean Donohue, Rick Smith, Dan Johnston, Larry and Vada DeWerd, Sung Wu, Tim and Sarah Kim, Jessica Choi, Sylva and Peter Lee, and Randi Johnson. Thank you so much for your support! I also want to thank the *Cambridge Journal of Education*, the *Peabody Journal of Education*, *Educational Policy*, and the *Interdisciplinary Journal of Research on Religion* for publishing earlier versions of my research, on which portions of several chapters of this book are based. I also want to thank presidents George W. Bush and Barack Obama, as well as former members of the Bill Clinton administration for inviting me to speak on these issues in various government forums, such as for the White House and various U.S. government departments.

    I am incredibly blessed to have been married 28 years to my wife Hyelee, whose support has been exemplary. Without her prayers and support, this work never could have been completed. I am blessed and honored to have three wonderful boys, whom I thank for their love and inspiration. I also want to thank God for giving me the strength and providence to complete this project. I am very grateful for His encouragement and strength.

Foreword

It is generally and correctly perceived that two of the greatest challenges facing the United States can be successfully met only if we get really serious about improving our K-12 education system ... and if our higher education system also stops coasting along complacently. The two areas of essential improvement are in some tension with one another: raising academic results into the range achieved by many of the nations with which we compete economically and scientifically, and at the same time reducing the gap in achievement between white and Asian students, on the one hand, and black, Latino, and Native American students, on the other. The danger, of course, is that a focus on high achievers will in fact widen that gap, leaving millions of youth condemned to academic failure and to being a burden rather than an asset to American society.

A third dimension of education to which serious attention should be directed is not mentioned so often in the public debates: it is that America's schools are no longer placing a priority on forming character and the qualities necessary to good citizenship. Less and less do schools offer a strong and positive culture that can counter the influence of the media, consumerism, and disillusionment with all ideals of the Good Life.

It is not that proposed remedies are lacking. In fact, the world of K-12 education, and to a growing extent that of higher education as well, is overrun with "solutions" that can cost billions and usually solve little. Most large school systems are immobilized by "policy churn" that leads to little serious improvement, often because of the covert or overt resistance of the adults in the system who resist change and accountability. Many small school systems are equally immobilized by complacency.

This is not intended to paint an altogether gloomy picture. I see many bright spots, including the flourishing of many hundreds of urban charter schools that are producing remarkable results. Some urban districts—New York City and Montgomery County, Maryland, are good examples—have become serious about reform.

It is the great merit of this book by Bill Jeynes that he draws attention, with data to back it up, to a success story that most policy specialists have chosen to ignore, that of faith-based private schools addressing all three of the challenges mentioned earlier: producing strong academic results, reducing the achievement gap, and placing a strong emphasis on character. Indeed, arguably these three outcomes are mutually reinforcing in good schools.

I will not attempt to sum up the arguments on the academic outcome advantage of faith-based schools made and supported in detail in Chapters 2 and 9 of this book. The reader is urged to confront the data that Jeynes presents and ask whether we have not been overlooking a threatened treasure, the thousands of Catholic and Protestant (and, increasingly, Jewish and Islamic) schools that are providing an excellent education, balancing academics and character, to American youth. And whether we are not supremely foolish to allow so many of these schools to close each year because of an unexamined assumption that they are not providing "public education" in the true sense of that term.

Jeynes informs us, early in Chapter 9, that the "results of the NELS dataset analysis indicate that (1) children in the lowest SES quartile who attend religious schools achieve at higher levels than do children in the lowest SES quartile who attend public schools and (2) children in the lowest SES quartile benefit from attending religious schools more than do students in the other SES quartiles. Low-SES students attending religious schools outperformed their counterparts in public schools on both standardized and nonstandardized measures." As for the racial achievement gap, he shows that, in faith-based schools, "African American and Latino students gained 2.5 percent more than white students for the Social Studies test and 1.8 percent more for the Science test. When SES was controlled for, African American and

Latino students gained 1.8 percent more than white students for the Social Studies test and 0.8 percent more for the Science test."

Such results have been reported by many others, of course, but it is a merit of Jeynes's book that he brings them together in a convenient and clearly argued form. Backing them up are historical and policy arguments that I will not seek to assess in this brief note, except to say that they identify accurately many of the issues about which we should be debating as we seek to confront the urgent challenges facing the American educational system, and the country itself.

Charles L. Glenn
Professor of Educational
Leadership and Policy Studies
Boston University

Chapter 1

School Choice: The Main Arguments
For and Against

Few educational issues have attracted as much attention in the past 30 years as school choice (Eberts & Hollenbeck, 2006; Gronberg & Jansen, 2006). School choice stands as an attractive concept largely because it appeals to three cherished desires of most Americans and Europeans: (1) *liberty*, the freedom for parents to choose a school for their children (Peterson, et al., 1996, 2006); (2) *control*, a sense by the parent of the possession of more power to determine the kind of school atmosphere and curriculum their child is exposed to; and (3) *educational quality*, those leaders that advocate choice attempt to sell the program on this point (Eberts & Hollenbeck, 2006; Gronberg & Jansen, 2006). A copious number of parents believe that with the ability to choose the finest elementary and secondary schools in their areas, their children will gain access to the best education (Lankford & Wyckoff, 2006; Wolfe, 2003). Yet, increasingly critics raise certain objections that vary from the concern that minority children would benefit the least to church and state issues (Fiske & Ladd, 2003; Wolfe, 2003).

There exist a number of definitions of school choice and debates about its structure that make it difficult to discuss this topic. Chubb and Moe (1990) declare that parental school choice must involve private schools in order to succeed. President Clinton contributed a great deal to the growth of public school choice (Jeynes, 2007a; Peterson, et al., 1996, 2006). American, British, and the world's educational leaders are struggling with the issue of the extent to which a system of choice should be employed and whether it should consider parental preferences versus societal needs (Jeynes, 2002a; Lankford & Wyckoff, 2006; Peterson, 2006).

Arguments For School Choice

Greater Freedom and Higher Achievement

One of the reasons school choice attracts so much attention involves the accompanying promise that school choice will bring increased school quality, as a result of the insertion of greater freedom into the education system. Milton Friedman (1994) makes this assertion: "Choice produces competition. Competition produces quality." As Caroline Hoxby says (2003, p. 1), "Milton Friedman is generally credited with spurring modern interest in school choice."

A lot of the argument for choice revolves around the consistently superior performance of private school students over their public school counterparts (Gronberg & Jansen, 2006). Studies have shown that religious schools, which make up a large percentage of private schools, on the average, provide a better education (as measured by test scores and the satisfaction of parents and children) than public schools (Bryk, Lee & Holland, 1993; Chubb & Moe, 1990; Coleman, Hoffer, & Kilgore, 1982; Jeynes, 2002b). Educational researchers frequently propose any number of reasons for the private school advantage. The reasons include stricter discipline, an emphasis on traditional values, more demanding academic standards, and the student selectivity that private schools exercise (Bryk, Lee & Holland, 1993; Jeynes, 2010a, 2010b).

The fact that greater school choice means, by definition, enhanced liberty attracts many people to the concept of school choice (Holmes, DeSimone & Rupp, 2006; Peterson, 2006). Paul Peterson (2006, p. 7) observes, "The core operations of most public schools are operated directly by the government. As a result, choices are limitations and competition constrained." A great deal of emotion saturates the issue of school choice and liberty. Because of this, the literature sometimes is a bit "charged" with emotion and apparent exaggeration (Gutman, 2003). On the one hand, opponents of choice warn against the excesses of privatization and especially church-sponsored privatization (Perry, 2003). On the other hand, supporters of choice warn against the price of cultural uniformity (Ravitch, 2000; Scalia, 1989).

To understand why school choice enjoys the extent of interest that it does, one must comprehend the extent to which many individuals feel frustrated with the lack of results that other reforms· produced (Gronberg & Jansen, 2006; Ravitch, 2000). Perhaps, most should consider it only natural that parents want to take matters into their own hands via greater choice. Whether school choice can actually deliver what parents desire constitutes an entirely different matter. The question of whether school choice will foster as much competition as its supporters claim appears crucial in determining the potential impact of choice (Gibbons & Silva, 2006; Wolfe, 2003).

Better Matches between Families and Schools

As it stands now, in most school districts across the country, parents send their children to a public school based on its proximity to their home (Jeynes, 2000a; Lankford & Wyckoff, 2006). The values of that particular school may or may not reflect the values of the family, but this is currently the way the system works. Indeed, it is likely that although under this type of scenario, there is some degree of overlap between the values cherished by the family and those practiced by the schools, it is also probable that there are major areas of dissonance (Egan, 2002; Engelhardt, 2013). It is likely the case that most contemporary Americans simply accept this fact. Nevertheless, for much of this nation's history, community schools formed the backbone of the nation's school system (Jeynes, 2007a, 2010a). Under this rubric, these community schools understood that it was their moral responsibility to support the values of the family and community, except in cases in which there were practices that were patently wrong (Egan, 2002; Holmes, 2001; Jeynes, 2007a, 2010a). These community schools were generally private because they were generally community based and church founded (Carter, 1826; Cremin, 1980; Jones, 1964).

It is also true, however, that many schools in the mid-1800s were a combination of private and public (Gangel & Benson, 1983; Jeynes, 2007a, 2012a). The transition that many schools made from private to public did not occur overnight (Bobbe, 1933; Cubberley, 1920). Instead, there were "charity schools" that were private schools that honored the heartfelt conviction at the time that anyone who wanted to go to school should be able to do so (Kliebard, 1969; Raitt & McGinn, 1987; Randell, 1988). The Puritans were the group that originally developed these schools (Jeynes, 2002a; Kliebard, 1969; McCallum, 1939). Their intention was to make these schools available to all children regardless of their race or gender (Dickey, 1954; Marshall & Manuel, 1977; Tewksbury, 1932). The Puritans emphasized this orientation to such a great degree at all levels of education that it is even stated in Harvard College's charter that the institution was founded to educate Native Americans as well as the European settlers.

Dartmouth College, another of the Ivy League colleges founded by the Puritans, was actually founded for the purpose of educating Native Americans (McCallum, 1939; Marshall & Manuel, 1977). In fact, the reason Dartmouth is located near the New Hampshire–Vermont border well away from most of the major population centers of New England is because this was one of the primary places where Native Americans dwelled (Dickey, 1954; McCallum, 1939; Wheelock, 1763). The Puritans wanted a college education to be more accessible to Native Americans and therefore, the idea was to build a university for the Native American community (Dickey, 1954; Marshall & Manuel, 1977). The Puritans believed so deeply in the idea of making schooling attainable to all who desired it that they specified that Native Americans were to attend both Harvard and Dartmouth free of charge (Dickey, 1954; Marshall & Manuel, 1977; Wheelock, 1763).

The Puritans made charity schools available to pupils on the basis of what a family could afford and in the vast majority of cases, this meant that the parents either paid nothing at all or very little (Jones, 1964). This was made possible by the generosity of individuals who had been blessed financially or were not particularly wealthy but were just very sacrificial in their giving (Eavey, 1964; Jones, 1964). It was also facilitated by the frugality of the Puritans who ran the schools. As one might imagine, over time the nation became enamored by such a generous school paradigm (Cremin, 1980). Consequently, charity schools became the main school rubric practiced by the nation to educate its people (Cornog, 1998). During the post–Revolutionary War period, charity schools grew exponentially (Curran, 1954; Eavey, 1964; Jones, 1964). Patriots such as John Jay, the first chief justice of the U.S. Supreme Court, and Alexander Hamilton, the first secretary of the Treasury, gave countless millions of dollars specifically to support charity schools for African Americans (Jay, 1891). This is particularly impressive when one remembers that $1 million was worth far more then than it is now. Indeed, charity schools became the most common way that African American children were educated (Bobbe, 1933; Bourne, 1870; Cornog, 1998; Cubberley, 1920; Woodson, 1968). Most of these charity schools were integrated, but some were segregated (Wilson, 1977; Woodson & Wesley, 1962).

In the mid-1800s, the pressure of more and more poor immigrants coming to the United States in a nation that was not yet especially wealthy caused an increasing number of these private charity schools, nearly all of which were funded by churches, to look to the addition of public funds to insure that all who desired to be educated could be (Bobbe, 1933; Bourne, 1870; Cornog, 1998; Cubberley, 1920). Gradually, as these charity schools accepted an increasingly higher percentage of their funds from government taxes, the church-based charity schools became public schools. Nevertheless, during the transition, which often took 20 years, the schools would often remain community based in their orientation (Eavey, 1964). As time went on, however, and public schools became the dominant educational paradigm in North America, schools became less and less community based and more monolithic in their structure. Increasingly, state and federal government leaders determined the core value system upheld by the public schools (Gatto, 2001). As a result, the belief system upheld by the public schools became more and more detached from that of the parents (Curran 1954; Jeynes, 2011).

The rate accelerated at which public schools became more attached to government officials and state and national officials rather than local communities during the 1920s and 1930s due a great deal to the influence of George Counts and John Dewey. In 1932, George Counts published the book entitled *Dare We Build a New Social Order?* In this work, Counts calls for educators to replace the authority once held by parents and become the primary influences on children (Counts, 1932). He believed that it was not proper for families and communities to continue to have the impact on children that they did. Rather, it was most appropriate that teachers enjoy that place.

John Dewey convinced many Americans that the Industrial Revolution required a change in educational philosophy (Dewey, 1902, 1910, 1915, 1920, 1990; McCluskey, 1958). To Dewey, the ultimate influence of the industrial revolution on education is that the role of parents and communities would be reduced and the power of the teachers and the state would be increased (Egan, 2002; Martin, 2002). In Dewey's view, teachers in their professionalism were to be regarded as such by communities and entrusted with the mental development of children. The implementation of Dewey's philosophy established a pattern in which educators became increasingly insistent on establishing their wills in the training of children, rather than working in cooperation with families and communities to reflect their values in the school room (Dunn, 1955; Kay & Fitzgerald, 1997; Jeynes & Littell, 2000; Lamb, 1997). Prior to Dewey, most Americans had viewed raising children as primarily the responsibility of the parent with supplementation on the part of the community (Jeynes, 2003a, 2005c, 2007b, 2012b). With Dewey's admonitions regarding the changing times, however, an increasing number of Americans viewed it as a mutual compact between the parents and the state (Egan, 2002; Jeynes, 2008c; Spring, 1997). Ultimately, Dewey believed that one of the responsibilities of the teacher was to direct children away room the values of their parents so that they could develop their own values (Jeynes, 2007a). It was healthier, in Dewey's view, for children to procure their values from their own experiences and those of their peers than it was for their values to be instilled in them from the convictions and beliefs of their parents (Egan, 2002; Jeynes, 2007a).

Naturally, it is not entirely possible to ascertain how much of the departure from the community-based school could be attributed to some of the realities of capitalism and how much could be blamed an emerging socialism of which John Dewey was a part (Etzioni, 1964; Jeynes, 2009; Micklethwart & Woodridge, 2009). Nevertheless, by the 1960s, Deweyism (by this time, nearly every teacher had been trained in Deweyism) likely was one of many contributing factors to educators viewing the family as having less of a decisive role in rearing well-adjusted children (Davis-Kean, 2005; Delgado-Gaitan, 2004; Dunn, 1955; Lamb, 1997).

The move toward a broader usage of standardized tests has also contributed to the growing disconnect between the school and the community (Jeynes, 2006a, 2011). Perrone (1990) avers that beginning in the early 1960s, American schools became obsessed with giving young students standardized tests, largely due to blocks of time that became available by removing the Bible, character education, and prayer from the public schools. From the early 1960s until 1990 the use of standardized tests in American schools grew by 20 percent per year (Perrone, 1990). The sudden change in trajectory toward one that emphasized standardized tests was advocated by Piagetian psychologists and increased the gap between the people who were running the schools and the people these schools were serving.

Economic Efficiency

Another reason that school choice is attractive is that it will likely promote increased economic efficiency. Caroline Hoxby (2003a) notes that the economic analysis of school choice really did not begin until 1994. Before this time, she claims that the debate suffered by being limited primarily to a political argument (Hoxby, 2003a). Critics of Hoxby believe that this assertion of hers is oversimplified and it likely is, but the essence of her assertion rings with a great deal of truth. That is, if the debate remains limited too much to political considerations, all Americans lose. Before the United States can reach logical solutions, leaders on both sides of the aisle must allow an open-minded civil debate in which the goal of helping the nation and her children is paramount (Coulson, 1999; Jeynes, 2000a, 2005b). Christian schools are able to operate at approximately 60 percent of the cost per student that public schools do (Hoxby, 2003c; Swift, 2003). Given that private Christian schools are so much more efficient than public schools, states would save money by implementing programs that pay for children to attend these schools instead of more expensive public ones (Hoxby, 2003c). And according to countless academic studies and syntheses combining the results of all the existing studies on the topic, even after accounting for differences in race and socioeconomic status, Christian school students outperform their public school counterparts in both academic and behavioral measures (Hoxby, 2003c; Jeynes, 2002a, 2012a, 2012h).

Nearly all of America's 50 states have faced major budget deficits in the past few years. Education spending, which consumes nearly 50 percent of many states' budgets, has helped swell those deficits. Much of that spending is unnecessary. Public schools overpay administrators, purchase high-tech equipment that is rarely used, and offer lavish perks to their employees. Like all monopolies, the American public school system is inefficient. This is one reason Christian schools are able to operate at roughly 60 percent of the cost per student that public schools do. What this all means is that the United States is spending almost twice as much on schooling as it should.

With this context in mind, it is very unfortunate that a large number America's faith-based private schools have shut their doors in recent years, while others face the dire prospect of closure. Sadly, many of these closures are taking place in inner cities, where so many Christian schools have made a determined effort to make a difference in their communities. Meanwhile, the percentage of American students attending *public schools*—90 percent—is at an all-time high. Given that faith-based schools produce better results for less money, this last statistic seems counterintuitive (Buckingham, 2011; Hoxby, 2004). It is surprising, then, that in recent elections no major presidential candidate ran on the issue of school choice. A well-thought-out school choice program that includes the participation of faith-based schools could be an efficacious means of helping balance budgets all across the country while introducing competition that would encourage public schools to become stronger and giving parents the opportunity to send their children to schools that provide an atmosphere that is more drug free and gang free than that offered by traditional public schools and public charter ones. School choice could therefore be good for taxpayers, parents, and children. Clearly, faith-based schools enjoy a decided advantage over their traditional public school and public charter school counterparts in terms of the academic outcomes produced with each dollar. Therefore, to whatever extent school choice would foster some degree of growth in religious school enrollment, overall economic efficiency will increase.

Parents Are Likely to Be More Satisfied

Much of the notion behind school choice is to yield a schooling system that is more sensitive to the desires of parents and children (Chubb & Moe, 1990; Jeynes, 2002a, 2002c). Critics of the public school system often charge that advances in public education will be limited because the schools are obliged to satisfy three groups in particular: the state, the federal government, and the teachers unions. As the curriculum across various states and the nation overall has become increasingly standardized and the public school has grown increasingly compelled to meet these standards, the criticism of the resulting rigidity has heightened (Jeynes, 2006a; Phelps, 2000). Families have become more and more concerned that they are merely cogs in an impenetrable system that is fundamentally driven by test scores. To be sure, test scores are one of the most reliable measures of knowledge and scholastic prowess (Jeynes, 2006a; Phelps, 2000). One cannot gainsay that grade point average (GPA) together with SAT scores represent the most reliable combination of predictive factors for college success (Baird, 1983; Jeynes, 2007a; Wirtz, 1977). Indeed, those who most adamantly oppose the use of the SAT may have received lower than expected SAT scores themselves. Nevertheless, there is a difference between respecting the contribution of such test scores and using them prudently versus becoming obsessed with them so that they becoming the driving force of any major government educational effort (Fry, 1998; Phelps, 2000). Families often believe that they have been lost in the midst of what has become a mechanical scholastic behemoth (Fry, 1998). Some believe that the implementation of school choice, especially the broad rubric of including private schools, will cause schools to be more family sensitive and less driven by standardized tests (Peterson & Hassel, 1998).

Arguments Against School Choice

It Might Reward More Highly Educated and/or Aggressive Parents

Few would argue against the assertion that school choice might benefit some families more than others. One of the most common claims is that choice would reward more highly educated and/or aggressive parents (Nicotera, Mendiburo, & Brends, 2011). Nevertheless, one should note two truths along these lines. First, nearly all choice programs currently underway in the United States are "targeted choice" programs, which purposely focus on families low in the educational and income strata and equally low in taking the initiative (Peterson, 2006). Hence, while such a claim might be true under normal circumstances, currently the precise opposite is true (Peterson, 2006).

Second, under any normal circumstances, more highly educated and/or aggressive parents will nearly always benefit the most. The question arises, however, whether programs should punish these more engaged parents or whether the United States should encourage higher levels of parental involvement than is currently the case

(Jeynes, 2005a, 2007b, 2012b). The answer seems obvious. And indeed, it is hard to imagine students taking the initiative unless parents are serving as a model in this respect. Sizer's (1984, p. 54) quote from *Horace's Compromise* ... is worthy of remembrance at this juncture: "No more important finding has emerged from the inquiries of our study than that the American high school student is all too often docile, compliant, and without initiative."

School Choice and Equity/Possible Segregation and Reduction of Diversity

One of the greatest concerns about school choice concerns its influence on equity. Even today, there persists a concern about whether school choice may favor the wealthy and the white majority.

Three specific potential problems concern the opponents of choice on this issue of equity. First, they believe that poor people would not receive sufficient information about the options available to make the most prudent choices (Nicotera, Mendiburo, & Brends, 2011; Stevens, dela Terre, & Johnson, 2011). Second, they also possess concerns about transportation. A plethora of poor people might prove unable to afford to pay for the transportation necessary to attend the school of their preference. New York City, which initiated what is primarily a *public* school choice program, faces this problem (Barbanel, 1992; Lee, 1993). Third, social scientists are concerned about whether producing educational markets is in the best interests of the public (Ball, 2003; Levin, 2006). Bridges (1994) even asserts that school choice has turned parents into "customers," when they should be viewed as "partners." Researchers have especially become concerned with equity issues in the United Kingdom, where parental school choice programs are already in place nationwide (Woods, Bayley, & Glatter, 1998). Equity concerns have become the center of attention because (1) there is a degree of evidence that certain inequities, by class and race, have arisen in the British education system (Ball, 2003) and (2) given that the United States does not yet have a full-scale choice program, advocates of parental choice have had more time to respond to their critics and adjust choice programs accordingly, before the choice programs go into effect (Jeynes, 2012a).

There are those that advocate choice who argue that choice would actually decrease inequity (Stevens, dela Terre, & Johnson, 2011; Walberg, 2007). Joseph Viteritti (2003) notes that all choice programs in the United States that include private school are "targeted choice" efforts aimed at helping those in need. He believes that this approach "helps counter class, racial, and educational biases in determining who benefits" (p. 25). In terms of inequity and integration, Walberg (2007, p. 49) notes, "Religious schools were initially ineligible to participate in Milwaukee's voucher program. That prohibition was subsequently lifted, and an evaluation of the program showed that Milwaukee's voucher accepting religious schools are better integrated than the city's public schools." Although the Milwaukee results have enjoyed the most publicity, the aggregated results regarding segregation of a number of school choice programs indicate a rather consistent pattern (Figlio & Page, 2003). That is, initially there was "a slight temporary increase in the segregation index. ... However, in the longer term, choice is also likely to be exercised by the less advantaged sections of any community" (Walberg, 2007, p. 51). Melba and Sanford Levinson's (2003) research also supports the notion that faith-based schools are often quite diverse and make it a priority to recruit children of color. Consequently, they note that religious schools are more racially integrated than public schools (p. 121).

In European systems, where school choice is practiced, it does appear that over time, the poor and uneducated sectors of society do tend to benefit somewhat more than other groups. For example, statistics from Germany indicate that choice helps minorities the most (Glenn, 1989). During the 1990–1997 period in England under the choice program, segregation decreased substantially (Walberg, 2007). In France, there exists more general evidence that choice benefits the working class the most (Glenn, 1989). Social scientists generally disagree about whether these results can be transferred to America (Chubb & Moe, 1990; Glenn, 1989). Nevertheless, meta-analyses and the examination of nationwide data sets indicate that students of color and those of low socioeconomic status benefit the most from attending private schools (Jeynes, 2002a, 2010b, 2012a).

Advocates of school choice also present evidence indicating that the self-selection activities of private schools do not discriminate against minorities. Moreover, researchers have a considerable amount of evidence to back up this claim. David Campbell (2006, p. 207) states, "Researchers have shown that Catholic schools are more racially integrated than public schools and that voucher programs do not have an adverse effect on integration." Daniel Patrick Moynihan (1989) presents the chart (Table 1.1).

Table 1.1   Percentage of Catholic and Public Schools Having the Listed
Proportions of Black Students (from Moynihan, 1989)

	Catholic Schools	**Public Schools**
Few blacks	30%	29%
Half black	31%	28%
Mostly black	22%	24%
All black	17%	19%
Mostly or all black	39%	43%

This chart demonstrates that Catholic schools are no more segregated than public schools. In recent years, choice programs have become more sensitive to the needs of poor and minority students. This may result, in part, from responding to the attacks of critics. It may also result from the fact that most private schools are religious. Catholic schools and other Christian schools believe their call and mission involves helping the poor and the oppressed.

One example in religious schools of increased sensitivity to minorities among choice initiatives is the Milwaukee voucher program (National School Boards Association, 2013). In fact, efforts in Cleveland, Dayton, Louisiana, Washington D.C., New Hampshire, Indianapolis, and Florida indicate that aiding children of color and those of low socioeconomic status has been a central focus in the inauguration of almost every school choice program that includes private schools (Howell, Wolf, Peterson, & Campbell, 2006; Nicotera, Mendiburo, & Brends, 2011).

Choice proponents also aver that their programs would increase equity and equal access to schooling both for children of color and those from families who are not well educated and of low socioeconomic status. They claim that first, under the current public school strategy, the vast majority of families must send their children to "neighborhood schools," which in impoverished areas are more likely to be underperforming (1) because of teachers who do not want to teach in these areas because of the risk of rape and other violent crimes that generally exist in these high-poverty vicinities, (2) because the culture of these locations generally is not scholastically oriented, and (3) because there are fewer financial resources, on average, both in the home and the school going to support education. Second, they contend that public school choice programs that exclude faith-based schools from participation also demonstrate some degree of sensitivity to students of color and those facing challenging circumstances. For example, the Minnesota public school program demonstrates some sensitivity. Nearly half of the students participating in the Minnesota choice program classify as "at-risk" youth. The state appears to be doing everything humanly possible to accommodate these at-risk young. There the state government pays for the transportation costs, which is one of the primary concerns of the poor. Not only do the schools provide childcare, but they also proactively urge parents to become more engaged in their children's schooling.

Another example is the public school choice program in Cambridge, Massachusetts. The Cambridge school district places within *every* school a branch of the centralized parent information center to facilitate family members making sound decisions (Nechyba, 2003; Walser, 1998). In addition, the Cambridge schools pay for the transportation costs associated with choice. Finally, Cambridge ensures that the individual choices people make do not increase the degree of segregation in the schools (Ladd, 2003; Nechyba, 2003; Walser, 1998). Each of these issues addressed by the Cambridge school system is of concern nationally, but also locally in Cambridge.

If school choice advocates are insensitive—as opponents of choice claim—one would not expect the intensity in the degree to which they address issues of concern to families of color and those that lack educational and financial resources, as well those expressed by the general populace on these matters. These examples of choice supporters attempting to remove obstacles in both the private and public sector defy the stereotype that school choice programs show insensitivity to the needs of poor and minority students. Contrary to the preconception that school choice would hurt some of the more vulnerable in society, polls quite consistently indicate that American people of color support the implementation of a voucher program by a wider margin than white people do (Jeynes, 2007a; Kirkpatrick, 1990; Nechyba, 2003). Moreover, African Americans generally favor the adoption of a voucher program more than any other racial group (Kirkpatrick, 1990; Jeynes, 2007a; Phi Beta Kappa/Gallup Poll, 2002). In a real sense, the observer should not be surprised by these results. African Americans and Latinos are more likely than other ethnic groups to declare that religion is an important part of their lives (Gallup, 2011; Winn, 2011). It would only follow that concurrently, these would be some of the people most desirous of sending their children to faith-based schools, which constitute the vast majority of U.S. private schools (Holt, 2000; Jeynes, 2000a; Stolberg, 2008).

As sensitive as school choice programs in the United States have become to the needs of minorities, one wonders about the degree to which this sensitivity could be expressed if more people participated in the programs. If a large number of students participated in choice programs, the cost of supplying transportation and information access for the benefit of the students could become exorbitant (Levin, 2006). Levin argues that public schools are so heavily subsidized that it is difficult for private schools to compete with them. Levin (2006, p. 24) even adds, "One reason why entrepreneurs have been reluctant to enter the schooling market is that they must compete against heavily subsidized public schools." It is certainly conceivable that if "choice enrollment" surged too much, it would become impractical to supply transportation and information. Some credit should go to the developers of a number of these school choice programs in the United States because they have manifested a good deal of responsiveness to the objections of their critics. Nevertheless, it is not clear whether this same level of efficiency could be maintained if the number of students attending the participating schools were to dramatically increase.

It is also unclear whether the sensitivity that local church leaders, community workers, and local politicians have shown to youth in need will extend to state and federal politicians, who have not always demonstrated that same kind of compassion. Unfortunately, these high-level politicians have been most interested in offering tax breaks or vouchers of approximately equal amounts to all Americans (Ladd, 2003; Nicotera, Mendiburo, & Brends, 2011). This generally creates soft underbelly to school choice initiatives in that many Americans would support giving financial breaks to the poor and middle class to enable them to send their children to faith-based schools. However, what a large number of the nation's citizenry find objectionable is giving tax breaks to the upper class (Nicotera, Mendiburo, & Brends, 2011; Stevens, dela Terre, & Johnson, 2011). Why should people making in excess of $200,000 each year receive a tax break to perhaps send their children to private school? When one considers the varying degrees of openness by the American public to the various choice proposals, based on how the financial tax breaks are distributed, it would certainly befit state and national politicians to yield on the issue of the distribution of tax breaks. It will probably be difficult to pass school choice legislation unless the poor receive a large tax break, the middle class a moderate one, and the wealthy none at all (Ladd, 2003; Jeynes, 2000a).

It should also be mentioned at this juncture that virtually no one in the choice movement maintains a perspective that families that do not utilize the public schools should not pay taxes to support these institutions. This is because choice advocates have an understanding that the nation's citizenry, as a whole, benefits from the existence of the public schools. That is, most people have a physician who attended public schools as well as a mechanic who received training there (Jeynes, 2007a). Rather, what these advocates argue is that it is only democratic and fair that those who do not utilize the public schools should pay less in the way of taxes (Peterson, 2003). This seems to be a perspective worthy of consideration, even by the naysayers, especially when one considers the unrelenting rise in tax rates to support public schools since 1872 and again beginning in the 1950s (King, 1964; Relland, 1997). In 1872, a key supreme court case in Kalamazoo, Michigan, upheld public taxation for high schools (King, 1964). This case forever reconfigured the balance of power between public and private schools. Before the Kalamazoo decision, private schools dominated high school enrollment by a margin of 2 to 1 (King, 1964). Within 20 years of the decision, public school enrollment had a 7 to 3 edge (King, 1964).

Church/State Issues

Some people present concerns that allowing tax breaks for individuals who choose to spend their money on private school education violates the "separation of church and state," which they claim appears in the U.S. Constitution. That concern emerges, of course, because the vast majority of private schools in the United States are faith-based schools. It should be noted, however, that separation of church and state never appears in the Constitution and was not used until early in the nineteenth century. Ironically, polls indicate that 65 percent of Americans believe that the phrase does occur in the First Amendment to the Constitution, and it is this misinformed majority that causes a great deal of consternation on this issue (Marshal,

1967). What the First Amendment to the Constitution actually does state is, "Congress shall make no law respecting an establishment of religion, or prohibiting the free exercise thereof" (U.S. Constitution, 1789). This phrase is generally referred to as the establishment clause. Sadly, many people do not realize that the key ideas in this statement deal with making sure the government does not establish one denomination as the official one of the United States, as was the case in many European nations of the time. That is, it guarantees the freedom of worship. Many Americans do not realize that it was churches that demanded James Madison, the Constitution's primary author, include the First Amendment, without which New York and Virginia would not have ratified the Constitution. In Virginia, where the Anglican Church was dominant, the Baptists and Presbyterians were often harassed by government representatives. Therefore, most Virginians would not support the Constitution unless an amendment was added guaranteeing freedom of religion. Most politicians understood that if these two heavily populated states refused to approve the document, other states would refuse as well and the Constitution would not be approved. The Baptists and Presbyterians were cognizant of the fact that they had the support of George Washington, who supported a specific guarantee of religious freedom. And because Washington—the most highly respected of the founders—backed them, they believed that Madison could eventually be convinced. Therefore, Washington and other government leaders convinced Madison to add the First Amendment to the Constitution.

To underscore the original purpose of the First Amendment, it is important to remember that the central argument in favor of its inclusion was to keep the government out of the affairs of the church rather than the other way around. Virtually all denominations at the time insisted on its inclusion as a matter of religious freedom (Estep, 1990; Haynes et al., 2003; Noll, 2002).

The phrase "separation of church and state" was never used until early in the nineteenth century, when Thomas Jefferson replied to a letter from the Danbury Baptists, who expressed concern that the Congregationalists were going to become the official denomination of the United States. People who raise the separation issue also are almost never aware that Jefferson greatly clarified his views of this phrase during his second presidential inaugural address. And his words are noteworthy, especially because he had a more liberal view in this case than the other founders.

In the second inaugural address of his presidency, Jefferson made it clear that it was not his view that the *entire* government should be separated by a wall from religious institutions (Jefferson, 1805). Instead, he believed that the *state government* rather than the *federal government* should be the institution, along with the church, to make religious proclamations such as fasting and calls for prayer. This perspective was consistent with Jefferson's overall view that the center of power should be at the state government level rather than at the federal government level (Hutson, 2008). Jefferson was the most prominent leader of the Democratic-Republican Party whose chief conviction was that there were great risks in retrogressing into a near-monarchy if too much power were concentrated in the central government (Cremin, 1976, 1980; Stephens, 1872). It is only consistent with his overall beliefs that he believed that religious proclamations should be undertaken by politicians at the state level rather than the federal level because he asserted that the overwhelming majority of government functions should take place at the state and not the federal level (Haynes et al., 2003). Jefferson averred in his second inaugural address that "religious exercises" should be "under the direction and discipline of state or church" (Jefferson, 1805, p. 11). Thomas Jefferson affirmed this conviction in a letter that he wrote to Samuel Miller in which he asserted "religious matters" were "reserved to the states" (Jefferson in Hutson, 2008, p. 80).

Jefferson not only made assertions indicating that religious declarations should indeed be made at the state level, but his actions made it quite patent that this was indeed his perspective. Jefferson as governor of Virginia was very active in announcing religious proclamations. When Jefferson served as president, however, he encouraged individual states to undertake these actions (Hutson, 2008). In 1779, for example, Governor Jefferson "issued a proclamation appointing a day of publick and solemn thanksgiving and prayer to Almighty God" (Jefferson, 1779, pp. 177–179).

Moreover, in the 1770s, Thomas Jefferson (1784, p. 59), together with James Madison, introduced a bill requiring that "Every minister of the gospel shall on each day so appointed attend and perform divine service and preach a sermon, or discourse, suited to the occasion in his church, on the pain of forfeiting fifty pounds for every failing, not having reasonable excuse." Although the Jefferson-Madison bill did not pass, the fact that they included a substantial fine for those ministers who did not comply demonstrates the extent to which Jefferson maintained that the state should be involved in stating various religious proclamations and practices. In addition, in 1776, Jefferson served on the Committee of Revisors that was given the responsibility of writing the revised code for "A Bill for Appointing Days of Public Fasting and Thanksgiving" (Jefferson, 1784).

The other founders who never used the phrase "separation of church and state" simply abided by the First Amendment. And therefore it appears that the founders, even Jefferson, believed in the First Amendment. They would therefore agree that it is the establishment clause that is the issue, that is, the government must not establish a certain religion or denomination as the official religion of the United States. Beyond that, constitutionally speaking, this issue is not really at the heart of the school choice debate.

Special Education Might Suffer

It is essential that educators be sensitive to the needs of youth with special needs. On the one hand, it is conceivable that school choice, if it is badly handled, could cause these children to receive a reduced level of funding and attention (Cullen & Rivkin, 2003). The reason is simply because even with the tax breaks or vouchers that might come with school choice that includes faith-based schools, the average funding per student at these religious private schools would almost certainly continue to be lower than at public schools (Jeynes & Beuttler, 2012). This is therefore a valid concern. To be sure, education at these faith-based schools, on average, is considerably more efficient than is the case in public schools (Cullen & Rivkin, 2003; Jeynes, 2012h). That is, on a dollar-per-dollar basis, religious schools draw out considerably more out of their students in terms of academic achievement and positive social behavior than is the case in public schools (Hoxby, 2003a, 2004). It is therefore possible that this trend could hold with special education as well (Cullen & Rivkin, 2003; Hoxby, 2003a, 2004). In other words, whatever disadvantage faith-based schools might face financially might be compensated for via their superior levels of efficiency (Cullen & Rivkin, 2003). Although this is possible, it is probably unwise to make the assumption that this advantage would be enough to compensate for the financial disadvantage (Cullen & Rivkin, 2003; Jeynes & Beuttler, 2012).

It is also possible, however, that school choice rather than hindering some opportunities for special needs students might actually increase them. Consequently, it is also conceivable that a school choice program, if implemented wisely, could actually enhance opportunities for special needs students because more affordable school options would be available for these students (Cullen & Rivkin, 2003; Hoxby, 2003a, 2004). Two possibilities are especially appealing along these lines. First, with a wider array of schools that would now be affordable, more schools might be able to specialize in meeting the needs of particular kinds of these students. Second, research indicates that many special needs students are best accommodated in a homeschooling environment (Barfield, 2002; Jeynes, 2012g; Linsenbach, 2003; Rivero, 2008). To the degree that school choice would also enable more parents to be able to afford homeschooling their children, the number of people engaging in this practice might also increase, enabling more special needs students to receive the personal and loving care that they really need to succeed (Jeynes, 2012g).

At this stage, it is therefore unclear how school choice might affect the instructional care that special needs children receive. What is clear, however, is that it is a worthy concern (Cullen & Rivkin, 2003). Beyond this, the impact of school choice on these children could go either way. That being the case, if school choice is implemented, it is essential that it be practiced in such a way that these children are aided even more and not less.

Public School Teacher Morale Might Decline

Ultimately, education must focus on what is best for the children and the nation as a whole. When one raises the issue of teacher morale, it is important to remember this. In addition, there are a plethora of other challenges that are dampening morale far more than the introduction of school choice. First, the fact that about 1,000 teachers require hospital or other medical attention each month because a student has assaulted them is of graver concern to teachers than the introduction of greater education choices for children (U.S. Department of Education, 1984; Wilson, Douglas, & Lyon, 2011).

In addition, the surge in the number of students disrespecting teachers by cussing them out in the classroom and the perception by teachers that they are left with few options for disciplining disruptive students are also pushing a dagger into the morale of teachers far more than what will be relatively limited school choice initiatives. With all due respect to those who raise this issue, they would do well to examine the body of research on what trends actually are dampening the morale of instructors.

Not Everyone Is For or Against School Choice

When one discusses school choice, there arises a need to understand that people cannot always quickly define those who debate the issue as arguing "for" or "against." Rather, there exists a vast array of opinions that constitute more of a continuum of opinions than anything else. Some people like Peterson (2006), and Hoxby (2003a) believe that choice represents that salient ingredient of success. Others, like Berliner and Biddle (1995), believe that choice will not address the problems of most students. Nevertheless, there are also many people whose views rest somewhere in between these two extremes on the continuum (Brighouse, 2003; Nicotera, Mendiburo, & Berends, 2011).

What the Results Show

In many respects, it is difficult to assess the results of school choice programs that include private schools, the vast majority of which are religious, because there are so few places in the United States that have actually experimented with a bona fide choice program that include private schools (Hanushek & Rivkin, 2003). Hanushek and Rivkin rightly note that too much of the academic debate surrounding school choice has focused on theoretical debates rather than real quantitative research and that this is not wise because it will cause leaders to premature conclusions. Nevertheless, it is prudent to at least examine the trends that seem to be there and determine what further analysis is necessary to arrive at more definite conclusions. With that in mind, the reader should note the following

The Low Participation Rate

The evidence appears sparse at this point, but those few places that practice a program of school choice suffer from a very low participation rate. This clearly is true for school choice programs that include private schools, but it is also ostensible for public school choice programs. Moreover, this phenomenon exists not only in the United States, but also worldwide (Jeynes, 2000a). Wherever one goes around the world, the participation rate is generally in the 10 percent to 15 percent range (Ball, 2003; Jeynes, 2000a). This fact is noteworthy because it is hard to conceive of a school reform having a monumental impact when the participation rate is that low (Jeynes, 2000a). And yes, this is a problem for school choice advocates who insist that embracing choice is somehow the key to ameliorating the American education system (Jeynes, 2002c). With these participation rates in mind, even if one admits that private religious schools have a real advantage over their public school counterparts, one needs to make a more realistic assessment and conclude that while school choice programs that include private schools may be *a key* to abetting improved student performance, it seems unlikely that they are *the key*.

Admittedly, choice proponents argue that one of the more latent, and yet real, benefits of these programs will be that the presence of competition from the private sector will, as the adage goes, "raise all ships." Yes, it is likely that in those areas where competition is especially intense, this will occur (Hoxby, 2003a). That is, competition will be highest in areas in which there is a plentitude of private religious schools or they are especially high in quality (Hoxby, 2003a). Nevertheless, with low participation rates, it is hard to imagine that as many ships will be as be raised as the optimists claim. The idea that low participation rates will limit the competitive benefits of school choice is supported by research both by Hoxby (2003c, 2004) and Hanushek and Rivken (2003), which indicates that the ship raising is most likely to take place when many schools are engaged in competition with each other. Reaching this conclusion does not mean that the government should desist from considering any effort to incorporate a school choice initiative. What it does mean, however, is that there is a need for a more realistic assessment of the extent of the benefits that inaugurating such a broad-scale program might yield (Jeynes, 2002c). Within this context, it seems prudent to view school choice as one branch in a set of, for example, half a dozen different reforms rather than constituting a singular answer in which almost no other solution is needed (Engelhardt, 2013; Jeynes, 2002a).

There are some economists who believe that allowing market solutions is the key to improving the quality of American schools

(Hoxby, 2003a). Hoxby and some other economists believe that making schooling more market based is the key to unleashing the type of choices that are the means through which the American education system can be improved. What is interesting, however, is that almost no educators believe increased choice is the reason students from private schools perform so well (Coleman, Hoffer, & Kilgore, 1982; Gatto, 2001). The fact that most researchers do not believe that choice represents the key ingredient that makes private schools work brings up an interesting weakness in the argument for choice. If choice is not the key ingredient in the success of private schools, how could it emerge as the key ingredient in the success of public schools?

> If choice is used as a cheap substitute for this more fundamental pursuit, then the prospects of turning around our public school system and dramatically improving the education of our children will be more remote than ever. (Roseberg, 1989)

Even many advocates of choice do not display that almost unbridled enthusiasm of Chubb and Moe (1990) or Milton Friedman (1994).

The reality is that school choice is an *external initiative*, that is, it is an answer that exists outside the public school system. To whatever extent it could, via competition and parental actions, lead to improved scholastic outcomes among youth, it is nevertheless an energy or force that exists outside the public school system. To be sure, there are a copious number of individuals who rejoice over this fact. They believe that the public school system has a dominant monopoly on schooling and the private educational system has essentially been brought to its knees by a taxation system that so completely supports the public schools that it is almost impossible for parents to afford to send their children to faith-based schools or other private schools (Jeynes, 2007a). These individuals believe that it would be far healthier for the ratio of public to private schools to be 80 percent to 20 percent or 75 percent to 25 percent rather than 92 percent to 8 percent, give or take a few percentage points (Jeynes & Beuttler, 2012). They contend that this kind of monopoly is not only unhealthy, but is probably even dangerous to the overall academic health of the school system and broader society (Egan, 2002; Gatto, 2001; Ravitch, 2000). They believe that such numbers undermine a democratic and diverse state and instead guarantee a move toward a *"one best system"* type of rubric that David Tyack (1974) in his seminal work of the same name warned was insalubrious. From the perspective of many, even those who do not necessary esteem the value of school choice programs, such skewed percentages are associated with socialist and communist societies rather than a democratic republic (Gatto, 2001; Ravitch, 2000). And while it may be argued that the United States is in the process of moving away from being a democratic republic, that is a debate for another day. But what is clear is that the American school system is dominated much more by government standards and public schools policies than has been historically evident in its past. And one is left to ponder the possibility of whether today's youth will lead the nation into higher degrees of socialism or even beyond, in part because they have been raised in a schooling environment in which the state and federal governments wield such inexorable power (Gatto, 2001).

But given that school choice programs are *external initiatives*, their ultimate influence on the public schools is likely to be somewhat limited (Engelhardt, 2013). Might they improve the overall quality of the American education system? That is clearly a real possibility (Glenn, 2000; Jeynes, 2002c). But whatever curative results might emerge would be largely due to the increased private school enrollment that would likely result (Chubb & Moe, 1990; Glenn, 1989). Although there is some evidence that the presence of greater competition from schools that are not traditional public schools (TPS) might cause or be related to improved scholastic out comes of nearby traditional public schools, this phenomenon would likely be secondary to the direct impact of a higher number of students attending faith-based schools (Glenn, 2000; Hoxby, 2003a, 2004).

If one looks at the evidence objectively, it is hard to imagine school choice having the huge impact that proponents envisage. On the other hand, opponents of school choice may exaggerate even more when they speak of school choice as an inexorable threat to the existence of public education (Doerr, 1996; Smith & Meier, 1995). It is implausible to believe that the private school sector could grow to anything more than 20 or 25 percent of the overall U.S. school population. To argue that to go from a virtual monopoly on K-12 schooling to a still prodigious oligopoly and then claim that school choice is a threat to the very existence of public school is disingenuous.

Nevertheless, it remains likely that school choice can have an impact of school achievement overall. Moreover, it is possible than such a program, via increased competition and other factors, could have a positive impact of public school achievement outcomes. It is clear, however, that at least for the foreseeable future, the vast majority of the nation's school children will continue to attend public schools. That being the case, it would seem that to raise the efficacy of public schools, more than an *external initiative* is needed (Ryan & Bohlin, 1998). There needs to be a movement generated from within the public schools themselves. It may be that faith-based schools or even the families from these schools may provide the examples of some of the paradigms needed to produce this change (Jeynes, 1999, 2003c). After all, religious schools are more likely to emphasize the moral traits that are often associated with higher achievement and better behavior (Jeynes, 1999, 2010c). Faith-based schools also place a great deal of emphasis on parental involvement, which is also related to strong school results (Jeynes, 2005c, 2007b).

The Limited Value of Looking at Public School Choice as an Indication of What a Broader School Choice Program Would Look Like

As one examines data that might indicate what the impact of a broad school choice program might look like, it is naturally tempting to look into the influence of public school choice programs, most of which include a strong emphasis on public charter schools. There are currently over 2 million American students enrolled in nearly 6,000 public charter schools in 40 states and the District of Columbia (Center for Education Reform, 2011; Toma & Zimmer, 2012). As one might imagine, Chubb and Moe (1990) have been among those most vigorously dissuading academics from doing this because they believe that the real key issue is whether we allow the private sector and the public sector to directly compete with one another. They state that if the American K-12 school system ever hopes to receive the same boost from competition that takes place at the collegiate level, then these two sectors competing against each other is an absolute necessity. Nevertheless, there is a sense in which Chubb and Moe (1990) opine that including a public school program is at least a step in the right direction.

With this in mind, it is wise to note some of the most salient remarks that have emerged from those who have been involved with such initiatives. Deborah W. Meier taught in East Harlem's District 4, where choice played a prominent role in attempts at school reform. District 4 witnessed a significant increase in academic achievement as a result of these reforms (Meier, 1992b). Meier (1992a) contends, "It would have been impossible to carry out this ambitious agenda without choice. Choice was the necessary, however insufficient, prerequisite." Over the past 20 or 25 years, Harlem's District 4 has in many respects risen as a hallmark of educational progress and achievement in the inner city. The praises that various teachers, administrators, community leaders, and other observers have directed toward Harlem's District 4 are quite numerous (Brighouse, 2003; Starling, 2010; Wagner & Vander Ark, 2001). With this in mind, however, they all point to choice as one factor among several that helped swing the district from an underperforming area to an exemplary one. Moreover, it should be noted that even Deborah Meier's comments are quite cautious in this regard. Although she and others acknowledge the fact that choice in various and sundry ways acted as a catalyst to ensure progress, it was not "sufficient." That is, many educators and researchers have pointed to the character of the leadership and the involvement of the parents as factors that helped insure that progress would be made (Jeynes, 2006a, 2010d; Ryan & Bohlin, 1998). It takes a person of conviction to know what should be done and then demonstrate the disciplined passion, integrity, and conviction to actually follow through with his or her words and make idealistic goals a reality (Jeynes, 2006a, 2010a). Those who comment on the successes of District 4 point this fact out with regularity. To make an analogous statement, Harvard, Princeton, Yale, Chicago, and Columbia provide the competition that they do because they have performed so well that they have been ranked as the top five universities in *U.S. News and World Report.* It is their high quality that makes them excellent competitors that encourage other institutions of higher learning to become better. Similarly, if one were to allow underperforming schools to be the only competitors in a school choice district, it is unlikely that choice would have that much of an impact on the overall school outcomes in the district.

A certain level of quality in the leadership, integrity, and commitment of the participating school officials and teachers is essential if choice is to have a real impact. This being the case, however, one can certainly argue that faith-based schools and other private schools ought to be included in any such choice program because on average, studies indicate that these schools produce better outcomes, even when adjusting for socioeconomic status, selectivity, and other variables (Jeynes, 2012a; Starling, 2010; Wagner & Vander Ark, 2001).

While it is true that examining the impact of public school choice as one indicator of what the impact of a broader program might look like yields some positive findings, using this method also divulges some potential concerns. Morris (1994), a retired director of local education authority (LEA) services, is concerned that market forces may overlook the needs of those unfairly treated by the system. For example, foreign families who are not familiar with how the American school system works might find it difficult to act as quickly with informed decisions as those who have resided in the United States for a long period of time (Brighouse, 2003; Wagner & Vander Ark, 2001). Such a conclusion does not eliminate choice from consideration, especially because most advocates have demonstrated that they are almost amazingly sensitive to the objections raised by opponents and make adjustments with sound alacrity (Jeynes, 2000a). Nevertheless, it is also important to understand that meeting the needs of these students should always be a core consideration.

More Research Is Needed

One of the greatest problems in assessing the effects of school choice abides in the lack of relevant data collected on its impact on children (Hanushek & Rivkin, 2003). In the United Kingdom there has been more research done on parental school choice than in America. Nevertheless, almost none of this research has examined the effects of school choice on scholastic outcomes. Gewirtz, Ball, and Bowe (1995) note, "Most of the empirical research is piecemeal and tends to be very specifically focused" (p. 3). Gewirtz, Ball, and Bowe therefore contend that much of the research on school choice has been "inadequate" (p. 6). There are some recent data indicating that school choice *may* positively impact academic achievement (Greene et al., 1996; Hoxby, 2003c, 2004; Peterson et al., 1996; Witte & Thorne, 1996), but overall the evidence is sparse. Hanushek and Rivkin (2003) assert that too many educational policies relating to choice are based on largely untested theoretical ideas and therefore, there is an element of presumptuousness and capriciousness to some of these policies.

There are four reasons a report card on school choice might contain more "incompletes" than definitive letter grades. First, the number of studies that social scientists have done measuring the impact of school choice is relatively small. Second, for those studies that have attempted to assess the effects of school choice, it is not clear whether this is in fact what has ultimately been measured. Many studies that have been done in the United Kingdome, for example, have focused on how choice affects: (1) the distribution of students among schools (Ball, 2003; Woods, Bagley, & Glatter, 1998); (2) what parents consider when making their choices (Woods, Bagley, & Glatter, 1998); and (3) grant-maintained schools (Ball, 2003; Bush, Coleman, & Glover, 1993). Third, the school choice debate has become so politicized that it has become hard to disentangle the research of many social scientists from their political views (Doerr, 1996; Salisbury & Tooley, 2007; Smith & Meier, 1995). Fourth, the dynamics of school choice are complex and difficult to examine (Brighouse, 2003).

The first point regarding the dearth of studies on school choice strongly relates to a chief exhortation of this text, that is, social scientists need to initiate more research on the effects of school choice. The second point, though, especially deserves mention. That is, even a plethora of new studies measuring the effects of school choice will yield little valuable information if there are problems with construct validity. This may especially become a problem when the analysts use large data sets on which to base their conclusions. In most cases, using samples from large nationwide data sets is preferable to using samples from localized populations (the latter method is more likely to suffer from problems dealing with randomization, experimenter bias, underrepresented groups, nationally representative samples, etc.). But using large nationwide data sets to assess the effects of school choice may simply result in comparing apples with oranges (Hoxby, 2003c). For often, studies assessing school choice simply compare the academic achievement of children participating in choice programs versus those that do not. This may sound like a logical procedure on the surface, but urban children are much more likely to participate in school choice programs than rural children. Rural children simply do not have access to level of choice that urban children have because even if there does exist another school for a rural child to attend, the extent of the choices available is far less. Therefore, assessing the effects of choice by comparing the academic achievement of children who participate in choice programs versus those who do not involves comparing one group of students (non-choice) that has a disproportionate number of rural children with another group of students (choice) that has a disproportionate number of urban children. Research indicates that these inner-city children, for example, are more likely to be poor and/or minority students than their rural counterparts (Hoxby, 2003c, 2004). Therefore, it seems likely that part or all of the difference between the choice and nonchoice groups may be a result of confounding variables at work in the analysis. Ultimately, the comparison groups should be choice students and nonchoice students from the same school district, rather than two groups of children often living in two entirely different parts of the country (or state). On the other hand, proponents of choice have some satisfaction because a difference in academic achievement emerged by the third year of the choice program. Nevertheless, one can argue that this may partially be a result of children that are struggling in their new schools, often dropping out of the project by the third year and leaving only those students who are doing reasonably well as the study's sample.

The third point regarding the political nature of the choice debate is particularly important to acknowledge if a person is to have any hope of coming to some objective conclusions about the effects of choice. To some degree, the debate is between liberals and conservatives. The debate over school choice is particularly portrayed this way in the United Kingdom (Ball, 2003; Smith & Meier, 1995). This may be because it was the conservatives who ultimately pushed through the current program of school choice (Ball, 2003; Gronberg & Jansen, 2006; Jeynes, 2000a). But there are too many exceptions to this generalization to characterize the debate in this way. Instead, often the debate is between those who serve in public education and those who are not in public education but depend on public education to reach their goals (parents, business leaders, etc.). By observing whether a social scientist serves (or has served) in public education, a person can almost predict what his or her conclusions will be regarding choice. With these facts in mind, there needs to be a redoubled effort of those participating in this debate to examine the matter of school choice with the utmost objectivity.

Choice in Today's Educational Context

Assessing the Evidence and the Debate

Four points appear relevant in making an assessment of the evidence, as well as the debate, regarding school choice. First, it appears unlikely that school choice will emerge as the grand source of reform that its advocates promise. The primary reason for this is that in all areas where a considerable choice program exists, the participation rate is low (Ball, 2003). As a result, few children will benefit from the program, and few schools will possess the incentive to change significantly. This does not mean, however, that the choice program has no merit.

Second, due to the inundation of political motives entering the choice debate and the low participation rates just mentioned, there exists insufficient experimentation to conclude that school choice (public or private school version) works (Doerr, 1996; Salisbury & Tooley, 2007; Smith & Meier, 1995). The U.S. Supreme Court has never ruled vouchers or public school choice unconstitutional (Berends, Cannata, & Goldring, 2011; Kirkpatrick, 1990). Therefore, there stands no reason why the United States should not conduct a wide experiment using choice. In the United Kingdom, most studies have focused on demographic, political, or equity factors, with only a small amount of attention placed on the effects on the academic results in children (Ball, 2003; Bush, Coleman, & Glover, 1993; Woods, Bagley, & Glatter, 1998). More experimentation on the academic aspects of school choice is needed in both the United Kingdom and the United States. A school choice program in Montclair, New Jersey, represents a program that closely approximates the type of school choice experiment that is necessary in the United States. Montclair decided to go with a 100 percent choice program, eliminating all neighborhood schools (Fitzgerald, 1991; Schneider, Teske, Marshall & Roch, 1997). From a financial viewpoint, the choice program experienced success, with its per student expenditures falling under the county average (Fitzgerald, 1991). And in a district that contains 50 percent minority students, May Lee Fitzgerald, the district superintendent, reports:

> Montclair High School sends 80 percent of its students on to two-to four-year college/universities. Its SAT scores rose 18 points last year and seven students were national merit semi-finalists. Its drop-out rate is under three percent. (Fitzgerald, 1991)

Reports like this one indicate that we should construct some choice programs designed specifically to answer many of the questions circulating in the school choice debate. I would propose that the federal and state governments work together with educators to construct public school choice programs for the purpose of experimentation in both the United States and the United Kingdom. There simply does not exist enough information presently to determine whether school choice programs raise achievement test scores. Nevertheless, we should note that no one argues that school choice *decreases* test scores. This fact alone warrants some attention.

Third, choice may emerge as a puissant means of raising the achievement of minority students. Contrary to my initial expectations, most programs of public school choice in the United States demonstrate considerable sensitivity to the needs of minorities. There is also little doubt that because of the state of many UK and U.S. urban schools, minorities in the inner city may need choice the most. There may even exist some justification for including private schools in choice, if the objective is to specifically help minorities. Evidence indicates that Catholic schools, for example, raise the achievement of African Americans even more than they do whites (Stolberg, 2008; Williams, 1983).

Fourth, a program of school choice that is sensitive to equity issues may not prove feasible monetarily. The small programs in the United States that exist now do show some sensitivity to minorities by providing transportation costs and other financial benefits. But if school choice expands, as it has in the United Kingdom, many school districts will face difficult choices. Total costs of transportation and making available information about choice will soar. Districts may be forced either to face a fiscal crisis or to cut back on some programs.

Overall, school choice possesses limited potential. Yet, the potential is sufficient enough to warrant a government-sponsored program of experimentation. And the potential is certainly substantial enough to investigate in a book such as this one.

Chapter 2

A Meta-Analysis Examining the Effects of Public, Faith-Based, and Public Charter Schools

Over the past 45 years, there has been a considerable amount of debate on the effects of faith-based schools and charter schools have on the academic achievement of children (Bryk, Lee, & Holland, 1993; Chubb & Moe, 1990; Coleman, Hoffer, & Kilgore, 1982; Garcia, Barber & Molnar, 2009). Different authors have come at this debate from a number of different angles. Sociologists such as James Coleman have focused on the social capital and cultural aspects of religious private education to explain much of the faith-based school advantage (Coleman, Hoffer, & Kilgore, 1982; Jeynes, 2003c). Bryk and his associates concurred with Coleman and this led the debate to the next logical step of asking whether there are certain moral dynamics and self-disciplinary practices extant in faith-based schools that can also be applied in part in the public sector (Bryk, Lee, & Holland, 1993; Jeynes, 2010). To be sure, these debates had a considerable impact on the school choice debate and also whether public schools could at least partially mimic some of the qualities that have made faith-based schools successful in terms of both scholastic outcomes and student behavior (Ireland, 2005). This has, in part, led to the popularity of public charter schools. Each public charter school exists under a separate charter that allows it to exhibit some of the flexibility that people do not normally associate with traditional public schools (TPS) (Bifulco & Ladd, 2006).

With increased debates mounting on the value of each of these schooling rubrics, one can easily overlook the broader picture. That is, the goal of Americans at large and educators specifically really is to improve the overall system of American education as a whole (Boyer, 1995). And if one is to realize this goal, it is valuable to lay aside one's own particular preferences and ask three simple questions: (1) how do these various rubrics (TPS, faith-based, and public charter) compare to one another; (2) what are the strengths and weaknesses of each of these paradigms; and (3) what might they learn from one another so that all these types of schools might benefit and so that the American system of elementary and secondary schooling can become stronger?

This meta-analysis will focus on the first of these questions but will also provide some foundational insights that will help establish an intelligent national discussion on the second and third questions.

Review of the Literature: The Journey Thus Far

There is little question that by the mid-1960s, the American system of elementary and secondary school education in many respects was much more monolithic than the system had ever been (Gatto, 2001). Specifically, by the mid-1960s and in every decade since that point, approximately 90 percent of school children in the United States attended public schools (U.S. Department of Education, 2011). Most Americans do not recall living in a nation in which other expressions of education, mostly in the private sector, enjoyed much more influence than they do now. Intellectually, most of the nation's citizenry understand that those who established the nation's first colleges and schools viewed education as the responsibility of the church much more than the state (Jeynes, 2007a; Stewart, 1969). Consequently, nearly a century and a half elapsed between the founding of Harvard College (1636) and the first government college in Georgia (1785). Beginning in the 1600s, religious charity schools became the primary mode of instruction to help insure that people (especially in the north) who desired to receive an education could receive one (Cornog, 1998). Students were asked to pay only what they could afford, and for 80 percent of the students, that meant they paid little or nothing. Charity schools thrived well into the mid-1800s, supported largely by a generous upper class that believed in giving back to society and an economically efficient system that was ultimately improved on by an Englishman named Joseph Lancaster (Cornog, 1998).

With the rise of immigration in the 1830s and 1840s, however, it became increasingly hard for religious charity schools to continue to charge little or no tuition (Bourne, 1870). Concurrently, public school advocates led by Horace Mann, Emma Willard, and Henry Barnard called for taxes to be raised to ensure a continued emphasis on educating as many children as possible (MacMullen, 1991). From about 1837 until the 1860s, many charity schools increasingly turned to tax money from governments to supplement charitable giving so that eventually many charity schools became public schools, and other new public schools were founded. Even by the Civil War, however, most Americans believed that education was a responsibility of the church and not the government. By 1861, seven of the original 13 states still did not have a state university, although they had a plentitude of Christian colleges (Tewksbury, 1932). Even by 1872, nearly 67 percent of American students attending high school attended a private school (Jeynes, 2007a; King, 1964). In 1872, a key supreme court case in Kalamazoo, Michigan, upheld public taxation for high schools (King, 1964). This decision set the stage for the number of public high schools to eventually exceed the number of private high schools and by 1892, about 70 percent of American high school students attended public schools (Jeynes, 2007a; King, 1964).

The percentage of the school population attending public schools continued to steadily rise through the remainder of the 1800s and into the 1900s. Public schools taught the Bible and allowed prayer, even as the Christian schools did (Westerhoff, 1982). In addition, with these facts in mind and with school taxes steadily rising and the formidable cost of tuition, parents increasingly sent their children to public schools (Grant, 2005). Generally, the wisdom of 90 percent American children attending public schools rather than private ones was not especially questioned until the infamous decline in most national and statewide test scores during the 1963–1980 period (Wirtz, 1977). However, at that time, nations that had ordered plenteous literature on American schooling suddenly reduced or ceased the ordering of materials on America's public school system (Jeynes, 2007a).

Beginning in the mid-1960s researchers took note of viable alternatives to traditional public schools (TPS). The U.S. Supreme Court's 1962 and 1963 decisions to remove voluntary prayer and Bible reading from public schools likely contributed to social scientists examining faith-based schools in particular. Especially to the extent that schools, in the advent of these decisions, were now hesitant to risk teaching character traits such as love, forgiveness, the golden rule, and turning the other cheek—which in the views of some were infused with Judeo-Christian values—some theorists believed that the absence of these teachings could have behavioral and academic effects (Jeynes, 1999, 2003c). Some believed that these teachings and expressions created a culture of love and self-discipline in the schools that might enhance achievement (Jeynes, 2003c, 2014; Wirtz, 1977). In terms of examining the religious school culture and discipline, probably no two researchers have done a more thorough job than James Coleman and Thomas Hoffer. In their book, *Public and Private High Schools: The Impact of Communities* (1987), Coleman and Hoffer use their examination of the High School and Beyond data set to expound on why they believe religious schools do possess high levels of social capital that enhances student performance and behavior (Coleman, Hoffer, & Kilgore, 1982. In other writings, Coleman (1988) further elaborates on this concept that is called the social capital theory. In this theory, Coleman posits that students attending religious schools have a higher degree of social capital invested into them. He argues that social capital represents the degree to which certain key members of a society invest their time, energy, wisdom, and knowledge in an individual or institution.

With the previously discussed findings in mind, some educators argued that some of the qualities most apparent in explaining the success of faith-based schools could be incorporated into the public school orientation (Hudolin, 1994). Under the guidance of Anthony Bryk, the Chicago public school system was one of the first to attempt to model several aspects of the Catholic school system (Bryk, Lee, & Holland, 1993; Hudolin, 1994). Although some character and other factors that contribute to the success of Catholic schools may be difficult to imitate, many social scientists believe that Catholic schools serve as a useful model for public schools (Bryk, Lee, & Holland, 1993; LePore & Warren, 1997; McEwen, Knipe, & Gallagher, 1997).

Importance of Determining Which School Paradigms Work Best and How They Can Learn from One Another

In the past two decades the debate has become even more complex as educators and politicians have considered the possibility that a greater level of competition should be allowed among schools to spur greater advancement. Perhaps the most notable of these arguments was propounded by Chubb and Moe (1990) in their work *Politics, Markets, and America's Schools*. In this work, the authors ask a very logical rhetorical question. That is, why is it that educators and world leaders almost universally acknowledge that the United States has the best system of university education in the world and yet concurrently these same experts agree that the American system of public elementary and secondary schools is mediocre at best. And indeed, if one looks at the world rankings with any degree of objectivity, on this point at least Chubb and Moe are quite correct. If one examines the world rankings of universities that have been regularly disseminated out of China, Great Britain, and Germany over the past 20 years, American universities dominate the list (BBC, 2010). There is fairly strong recognition that if one states that he or she is a graduate of Harvard University, for example, it is almost equivalent to saying that one attended the best university in the world (BBC, 2010). The only real competition that Harvard, Princeton, and Yale receive for the top slots have generally come from Cambridge and Oxford in England (BBC, 2010). Equally impressive is the fact that universities such as Columbia, MIT, Stanford, Duke, Dartmouth, and Chicago are usually in the world's top six to 15 (BBC, 2010). Chubb and Moe answer their question by asserting that American public schools do not possess a good reputation because there is so little competition in the elementary and secondary school sphere when compared to universities. Technically, Chubb and Moe insist that private schools be allowed to compete against public schools but in the limitations of the real world, Presidents George H. W. Bush and Bill Clinton especially embraced the idea of competition and advocated the establishment and expansion of charter schools.

The notion that there may be better alternatives to the TPS rubric, most notably religious private schools and charter schools, has received a great deal of attention because the number of charter schools in the United States has been surging. There is an ongoing debate regarding whether students from schools using these alternatives to the TPS paradigm perform better in school. Some researchers believe there is no difference, and others assert that students from religious schools outperform public school students simply because public schools have a high percentage of low-SES and racial minority children (Baker, 1999). Moynihan (1989), however, presents evidence suggesting that the racial distribution of students in religious schools is similar to that found in public schools.

As important as this debate is, there has never been a meta-analysis undertaken that collectively considers TPS, public charter schools, and faith-based schools. A meta-analysis statistically combines all the relevant existing studies on a given subject to determine the aggregated results of said research. A meta-analysis is a quantitative approach to statistically summarizing the body of research on a given topic and therefore is extremely practical and useful for educators, academics, government leaders, parents, and students who certainly do not have time to read all of these individual studies but want insight into what the overall body of research indicates. Clearly, enough studies have been done on these educational paradigms to make a meta-analysis on this topic very valuable.

Three Research Questions Addressed in This Study

Therefore, three research questions that are especially pertinent to parents, educators, and government leaders will rest at the heart of this meta-analysis. The first analysis determines the effect sizes by school types (i.e., religious private and public charter versus traditional public schools). This approach does not utilize sophisticated controls that might change the effect sizes; instead, it is designed to obtain a sense of what the overall effects of these schools actually is (research question 1). The second analysis assesses effect sizes using sophisticated controls to get an idea of the influence of these schools when certain other factors such as socioeconomic status, race, and individual history are considered in the analysis (research question 2). The third analysis examines the association between practices in these schools with student achievement (research question 3).

Methods

Analytical Approach

This meta-analysis examines the relationship between the types of school (TPS, religious, and public charter) and K-12 student achievement. The procedures employed to conduct the meta-analysis are outlined under this heading ("Analytical Approach") and the following headings: "Data Collection Method," "Statistical Methods and

Effect Size Statistic," "Study Quality Rating," and "Defining of Variables." Three research questions were addressed. The first analysis determined the effect sizes school types (i.e., religious private and public charter versus traditional public schools) (research question 1). The second analysis assessed if effect sizes different for studies using sophisticated versus less sophisticated controls (research question 2). The third analysis examined the association between practices in these schools with student achievement (research question 3).

Each study included in this meta-analysis met the following criteria:

1. It needed to examine school type in a way that could be conceptually and statistically distinguished from other primary variables under consideration. For example, if a study examined schools generically or if two types of schools were somehow combined (e.g., semireligious with charter), and the influence of school type could not be statistically isolated from the other features, the study was not included in the analysis.

2. It needed to include a sufficient amount of statistical information to determine effect sizes. That is, a study needed to contain enough information so that test statistics, such as those resulting from a t-test, analysis of variance, and so forth, were either provided in the study or could be determined from the means and measures of variance listed in the study.

3. If the study used a control group, it had to qualify as a true control group and therefore be a fair and accurate means of comparison. Moreover, if the research utilized a control group at some times but not others, only the former comparisons were included in the meta-analysis.

4. The study could be a published or unpublished study. This was to reduce the likelihood of publication bias.

Due to the nature of the criteria listed, qualitative studies were not included in the analysis. Although qualitative studies are definitely valuable, they are difficult to code for quantitative purposes, and any attempt to do so might bias the results of the meta-analysis.

Data Collection Method (Coding and Rater Reliability)

To obtain the studies used in the meta-analysis, a search was performed using every major social science research database (e.g., Psych Info, ERIC, Dissertation Abstracts International,

Wilson Periodicals, Sociological Abstracts), totaling 60 databases, to find studies examining the relationship between school type (TPS, religious, and public charter) and the academic achievement of children from prekindergarten through twelfth grade. The search terms included *religious schools, achievement, Christian schools, Evangelical schools, Jewish schools, Lutheran schools, charter schools, competition, public school choice, magnet schools, community schools, neighborhood schools, Protestant schools, Islamic schools, raising achievement, faith-based schools, socioeconomic, urban schools, urban education,* and many other similar terms. Reference sections from journal articles on parental involvement programs were also examined to find additional research articles. Emails were also sent to each of the education department chairs of the over 100 Research 1 universities in the United States asking them if there were any faculty in their department who had either recently completed or were just about to complete a study examining the relationship between school type and student achievement and behavior. Although this comprehensive search yielded hundreds of articles and papers on school types and achievement, nearly all of these articles were not quantitative in nature. The research team obtained a total of over 148 studies that addressed the relationship under study and found 90 studies that had a sufficient degree of quantitative data to include in this meta-analysis.

A number of different characteristics of each study were included for use in this study. These characteristics included (a) report characteristics, (b) sample characteristics, (c) intervention type, (d) the research design, (e) the grade level or age of the students, (f) the outcome and predictor variables, (g) the length (in weeks) of the school type assessment, (h) the attrition rate, and (i) the estimate of the relationship between school type and academic achievement. Two coders, who had been coding for at least 10 years, coded the studies on these characteristics and had 96 percent agreement on their coding of the following study characteristics.

Report characteristics. Each study entry began with the name of the author of the study, then the year the study was recorded, followed by the type of research report. Research reports were defined either as a journal article; book; book chapter; dissertation; master's thesis; government, school, or private report; conference paper; or other type of report.

Sample characteristics included the number of students sampled, their locations, and how they were selected, for example, via random selection, stratified random selection, or advertisement.

Intervention type. The experimental or procedural manipulation used, if any, was recorded to determine the effects of school type on student achievement.

Research design. The studies in this meta-analysis were categorized into three basic types of designs. First noted were the studies that employed some type of manipulations to assess the effects of the three school types under study.

The second type of design included studies that took cross-sectional measures of the effect of a school type without utilizing any type of manipulation. The third type of design involved the calculation of a correlation coefficient between the school type and student educational outcomes.

For studies that employed a manipulation to measure the effects of school type program, the following were recorded: (a) the length, frequency, duration, and total number of training sessions; (b) the method of training (workshop, individual meetings, phone calls, videotape, email communication, newsletter); (c) the type of behavioral or achievement-related outcome measure (e.g., standardized achievement test, nonstandardized achievement test, class grades); (d) the unit of analysis (individual student or classroom) at which the effect size was calculated; and (e) the magnitude of the relationship between school type and student achievement.

For the cross-sectional studies and correlation studies, if they were available, the following were also recorded: (a) the socioeconomic status of participants in the sample and (b) the types of behavioral and academic measures that were used.

The grade level or age of the students was coded, including means and standard deviations when they were available.

The outcome and predictor variables from each study were coded to include the different ways that achievement was measured.

Attrition rate. When available, the attrition rate of each study was coded.

The estimate of the relationship between school type and student achievement. The process of the effect size estimation is described in the next section.

Statistical Methods and the Effect Size Statistic

Effect sizes were computed from data in such forms as t-tests, F tests, p levels, frequencies, and r-values via conversion formulas provided by Glass and colleagues (Glass, McGaw, & Smith, 1981). When results were not significant, studies sometimes reported only a significance level. In the unusual case that the direction of these not significant results was not available, the effect size was calculated to be zero.

For studies with manipulations, I used the standardized mean difference to estimate the effect of school type. The d-index (Cohen, 1988) is a scale-free measure of the separation between two group means. Calculating the d-index for any comparison involves dividing the difference between the two group means by either their average standard deviation or by the standard deviation of the control group. In the meta-analysis, I subtracted the experimental group mean from the control group mean and divided the difference by their average standard deviation. Hence, positive effect sizes indicated that various factors were successful in reducing the achievement gap. As a supplement to these analyses, the Hedges' "g" measure of effect size was used (Hedges, 1981). Since it employed the pooled standard deviation in the denominator, it customarily provided a more conservative estimate of effect size. Hedges also provided a correction factor that helped to adjust for the impact of small samples.

For studies that involved cross-sectional measures of the relationship between school type and achievement, the following procedures were undertaken. For those studies that attempted to statistically equate students on other variables, the preferred measure of relationship strength was the standardized beta-weight, b. These parameters were determined from the output of multiple regression analyses. If beta-weights could not be obtained from study reports, the most similar measures of effect (e.g., unstandardized regression weights) were retrieved.

For studies that involved cross-sectional measures but included no attempt to statistically equate students on third variables, the results from the t-tests, F tests, and correlation studies provided by the researchers in the study were used. Probability values were used as a basis for computation only if the researchers did not supply any information on the test statistics just mentioned.

Calculating average effect sizes. A weighting procedure was used to calculate average effect sizes across all the comparisons. First, each independent effect size was multiplied by the inverse of its variance. The sum of these products was then divided by the sum of the inverses. Then, 95 percent confidence intervals were calculated. As Hedges and Vevea (1998) recommend, all the analyses were conducted using fixed-error assumptions in one analysis and applied random-error assumptions in the other. The numerical results listed in this chapter are based on the more conservative random-error assumptions, unless otherwise noted. However, it was noted in the text when the fixed-error results differed considerably from those using the random-error assumptions.

If there was more than one effect size presented in the results section, the effect size that was chosen was based on that which referred to: (a) the overall sample and (b) the purest measure of school type. In the case of results that included clear statistical outliers, the presence of these outliers was acknowledged and then supplemental analyses were run without such an outlier to estimate the degree to which the presence of an outlier might have affected the results.

Tests of homogeneity were completed on the school type variables to gain a sense of the consistency of specific school type measures across studies.

Study Quality Rating

Two researchers coded the studies independently for quality, the presence of randomization, and whether the schools being examined satisfied definitional criteria for that school type. Study quality and the use of random samples were graded on a 0 (lowest) to 3 (highest) scale. Quality was determined using the following:

(1) Did it use randomization of assignment? (2) Did it avoid mono-method bias? (3) Did it avoid mono-operation bias? (4) Did it avoid selection bias? (5) Did it use a specific definition of school type?

We calculated inter-rater reliability by computing percentage of agreement on school type, issues of randomization, and quality of the study. Inter-rater reliability was 100 percent for school type, 92 percent for the quality of the study, 95 percent for randomization, 96 percent for avoiding mono-method bias, 94 percent for avoiding mono-operation bias, 92 percent for avoiding selection bias.

Two supplementary analyses were done to include first, only those studies with quality ratings of 2 and 3 and second, only those studies with quality ratings of 1–3.

Defining Variables

For the purposes of this study, attending a *religious school (faith-based school)* was defined as a student attending a private school that was sponsored by a religious group and was defined to meet certain religious and educational goals. A *charter school* was defined as a public state-legislated school that operated independently from the local school board and under a separate charter.

Regarding the factors that will be used to assess some of the distinguishing factors (strengths and weaknesses) between public and religious schools, the following definitions were utilized.

Taking harder courses. Defined as students being more likely to take higher-level courses such as Advanced Placement (AP) and honors courses, when compared to students at their same academic levels.

High expectations. Defined teachers in this manner when they anticipated that students could achieve and accomplish at higher levels, when compared to teachers who instructed students at the same academic levels in other schools.

Achievement gap. For the purposes of this study, the achievement gap was defined as the difference in academic achievement that exists between the average white student and the average African American and/or Latino student.

Classroom flexibility. The degree to which students reported that they could engage in classroom discussions that took place in class or could easily choose electives as their course choices.

Types of Analyses and Models Utilized

Two sets of statistical procedures were done to distinguish between studies. First, one analysis distinguished between those analyses that included sophisticated controls in their analyses (e.g., socioeconomic status, race, and gender) and those studies that did not. This was the primary way that studies were distinguished when comparing school types. Second, supplementary analyses were undertaken to distinguish between two models researchers utilized in their studies. The first model, Model A, included all the studies that examined the impact of religious versus public schools. The second model, Model B, looked at a similar sample of studies but excluded those studies controlling for some of the educational emphases that are often used to explain differences in achievement. These studies were excluded in Model B because if a study controlled for some of the specific educational emphases that often explain the academic differences, they would tend to understate differences that exist between religious and public schools. Specifically, studies were excluded from Model B if they controlled for whether a school had a high percentage of students on the academic track and if they controlled for parental involvement. The problem with controlling for these variables is that many social scientists believe the fact that religious schools insist that more of their students be on the academic track and that parents be strongly involved in education are two of the reasons religious students outperform their counterparts in public schools (Gamoran, 1992; Sander, 1996). Although for the purposes of this meta-analysis academics were the primary focus, behavioral variables were also examined.

Results

Table 2.1 lists the year of the study, some descriptive information, and overall effect size for studies examining the impact of religious schools and charter schools, versus their traditional public school (TPS) counterparts, on academic achievement. The studies are distinguished on the basis of whether the study examined the effects of religious schools or charter schools (or both), when compared to public schools and also whether or not they included or not sophisticated controls. Table 2.1 lists the effects sizes of the 90 studies in descending order. Table 2.1 includes the findings for both research questions 1 and 2, where applicable, in the same table.

The results presented here used analyses based on random-error assumptions. The rationale for presenting these results rather than those using fixed-error assumptions is to utilize analyses that will yield more conservative effect sizes. As one would expect, the analyses based on fixed-error assumptions yielded somewhat larger effect sizes in the case of religious schools, although there was virtually no difference in the case of charter schools. Table 2.1 indicates that the effects for religious schools ranged from +.68 to −.07 standard deviation units, with only one of the studies indicating a negative relationship between attending a faith-based school and educational outcomes. The effects for charter schools showed a considerably greater variation, spanning from +.75 to −.87 standard deviation units. In the case of charter schools, 53 percent of the studies indicated a negative

Table 2.1 List of Studies Used in the Meta-Analysis for Religious Schools, Public Charter Schools, and Traditional Public Schools (TPS), the Year of the Study, the Effects, and the Study Distinctions for the Various Studies

Study	Year	Effect Sizes for Religious Schools without Sophisticated Controls	Effect Sizes for Religious Schools with Sophisticated Controls	Effect Sizes for Charter Schools without Sophisticated Controls	Effect Sizes for Charter Schools with Sophisticated Controls	Study Distinctions
Fass-Holmes et al.	1996			+.75		Examined San Diego charter schools
Graetz	1990	+.68				Australian study of over 3,000 students
Keith & Page	1985	+.58	+.31			Examined children of color
McEwan	2001	+.57				South American study
McDonald et al.	2007			+.54		Examined 3 inner city sites
Lee & Bryk	1989	+.50	+.10			Examined HSB Data Set
Lee	1986	+.44	+.10			Examined HSB Data Set
Hoffer	1998	+.44	+.04			Examined NELS Data Set
Lee	1985a	+.38	+.12			Examined HSB Data Set
Hoffer, Greeley, & Coleman	1985	+.36	+.20			Examined HSB Data Set
Alexander & Pallas	1983	+.36	+.20			Examined HSB & NLS Data Sets
Jeynes	2002b	+.35	+.19			Examined NELS Data Set
Raudenbush & Bryk	1986	+.33	+.27			Examined HSB Data Set
Lee & Smith	1993	+.33				Examined NLS Data Set
Hoffer, Greeley, & Coleman	1987	+.32	+.18			Examined HSB Data Set

(continued)

Table 2.1 *(Continued)*

Study	Year	Effect Sizes for Religious Schools without Sophisticated Controls	Effect Sizes for Religious Schools with Sophisticated Controls	Effect Sizes for Charter Schools without Sophisticated Controls	Effect Sizes for Charter Schools with Sophisticated Controls	Study Distinctions
Coleman, Hoffer, & Kilgore	1981	+.30	+.20			Examined HSB Data Set
Coleman, Hoffer, & Kilgore	1982	+.28	+.19			Examined nationwide data sets
Shokraii	1997	+.26				Comparisons made in Washington D.C.
Goldberger & Cain	1982	+.26				Examined HSB Data Set
Regnerus	2000		+.25			Examined subset of NELS Data Set
Lee, Chen, & Smerdon	1996	+.25				Examined NELS Data Set
Lauren	2009			+.23	+.07	Examined Chicago charter schools
Taylor et al.	1994	+.23				Examined African American students
Lee & Stewart	1989	+.22				Examined NAEP Data Set
Bauernfeind & Blumenfeld	1963		+.22			Matched students
Lubienski & Lubienski	2006	+.22	+.03	−.06	+.05	NAEP Data Set
Prince	1960	+.21				Assessed 1,197 High school freshman & seniors
Johnson	1999	+.20				Examined African American students
Bennett	2009			+.20		Examined Arizona charter schools at 4 grade levels

(continued)

Table 2.1 *(Continued)*

Study	Year	Effect Sizes for Religious Schools without Sophisticated Controls	Effect Sizes for Religious Schools with Sophisticated Controls	Effect Sizes for Charter Schools without Sophisticated Controls	Effect Sizes for Charter Schools with Sophisticated Controls	Study Distinctions
Jeynes	2002e		+.19			Examined NELS Data Set
Lee	1985b	+.18				Examined NAEP Data Set
Perie, Vanneman, & Goldstein	2005	+.17				Examined NAEP Data Set
Weaver	1970	+.16				Examined Latino students
Witte, Wolf, Dean & Carlson	2011			+.16	+.05	Examined Milwaukee charter schools
Marsch & Grayson	1990		+.16			Examined HSB Data Set
Sutton & de Diveira	1995	+.15				Examines critical thinking skills
Kamienski	2011			+.14		Examined Chicago charter schools
Riordan	1985	+.14	+.12			Examined NLS Data Set
Wolf et al.	2009			+.13		Examined students who participated in DC Opportunity Scholarship Program
Booker et al.	2007			+.13		Examined Texas charter schools
Mok & Flynn	1998		+.12			Studied a large sample of Catholic schools in Australia
Witte et al.	2007			+.11		Examined Milwaukee charter schools
Brutsaert	1998		+.10			Examined elementary schools in Belgium

(continued)

Table 2.1 *(Continued)*

Study	Year	Effect Sizes for Religious Schools without Sophisticated Controls	Effect Sizes for Religious Schools with Sophisticated Controls	Effect Sizes for Charter Schools without Sophisticated Controls	Effect Sizes for Charter Schools with Sophisticated Controls	Study Distinctions
Bryk & Thum	1998		+.10			Examined HSB Data Set
Marsch	1991		+.10			Examined HSB Data Set
Beltz	1980	+.10				Focused on Seventh Day Adventist
Sass	2006				+.08	Examined Florida charter schools
Alexander & Pallas	1985	+.08				Examined HSB Data Set
Schindler	2008	+.08				European study
Myers	2007	+.08				Examined 8th graders
Corten & Dronkers	2006	+.08				European study
Witte, Wolf & Dean	2011				+.06	Examined Milwaukee charter schools
Hoxby	2004				+.06	Compared charter and public schools nationwide in comparable neighborhoods
Bettinger	2005			+.06	−.20	Examined Michigan charter schools
Bodenhausen	1989	+.05				Examined 272 schools in California
Williams & Carpenter	1990		+.05			Australian study
Willms	1985		+.05			Examined HSB Data Set
Fitzgerald	2000			+.04	+.01	Examined Colorado charter schools

(continued)

Table 2.1 (*Continued*)

Study	Year	Effect Sizes for Religious Schools without Sophisticated Controls	Effect Sizes for Religious Schools with Sophisticated Controls	Effect Sizes for Charter Schools without Sophisticated Controls	Effect Sizes for Charter Schools with Sophisticated Controls	Study Distinctions
Lee & Smith	1995		+.03			Examined NELS Data Set
Morgan	1983		+.03			Examined NLS Data Sets
Miron	2005			+.03		Examined charter schools in Connecticut
Willms	1982		+.03			Examined HSB Data Set
Mora & Escardibul	2008	+.03				European study
Noell	1982		+.02			Examined HSB Data Set
Barr et al.	2006			+.02		Examined charter schools in Newark
Carpenter	1985		+.02			Examined religious schools in Australia
Garcia, Barber, & Molnar	2009			+.02		Examined Arizona charter schools
Sassenrath, Croce, & Penaloza	1984		+.00			Sample of 98 matched students
Plucker, Makel, & Rapp	2007			.00		Examined Georgia charter schools
Berends et al.	2010			.00	−.05	Examined charter schools in several states
Schneider	1965	.00				Examined 214 students' college performance
Young & Fraser	1990		.00			Study done in Western Australia
Gleason et al.	2001			−.01		Examined charter schools in 15 states

(*continued*)

Table 2.1 *(Continued)*

Study	Year	Effect Sizes for Religious Schools without Sophisticated Controls	Effect Sizes for Religious Schools with Sophisticated Controls	Effect Sizes for Charter Schools without Sophisticated Controls	Effect Sizes for Charter Schools with Sophisticated Controls	Study Distinctions
Zimmer et al.	2008			−.01		Examined Philadelphia charter schools
Imberman	2011a			−.04		Examined both academic and behavioral factors
Zimmer & Buddin	2007				−.04	Examined California charter schools
Miron, Nelson, & Risley	2002			−.04		Examined Pennsylvania charter schools
Bifulco & Ladd	2006			−.05		Examined North Carolina charter schools
Lange et al.	1998			−.06		Examined Minnesota charter schools
Robelen	2008			−.07		Examined NAEP data
Imberman	2011b			−.07		Examined both academic and behavioral factors
Payne & Ford	1977	−.07				European sample
Lubienski & Lubienski	2007				−.08	Examined 300,000 4th & 8th grade students
Nelson & Van Meter	2003			−.09		Examined charter schools run by Mosaica
DeLuca & Hinshaws	2006			−.12		Compared 159 schools
Braun, Jenkins, & Gregg	2006			−.17	−.14	Examined NAEP data set

(continued)

Table 2.1 (*Continued*)

Study	Year	Effect Sizes for Religious Schools without Sophisticated Controls	Effect Sizes for Religious Schools with Sophisticated Controls	Effect Sizes for Charter Schools without Sophisticated Controls	Effect Sizes for Charter Schools with Sophisticated Controls	Study Distinctions
Barnett	2011			−.21		Examined Ohio charter schools at 3 grade levels
Eberts & Hollenbeck	2001			−.22		Examined Michigan charter schools
Buddin & Zimmer	2005			−.25	−.13	Examined SAT9 data
Hinojosa	2009			−.87		Examined Texas elementary charter schools

association between charter schools and education outcomes, when compared to students attending traditional public schools (TPS). The difference between the highest and lowest effects for religious schools (.75 standard deviation units) was considerably smaller than for charter schools (1.62 standard deviation units).

In Table 2.2 are listed findings regarding the studies included in this meta-analysis, as well as the correlations between the quality of the study and whether a random sample was used on the one hand and the year the study was done and the overall effect ("d") on the other. The results listed in Table 2.2 indicate that the mean year of the studies examined was 1995.1. The average quality rating for all the studies examined, using the 0 (lowest) to 3 (highest) scale was 2.17. This rating would indicate a pretty high average quality rating, with 1.5 considered about average. The ratings for the extent a random sample was used (which was also one component of the quality rating) was 1.81 for the studies overall. Although numerically speaking, higher-quality studies were slightly associated with positive effect sizes, this amount (.12, p > .05), did not reach statistical significance. The correlation between using a random sample and positive effect sizes was also not statistically significant (.06, p > .05).

Table 2.3 indicates the effects for students attending religious schools and public charter schools, examining academic achievement

overall and standardized tests specifically, as well as behavioral outcomes. All of the effect size measures for religious schools were
statistically significant. In contrast, none of the effect sizes for public
charter schools were statistically significant in *either* the positive *or* negative direction. For both U.S. and foreign schools combined, the effect
sizes for religious schools for both Models A and B were .26 standard
deviation units for all measures of academic achievement combined

Table 2.2 Means for Measures Assessing the Quality of Study, whether a
Random Sample Was Used, Year of Study, and Sample Size for the 90
Studies Included in the Meta-Analysis

	Mean	Number of Studies in Each Category	Range	Correlation Coefficient
Year of Study	1995.1	2002+ = 39 1992–2001 = 18 1982–1991 = 26 1972–1981 = 3 before 1972 = 4	1960–2011	
Quality of Study	2.17	3 = 47 2 = 18 1 = 18 0 = 7	0–3	
Random Sample Used	1.81	3 = 25 2 = 30 1 = 28 0 = 7	0–3	
Correlation between Quality of Study and Effect Size				.12
Correlation between Study Year and Effect Size				.06

Note for correlation coefficients: * = p < .05, ** = p < .01. Otherwise, the correlation
coefficient was not statistically significant

and .27 for standardized tests specifically (p < .01). For American schools alone, the effect sizes were somewhat higher. For both Models A and B, for overall achievement, the effect sizes were .28 and for all measures of academic achievement combined and they were .29 standard deviation units for standardized tests specifically (p < .01). For those studies that used sophisticated controls, the effect sizes were smaller but were still statistically significant at the .05 level of probability. For U.S. and foreign schools combined, the effect sizes for religious schools for Models B and A were .14 (p < .05) and .12 (p < .05) standard deviation units, respectively, for all measures of academic achievement combined and .15 (p < .05) and .13 (p < .05) for standardized tests. For U.S. schools alone, the effect sizes were somewhat higher. In this case, the effect sizes for religious schools for Models B and A were .15 (p < .05) and .13 (p < .05) standard deviation units, respectively, for all measures of academic achievement combined and .16 (p < .05) and .14 (p < .05) for standardized tests.

Analyses were also done excluding the two studies undertaken by the author. These studies both involved utilizing the National Education Longitudinal Study (NELS) data set. The exclusion of these two studies did not affect the statistical significance levels of the meta-analysis and had little or no impact on the effect sizes, with the smallest impact being .00 of a standard deviation unit change and the largest impact being .01 of a standard deviation unit change. In the case of analyses that did not include sophisticated controls, for U.S. and foreign schools combined, the effect sizes for religious schools for Model B were .26 standard deviation units for all measures of academic achievement combined and .26 for standardized tests specifically (p < .01). When sophisticated controls were included, the effect sizes were for all measures of academic achievement combined and .13 (p < .05) and .14 (p < .05) for standardized tests.

For behavioral outcomes, students from faith-based schools were more likely to show more positive behavior than their counterparts in traditional public schools. For those studies that did not utilize sophisticated controls, the effect size was .35 (p < .01) of a standard deviation unit. For those studies that did utilize sophisticated controls, the effect size was .34 (p < .01) of a standard deviation unit.

In the case of charter schools, no statistically significant differences emerged. All the studies that were done on charter schools focused on U.S. schools. When the studies did not use sophisticated controls, the effect sizes were near zero, at .01, and when there were sophisticated controls employed, the effect sizes were slightly negative, but not to a statistically significant degree, at −.03.

Table 2.4 reflects the same analyses undertaken in Table 3 except includes only those studies rated 2–3 in quality. Analyses were also undertaken, including only those studies rated 1–3 in quality, but as one might expect, because there were so few studies rated 0 in quality that the results were almost identical to those presented in Table 2.3. Using the higher quality (2–3) studies, the effect sizes for religious schools were somewhat higher than those in Table 2.3. All of them rose in the range of .01 to .02 standard deviation units. But none of them rose to a degree sufficient to increase the level of statistical significance. For U.S. and foreign schools combined, where sophisticated controls were not employed, the effect sizes for religious schools for Model B was .28 standard deviation units for all measures of academic achievement combined and .29 for standardized tests specifically (p < .01). For U.S. schools alone, the effect sizes were somewhat higher. For Model B, for overall achievement, the effect size was .30 and for standardized tests specifically it was .31 standard deviation units (p < .01). For U.S. and foreign schools combined, studies that used sophisticated controls for Model B yielded an effect size of .15 (p < .05) for all measures of academic achievement combined and .16 (p < .05) standard deviation units for standardized tests. For U.S. school studies that used sophisticated controls, for Model B, the effects were .16 (p < .05) for all measures of academic achievement combined and .17 (p < .05) standard deviation units for standardized tests.

For behavioral outcomes, assessing only the studies rated 2 and 3 in the analysis did not change any of the effect sizes. The effect sizes remained .35 (p < .01) of a standard deviation unit for those analyses that did not utilize sophisticated controls and .34 (p < .01) of a standard deviation unit for those studies that did use sophisticated controls.

For charter schools, including only the studies rated 2 and 3 in the analysis did not change any of the effect sizes, when rounded to the nearest hundredth. This is largely because so many of the studies of charter schools were rated 2 and were similar to each other in quality.

Table 2.5 addresses the results of comparisons that are even more specific than those focused on in Tables 2.3 and 2.4. Table 2.5 examines comparisons at the elementary and secondary level, as well as for African American and Latino students. The pattern for Table 2.5 was

Table 2.3 Effect Sizes for Religious School Students and Public Charter School Students Compared to Their Counterparts in Traditional Public Schools (TPS) for the 90 Studies in the Meta-Analysis; Effect Sizes Include Those for Overall Achievement and for Standardized Tests

	Religious Schools Overall Academic Achievement	Religious Schools Achievement on Standardized Tests	Charter Schools Overall Academic Achievement	Charter Schools Achievement on Standardized Tests
U.S. and Foreign Without Sophisticated Controls Using Model B	.26** (.07, .45)	.27** (.07, .47)	.01[a]	.01[a]
U.S. and Foreign Without Sophisticated Controls Using Model A	.26** (.06, .46)	.27** (.07, .47)	.01[a]	.01[a]
American Schools Without Sophisticated Controls Using Model B	.28** (.08, .48)	.29** (.08, .50)	.01[a]	.01[a]
American Schools Without Sophisticated Controls Using Model A	.28** (.07, .49)	.29** (.08, .50)	.01[a]	.01[a]
U.S. and Foreign Using Sophisticated Controls Using Model B	.14* (.02, .26)	.15* (.03, .27)	−.03[a]	−.03[a]
U.S. and Foreign Using Sophisticated Controls Using Model B	.12* (.01, .23)	.13* (.02, .24)	−.03[a]	−.03[a]
U.S. and Foreign Using Sophisticated Controls Using Model A	.15* (.03, .27)	.16* (.03, .29)	−.03[a]	−.03[a]

American Schools Using Sophisticated Controls Using Model B	.13* (.01, .25)	.14* (.02, .26)	−.03[a]
American Schools Using Sophisticated Controls Using Model A	.26** (.06, .46)	.26** (.06, .46)	.01[a]
U.S. and Foreign Without Sophisticated Controls Using Model B Excluding author's 2 studies	.13* (.01, .25)	.14* (.02, .26)	−.03[a]
U.S. and Foreign Using Sophisticated Controls Using Model B Excluding author's 2 studies	.35** (.11, .59)	.34** (.10, .58)	Not applicable
Behavioral Measures		Not applicable	Not applicable

Note: a = All the charter schools were in the United States.
* = $p < .05$
** = $p < .01$

Table 2.4 Effect Sizes (ES) for Religious School Students and Public Charter School Students Compared to Their Counterparts in Traditional Public Schools (TPS) for the Studies Rated 2–3 in Quality ($N = 65$); Effect Sizes Include Those for Overall Achievement and for Standardized Tests

	Religious Schools Overall Academic Achievement	Religious Schools Achievement on Standardized Tests	Charter Schools Overall Academic Achievement	Charter Schools Achievement on Standardized Tests
U.S. and Foreign Without Sophisticated Controls Using Model B	.28** (.08, .48)	.29** (.09, .49)	.01[a]	.01[a]
U.S. and Foreign Without Sophisticated Controls Using Model A	.28** (.07, .49)	.29** (.08, .50)	.01[a]	.01[a]
American Schools Without Sophisticated Controls Using Model B	.30** (.09, .51)	.31** (.09, .53)	.01[a]	.01[a]
American Schools Without Sophisticated Controls Using Model A	.30** (.09, .51)	.31** (.09, .53)	.01[a]	.01[a]
U.S. and Foreign Using Sophisticated Controls Using Model B	.15* (.02, .28)	.16* (.03, .29)	−.03[a]	−.03[a]
U.S. and Foreign Using Sophisticated Controls Using Model A	.13* (.01, .25)	.14* (.02, .26)	−.03[a]	−.03[a]

American Schools Using Sophisticated Controls Using Model B	.16* (.03, .29)	.17* (.03, .31)	−.03[a]	−.03[a]
American Schools Using Sophisticated Controls Using Model A	.14* (.01, .27)	.15* (.02, .28)	−.03[a]	−.03[a]
U.S. and Foreign Without Sophisticated Controls Using Model B excluding author's 2 studies	.28** (.06, .50)	.29** (.06, .50)	.01[a]	.01[a]
U.S. and Foreign Using Sophisticated Controls Using Model B Excluding author's 2 studies	.14* (.01, .27)	.15* (.02, .28)	−.03[a]	−.03[a]
Behavioral Measures	.35** (.11, .59)	.34** (.10, .58)	Not applicable	Not applicable

Note: a = All the charter schools were in the United States
$*$ = $p < .05$
$**$ = $p < .01$

Table 2.5 Effect Sizes for Religious School Students and Public Charter School Students, at Different Grade Levels and for Different Ethnicities, Compared to Their Counterparts in Traditional Public Schools for the 90 Studies in the Meta-Analysis. Results Listed for Overall Achievement and for Standardized Tests

	Religious Schools Overall Academic Achievement	Religious Schools Achievement on Standardized Tests	Charter Schools Overall Academic Achievement	Charter Schools Achievement on Standardized Tests
American Elementary Schools without Sophisticated Controls using Model B	.27[**] (.07, .47)	.28[**] (.08, .48)	−.04[a]	−.04[a]
American Elementary Schools without Sophisticated Controls using Model A	.27[**] (.07, .47)	.28[**] (.08, .48)	−.04[a]	−.04[a]
American Secondary Schools without Sophisticated Controls using Model B	.29[**] (.09, .49)	.30[**] (.09, .51)	.06[a]	.06[a]
American Secondary Schools without Sophisticated Controls using Model A	.29[**] (.09, .49)	.30[**] (.09, .51)	.06[a]	.06[a]
American Elementary Schools with Sophisticated Controls using Model B	.14[*] (.03, .25)	.15[*] (.03, .27)	−.06[a]	−.06[a]

58

American Elementary Schools with Sophisticated Controls using Model A	.12[*] (.01, .23)	.13[*] (.02, .24)	–.06[a]
American Secondary Schools with Sophisticated Controls using Model B	.16[*] (.03, .29)	.17[*] (.03, .31)	.00[a]
American Secondary Schools with Sophisticated Controls using Model A	.14[*] (.01, .27)	.15[*] (.01, .29)	.00[a]
African American and Latino Students without Sophisticated Controls using Model B	.35[**] (.11, .59)	.39[**] (.12, .66)	.01[a]
African American and Latino Students with Sophisticated Controls using Model B	.18[*] (.03, .33)	.21[*] (.06, .36)	–.03[a]

Note: a = All the charter schools were in the United States
[*] = $p < .05$
[**] = $p < .01$

similar to that of Tables 2.3 and 2.4 in that all of the effect size measures for religious schools were statistically significant. In contrast, none of the effect sizes for public charter schools were statistically significant in *either* the positive *or* negative direction. Numerically speaking, the effect sizes for secondary school students attending religious schools were slightly higher than for those attending elementary schools, but these differences were not statistically significant. For U.S. elementary schools, when sophisticated controls were not used, the effect sizes for religious schools for both Models A and B were .27 standard deviation units for all measures of academic achievement combined and .28 for standardized tests specifically (p < .01). For U.S. secondary schools, the effect sizes were somewhat higher. For both Models A and B for overall achievement, the effect sizes were .29, and for standardized tests specifically, they were .30 standard deviation units (p < .01). For those studies that used sophisticated controls, the effect sizes were smaller and were still statistically significant, but at the .05 level of probability. For elementary schools, the effect sizes for religious schools for Models B and A were .14 (p < .05) and .12 (p < .05) standard deviation units, respectively, for all measures of academic achievement combined and .15 (p < .05) and .13 (p < .05) for standardized tests. For secondary schools, the effect sizes were somewhat higher. In this case, the effect sizes for religious schools for Models B and A were .16 (p < .05) and .14 (p < .05) standard deviation units, respectively, for all measures of academic achievement combined and .17 (p < .05) and .15 (p < .05) for standardized tests.

Among African American and Latino students, the effects sizes for attending religious schools were .35 (p < .01) for overall academic achievement and .39 (p < .01) for standardized tests, when there were not sophisticated controls employed. When sophisticated controls were applied, the effects sizes for African American and Latino students attending religious schools rather than public schools were .18 (p < .05) for overall academic achievement and .21 (p < .05) for standardized tests.

In the case of charter schools, once again, no statistically significant differences emerged. When no sophisticated controls were employed, the effect sizes for elementary and secondary schools were −.04 (p > .05) and .06 (p > .05), respectively. When sophisticated controls were used, the effect sizes for elementary and secondary schools were −.06 (p > .05) and .00 (p > .05), respectively.

Table 2.6 Effect Sizes Indicating Strengths and Weaknesses of Religious Private Schools and Traditional Public Schools for the 90 Studies

Variables Examined	Overall Effect Size	Effect Size for without Sophisticated Controls	Effect Size for without Sophisticated Controls
Taking harder courses	.19*	.22*	.17*
High expectations	.20*	.23*	.17*
Reduction of Achievement Gap	.10*	.15*	.07
Classroom flexibility	−.15*	−.16*	−.14*

Note:
* = $p < .05$
** = $p < .01$

The third research question regarding the association between practices in faith-based and public schools is addressed in Table 2.6. For three of the four practices examined, the effect sizes favored students attending faith-based private schools. When sophisticated controls were not used in the study, the effect sizes favoring children from faith-based private schools were .22 (p < .05) for taking harder courses, .23 (p < .05) for teachers having high expectations of their students, and .15 (p < .05) for a reduction in the achievement gap (between white students and African American and Latino students). When sophisticated controls were used in the study, the effect sizes favoring children from faith-based private schools were .17 (p < .05) for taking harder courses and .20 (p < .05) for teachers having high expectations of their students. The effect size for a reduction in the achievement gap was no longer statistically significant at .07 (p > .05), although it was numerically in the same direction as the effect size without the use of sophisticated controls. For all the studies combined, the effect sizes favoring children from faith-based private schools were .19 (p < .05) for taking harder courses, .20 (p < .05) for teachers having high expectations of their students, and .10 (p < .05) for a reduction in the achievement gap.

In contrast, the results for classroom flexibility, as defined in the "Methods" section, showed an advantage for traditional public school (TPS) students when compared to their counterparts attending faith-based private schools. When sophisticated controls were not used in the study, the effect size favoring children from public schools was −.16 (p < .05). When sophisticated controls were used in the study and for all the studies combined, the results were similar at −.14 (p < .05) and −.15 (p < .05), respectively.

Discussion

The results of the study suggest rather mixed results for schools that are not traditional public schools (TPS). This meta-analysis indicates that students who attend religious schools perform better than their counterparts who are in public schools. They achieve better both in terms of academic and behavioral outcomes at statistically significant levels. In contrast, youth attending charter schools on average did not do any better than their counterparts in traditional public schools.

First and Second Research Questions

The findings for the first research question indicated that the effect sizes for religious schools tended to be slightly over a quarter of a standard deviation unit favoring these schools in academic measures and .35 of a standard deviation unit for behavioral measures. For the second research question, which utilized sophisticated controls, the religious school advantage tended to be reduced to just below .15 standard deviation units for academic measures. However, for behavioral measures, it remained above one-third of a standard deviation unit. Statistically different results emerge even when sophisticated controls are used that consider the influence of socioeconomic status (SES), selectivity, and other factors. Although the differences vary somewhat depending on the age of the students and the measure utilized, the overall academic difference for all the studies combined appears to be approximately two-tenths of a standard deviation, favoring faith-based private schools. The behavioral measures, on the other hand, were roughly the same whether or not sophisticated controls were used, at nearly .35 of a standard deviation unit.

In contrast, statistically significant differences did not emerge when students in public charter schools were compared with children

YBP Library Services

JEYNES, WILLIAM.

SCHOOL CHOICE: A BALANCED APPROACH.

                   Cloth   246 P.
SANTA BARBARA: PRAEGER, 2014

AUTH: CALIFORNIA STATE U, LONG BEACH. COMPARATIVE
STUDY OF PUBLIC, CHARTER, & FAITH-BASED SCHOOLS.
  LCCN 2013046859
  ISBN 1440828350   **Library PO#** AP-BOOKS

	List	48.00	USD
395 NATIONAL UNIVERSITY LIBRAR	Disc	.0%	
App. Date 4/29/15 SOE-K12 8214-11	Net	48.00	USD

SUBJ: 1. SCHOOL CHOICE--U.S. 2. ALTERNATIVE
EDUCATION--U.S.

CLASS LB1027.9   DEWEY# 379.111   LEVEL ADV-AC

in traditional public schools. Not only were the differences not statistically significant, but the differences were very close to zero, and there appeared to be no hint at a general direction that for some reason might not have reached statistical significance.

These results clearly have significance in their own right, but the findings also have ramifications for the school choice debate. Over the past several decades, the school choice debate has emerged as one of the most intriguing discussions in education (Chubb & Moe, 1990; Jeynes, 2000, 2014). There is little question that two simultaneous realities caused the school choice debate to intensify. First, student achievement in public schools dropped 17 consecutive years from 1963 to 1980 (U.S. Department of Education, 2011). Second, taxes to support American public schools soared from the 1950s until the present time, far outpacing rises in inflation (U.S. Department of Education, 2011). This made private schools unaffordable for myriad citizens who otherwise would have utilized them (Glenn, 2011; Peterson, 2006; Wells, 2002). As a result, the calls increased for some relief from the tax burden imposed on American parents (Chubb & Moe, 1990; Peterson, 2006; Wells, 2002).

Moreover, this deliberation has reached such intense levels that school choice became a central topic of conversation among many of America's foremost leaders (Jeynes, 2007a; Glenn, 2011; Wells, 2002). At earlier stages in this debate, most of the focus was on the effects of youth attending faith-based schools versus those attending TPS, controlling for SES and other factors (Bryk, Lee, & Holland, 1993; Chubb & Moe, 1990; Jeynes, 2003c). Nevertheless, Presidents H. W. Bush and Clinton concluded that a strategy of limiting school choice to the public sector was an easier and less complex way of incorporating the benefits of additional competition (Jeynes, 2007a; Glenn, 2011; Wells, 2002). Consequently, the nation inaugurated a public school choice program that was designed to incorporate at least some of the recommendations of Chubb and Moe and others to make the U.S. school system more competitive. This decision, made by President Bush and especially President Clinton, caused the number of charter and magnet schools to surge (Imberman, 2011a). Concurrently, however, there was a considerable decrease in the percentage of students attending faith-based schools, particularly in the inner city (White House, 2008). Once again, parents point to the rising rates of taxation to support American public schools as one of the primary reasons for this trend (Glenn, 2011; Wells, 2002).

Given that a meta-analysis essentially quantifiably summarizes the existing body of research, there are some reasons for both encouragement and concern based on the results of this study. In terms of encouragement, there are several findings that should either inspire or at least calm those individuals most concerned about the state of American education. First, the faith-based sector appears to produce students that have pretty strong academic and behavioral outcomes. *One* should be able rejoice if any major sector of education appears to be benefiting students. Second, the faith-based sector appears to be associated with high scholastic outcomes even though it costs far less per student to school children than any of the other competing sectors.

Third, these results suggest that educators would be wise to at least investigate the possibility of expanding school choice programs to include the private sector, not only with educational and behavioral outcomes in mind, but also as a means of alleviating budgetary pressures that are commonly exerted upon various levels of government. The reality is that educational expenditures often represent about half of state and local government outlays at the state and local level (California State Government, 2006). As a result, the current budgetary crisis that pervades virtually every level of the U.S. government is indubitably impacting the quality of instruction that is available to all American students (U.S. Department of Education, 2011). Ultimately, numerous Americans could be faced with a very difficult quandary. That is, they must either become resolved to the notion that their children are bound to experience a steady decline in educational standards until America's budgetary problems are resolved, or they can open up their minds to a greater diversity of schooling options than is presently available. As difficult a situation as this might be, one can argue that it is inevitable.

Admittedly, the public sector maintains almost a monopoly on the institutional training and preparation of the nation's youth, and that is too considerable a level of dominance for any institution to be expected to uphold. In addition, in a nation that espouses diversity and variety as much as it supposedly does, there is a certain degree of irony that public educators are often so resistant to various and sundry expressions of nonpublic instruction (Glenn, 2011; Jeynes, 1999). Sometimes it takes crises to cause people to open up their minds to tolerate and embrace other ideas (Gatto, 2001; Jeynes, 2007a). Perhaps with the threat of almost perpetual budget deficits facing federal and state governments for as far as forecasters can see, the idea that there are others who would like to help educate the nation's children, who can potentially alleviate some of these fiscal tensions, may not seem so distasteful. It may also be that as public instructors allow those in the faith-based sector a place at the table, in terms of formulating government policy, it might make it easier for teachers in the private sector to have a more open attitude toward those in the public sector as well.

Equally true, however, is that these results also raise certain concerns. First, this meta-analysis accentuates the fact that TPS are likely not satisfying the expectations of many American parents. The TPS rubric does not fare particularly well when compared to religious schools or public charter institutions. Public school student achievement trails that of their counterparts in faith-based schools and is no better than that of youth in charter schools. These results are especially disconcerting when one considers that students in TPS receive far more funding than youth in religious schools generally and somewhat more than those in charter schools (U.S. Department of Education, 2011). In fact, the gap between public and faith-based schools is so great that even students in inner-city public schools receive considerably more education funding than the average student at a religious school (Glenn, 2011; U.S. Department of Education, 2011). This is particularly worthy of note because countless public school advocates point to inadequate funding as the primary reason inner-city children underperform (Berliner & Biddle, 1995; Bracey, 1997). This is not stated to discourage additional funding for education, but it does appear to support the idea of educational efficiency (Glenn, 2011; Jeynes, 1999; Peterson, 2006). That is, how well school and government officials spend money may be more important than how much is spent (Jeynes, 2008). These financial facts, in conjunction with the results of this meta-analysis, also suggest that there are likely factors beyond money that explain the religious school advantage in achievement (Jeynes, 1999, 2002a, 2003c).

Third Research Question

The third research question regarding the association between practices in faith-based and public schools is worthy of much discussion. In the case of three of the four practices examined, the effect sizes favored students attending faith-based private schools. Nevertheless, the one area where traditional public schools held an advantage (classroom flexibility) is also thought provoking. From the meta-analysis, it appears that teachers from faith-based schools are more demanding and expect higher levels of attainment from their students who are of equal status scholastically. In addition, it appears that the achievement gap is narrower at faith-based schools than it is at traditional public schools. It is conceivable that these three variables may overlap to some extent. That is, the achievement gap might be narrower at faith-based schools, in part because religious educators are more likely to believe that children, no matter what their color and background, can achieve and reach great potential. Consequently, they are more likely to have high expectations and insist that these students take demanding courses.

In spite of the possible hypothesis just presented, giving some elaboration on why these findings emerged, there are copious alternative explanations. For example, Sander (1996) asserts that one reason African Americans perform better in religious schools is that Catholics and other Christians are more likely to see people as equal because they are made in the image of God. Others argue that a sense of purpose in life, which is often associated with faith, is a plausible explanation for the high standards common in faith-based schools (Jeynes, 2003c; McKnight, 2003). Still other social scientists point to Weber's notion of an ethic of a strong motivation to work hard as a means of showing love to others and fulfilling a heavenly calling as possible explanations (Jeynes, 1999, 2003c). An alternative view, given by some, is that religious schools promote parental involvement more than public schools do (Bryk, Lee & Holland, 1993; Coleman, 1988; Coleman, Hoffer, & Kilgore, 1982). One might ask why it is that religious schools are more likely to be associated with parental involvement and also caring teachers. Coleman asserts that religious and public schools have very different orientations that result in religious school students eventually being endowed with higher levels of social capital.

One problem that emerges when studying the effects of religious schools, however, is that increasingly, researchers try to control for the very qualities that likely contribute to the academic advantage enjoyed by youth from faith-based schools. Some studies control for whether students took more demanding courses, had teachers with higher standards, and had the self-reliant attitudes that religious people often possess that lead them to refuse to take government help or what some term "handouts." Some studies examining high school achievement also control for "past achievement," but if attending religious schools for eight or nine years, for example, is largely responsible for producing that achievement edge, it seems ill advised—to say the least—to control for past achievement in such a simplistic way. In addition, should social scientists have blanket controls for parental involvement and whether students are English language learners, but faith-based schools go to great lengths to involve parents and help their students master English.

This meta-analysis attempted to use Models A and B to adjust to the tendency for certain studies to "overcontrol" for variables that likely explained, in part, the faith-based advantage.

Nevertheless, this meta-analysis quite possibly still understated the effects of faith-based schools to some degree. This possibility may be increased somewhat by the decision to report effects sizes using a random effects model rather than a fixed effects model. The former approach tends to yield more conservative effect sizes than in the latter case. However, it should be noted that in the case of this meta-analysis, the differences between these two models were not especially large for faith-based schools and were almost nonexistent in the case of public charter institutions. It should be noted, however, that there is perhaps greater wisdom in understating the effects of a given instructional paradigm than in possibly overstating its influence.

It should also be noted that in terms of classroom flexibility, traditional public schools had the edge over faith-based ones. Public school students believed that they had more opportunity to engage in classroom discussion and choose elective courses than their counterparts in religious schools. The difference in the perception of access to elective courses in public schools is probably pretty accurate. By their sheer enrollment advantage and employment base, it seems intuitive that public schools might possess a greater inherent ability to offer a wider array of classes to their students (Gatto, 2001). Concurrent to this reality, though, is the fact that by emphasizing the basics, a strong academic foundation, and more advanced courses than one typically finds in public schools, that focus will tend to yield intellectual advancement in key subjects and a curriculum that emphasizes preparation for the real world (Coleman, 1988; Gatto, 2001). Indeed, some social scientists have pointed out that a child-centered curriculum filled with a plethora of electives may not best serve the long-term interests of the children; thus, a preparation-centered curriculum might be more appropriate. While one might argue whether there is room for a centrist position in this debate, the meta-analytic data suggest that public schools have a Deweyian child-centered approach versus the preparation-centered orientation espoused by most faith-based schools.

To be sure, faith-based teachers might be more inclined to embrace certain aspects of classroom flexibility more than others (Boyer, 1995; Gatto, 2001). That is, to the extent that traditional public schools are more likely to encourage class discussion, religious instructors might find that this component of classroom flexibility might be worthy of emulation. Although technically one might argue that a large amount of time spent on classroom discussion runs the risk of a de facto reduction in instruction time, one would think this does not necessarily have to be the case if the discussion is specifically designed to: (1) complement the material taught and (2) occur at intervals of time in which students would absorb more if there were a brief respite from the usual instruction time (Boyer, 1995).

Thoughts for Consideration

What this meta-analysis, and the studies that follow, suggests is that faith-based schools and public schools of various types have something to learn from one another. And to the degree that is the case, there is something to be said for viewing education more holistically than hoping the best for one's own sector and considerably less than that for competing sectors. The nation's children likely deserve better. It would seem that both the public and the private sector can learn from one another, work more cooperatively, and together build a better American school system. For their part, it would seem that public school advocates, including many academics, might do well to admit some of the advantages maintained by faith-based schools and see to what extent some of their strengths can be emulated. Similarly, faith-based schools might do relatively well comparatively speaking, but greater classroom flexibility would likely make their school systems that much better.

Limitations of Study

The primary limitation of this meta-analysis, or any meta-analysis, is that it is restricted to analyzing the existing body of literature. Therefore, even if the researcher conducting the quantitative integrations sees ways the studies included could have been improved, there is no way to implement those changes. A second limitation of a meta-analysis is that the social scientist is limited to addressing the same research questions addressed in the aggregated studies. One can address only the questions that have been asked by researchers and cannot fully manipulate the variables in the same way as if he or she were conducting an original study.

Recommendations for Further Research

There is clearly more that the academic community needs to know regarding the effects of charter schools and religious private schools, in particular. For example, Hoxby (2003a) as well as Carpenter and Medina (2011) argue that in school districts with a relatively large number of charter schools, the presence of charter schools causes a more competitive environment. Consequently, they assert that there is evidence that the educational outcomes of other public schools rise. One might recall that Chubb and Moe (1990) argued that if private schools are allowed to compete with public schools, via school choice programs, it would cause public schools to raise their standards and perform at higher levels academically. The assumption by Chubb and Moe, however, is that this would occur because students from faith-based and other private schools achieved at such high levels. It is not intuitive, however, that public charter schools would cause TPS students to increase their educational outcomes. Most studies indicate that the presence of charter schools does not raise student achievement in the TPS environment (Bifulco & Ladd, 2005). Nevertheless, the hypothesis advanced by Hoxby (2003a) is interesting and worthy of further examination. Even if Hoxby is incorrect and charter schools, because they tend to post less than impressive results, have no competitive effect on TPS students, her logic might apply to faith-based schools, if they were allowed via school choice to increase in number.

Second, to the extent that this study suggests that faith-based schools and public schools have qualities to learn from one another, it would be interesting to undertake research designed to examine if there are measurable benefits from educators viewing education more holistically and working together to try to make American schooling overall more effective in accomplishing its goals. To be sure, this recommendation opens up a broad range of research ideas, from both

sectors working together to fulfill common objectives to implementing ideas that the other sector does well to actually functioning as a
collaborative supporter rather than a competitor who might actually
want something less than the best for the other sector. This recommendation for further research could radically change the way many
people perceive the American educational landscape.

A third suggestion is based on a statement made by Paul Hill
(2005, p. 141), who notes, "Growth can bring dangers if choice [is]
implemented carelessly." This would seem to be a logical statement.
But what constitutes a carefully planned choice system, especially
when so few that include faith-based schools have even been implemented? It would seem reasonable to assert that all of the claims on
either side of the choice debate that would include private schools
are mostly hypothetical and have limited merit, unless the nation
ceases to be so reluctant to at least experiment with the idea in
selected cities throughout the country. After decades of debate on
this issue, the time has come to at least experiment to see what hope,
if any, school choice programs might have for the quality of
American schooling (Jeynes, 2000). And the truth of the matter is
that academics, educators, parents, and other leaders should care
what the answer is, if in fact they view schooling holistically.

Conclusion

There are several conclusions one can reach from this meta-analysis
that are worthy of special attention. First, educators would be unwise
to dismiss the contributions of faith-based schools. There is certainly
a substantial enough body of knowledge available, as reflected in this
meta-analysis, demonstrating that faith-based schools contribute something vital to the academic well-being of millions of American students.
Even if one is not particularly religious, faith-based schools should
therefore be a source of national joy rather than a target of resentment
or of reluctant resignation. The United States is a nation that claims to
celebrate diversity. And if it is to conduct itself in a way that is consistent with that claim, it needs to also be tolerant of the presence and
successes of faith-based schools (Bryk, Lee, & Holland, 1993). And
indeed, to the degree that there is evidence that faith-based schools
are more like to reduce the racial and socioeconomic (SES) achievement gaps, Americans should rejoice that this is taking place without

regard to whether the gap is being bridged in a faith-based or public school.

Second, there is evidence that public and faith-based schools can indeed learn from each other. There are certain areas where faith-based schools flourish and others where public schools excel. Religious school educators tend to have high expectations and insist that their students take an advanced course load, whereas public schools are more likely to encourage classroom discussion and the taking of elective courses. It is plausible that teachers from both sectors would do well to learn from these successful practices in the other sector and learn from them.

Third, as much as there has been a major government push to encourage the establishment and continuance of public charter schools, it is not clear whether the push toward charter schools is a wise use of time and effort given that it appears that these students, on average, do not show any scholastic benefit. Perhaps its time to examine alternative means of improving American schools, including extending school choice to include the private sector, most of which is comprised of faith-based schools.

Fourth, faith-based educators should have a seat at the table. It is apparent that these schools contribute important educational attributes. And to actively oppose them not only discourages educational diversity, but also diminishes prospects for the nation's schooling system. Both faith-based schools and public institutions have a prodigious array of ideas that could potentially strengthen the American education system. Leaders and families in the United States have every reason to encourage increased communication and cooperation between these two sectors.

It is not in the best interests of America's children for public school educators to hope that the public sector's advantage will go from 90 percent of the nation's schoolchildren to 100 percent. Nor does it benefit the country for those in the private sector to think that the struggles of the public sector are not important.

This meta-analysis should cause us to ask some very practical questions that ultimately could cause the exercise of greater wisdom and cooperation in American education. One might also hope that the results of this meta-analysis will provide greater insight into the increased diversity that many Americans clearly desire in their schools. Concurrently, these data will also provide guidance so that the greater diversity can also increase student achievement.

Chapter 3

The History of School Choice Programs

Herbert Walberg (2007, p. 61) beautifully contextualizes the current school choice movement when he states, "For two centuries, private schools were the dominant form of American K-12 schooling. From the founding of the first colonies through the middle of the 19th centuries, most schools were privately owned, privately managed and funded by tuition and government subsidies." Walberg is also careful to note that through this period during which religious schools were dominant, the northern states had the highest literacy rate in the world. Nevertheless, most of the school choice programs have received the most attention in recent years have been *public* school choice programs.

Public School Choice in the United States

Some of the Most Prominent Public School Choice Programs

Minnesota

When most educators think of public school choice, Minnesota is often the first program to come to mind. Minnesota, for example, practices three kinds of school choice programs. Minnesota initiated the nation's first statewide public school choice program in 1992 (Toma & Zimmer, 2012). About 40,000 students participate in the public charter school program out of the over 2 million American students who are enrolled in public charter schools nationwide (Toma & Zimmer, 2012). Choice advocates often refer to the choice program in Minnesota as a model, and the state has won awards for its charter school programs (Toma & Zimmer, 2012). Public school choice programs that exclude faith-based schools from participation also demonstrate some degree of sensitivity to students of color and those of low socioeconomic status. The Minnesota public school program is one such example of this sensitivity. Nearly half of the students participating in the Minnesota choice program are classified as "at-risk" students. The state appears to bend over backward to accommodate these at-risk students. The Minnesota state government pays for their transportation costs, which is one of the major concerns of the poor. Not only do the schools provide childcare, but they also proactively exhort parents to become more engaged in their children's schooling (Toma & Zimmer, 2012).

Cambridge

Along similar lines, the public school choice program in Cambridge, Massachusetts, also addresses the primary concerns of the parents of poor people and minorities. As was mentioned in Chapter 1, the Cambridge plan includes a centralized parent information center, pays for the transportation costs associated with choice, and ensures that choice does not increase segregation in the schools (Nechyba, 2003; Walser, 1998).

These examples in both the private and public sector defy the stereotype that school choice programs show insensitivity to the needs of poor and minority students. In fact, the notion that school choice would hurt minorities carries with it a certain degree of irony. According to Harvard and Gallup polls, American people of color favor the adoption of a voucher program by a significantly wider margin than white people do (Harvard Poll, 2007; Kirkpatrick, 1990; Phi Beta Kappa/Gallup Poll, 2002). Moreover, African Americans favor the adoption of a voucher program more than any other racial group (Harvard Poll, 2007; Kirkpatrick, 1990; Phi Beta Kappa/Gallup Poll, 2002).

Harlem

Harlem inaugurated a plan for school choice in the 1970s, when New York City's District 4 in East Harlem ranked last out of the city's 32 school districts and encompassed neighborhoods that were some of the city's poorest (Fliegel & MacGuire, 1994). By the mid- to late 1980s, District 4 had jumped to fifteenth in reading achievement among the city's school districts (Sullivan, 2003). Moreover, the percentage of students reading at grade level surged from 15 percent in 1974 to 62 percent by 1988 (Sullivan, 2003). The turnaround was significant enough for some educators to call the improvement, the "miracle in East Harlem" (Fliegel & MacGuire, 1994).

Charter Schools

Arizona

One must not assume that all charter school programs are equal. There is a considerable amount of variation by location. As Caroline Hoxby (2006, p. 201) notes, "Arizona's charter school law, passed in 1994, is widely regarded as the friendliest to charter schools." It also appears that there are other realities that impact the efficacy of public school choice. For example, Hanushek and Rivkin (2003, p. 23) say that "school choice is more meaningful to metropolitan students than rural students."

Various Cities

Charter schools became quite popular, especially beginning under the Bill Clinton administration, beginning in January 1993 (Brighouse, 2003). They have only increased in popularity under the Barack Obama administration's Race to the Top program (Berends, Cannata, & Goldring, 2011). In fact, many supporters of the voucher and tax break approach to school choice have been critical of Obama for advocating public school choice while concurrently dismantling any choice programs involving the private sector (Wolf et al., 2011). Indeed, via pressure from Senator Dick Durbin from Illinois, Obama did phase out the Washington, DC, voucher program, which by nearly all accounts had been quite successful in helping children of color and financially strained families (Wolf et al., 2011).

Voucher/Tax Credit Programs

Alum Rock, California

The Alum Rock experiment has more in common with the Milwaukee and Cleveland efforts, which are also examined in this chapter, than it does with the public school choice initiatives and charter schools because it involved vouchers and private schools. It covered a five-year period and was federally funded. When the program began in 1972, it was already shrouded with controversy. Shortly before the inauguration of the Alum Rock project, the Representative Assembly of the National Educational Association at its annual meeting in San Francisco adopted a resolution that opposed tuition vouchers (Kirkpatrick, 1990). But to many people's surprise, initial reports about the experiment proved quite good, and some educators even rated it an "A" due to less absenteeism and vandalism, greater educational variety, and more enthusiasm for school (Kirkpatrick, 1990).

A summary of the opinions of teachers and parents demonstrated an overall positive impression. Ninety-six of the teachers said the voucher program enabled them to exercise innovative ideas more frequently. Ninety-five of the parents liked the idea of choosing schools, and 75 percent of the parents thought their children would receive a better education as a result (Kirkpatrick, 1990). These kinds of results are particularly salient because—as Hatcher (1994), Brighouse (2003), and Diem and Walter (2011) note—teachers must buy into choice for choice to work.

Although those familiar with the Alum Rock voucher experiment lauded the initial result, once the five-year voucher program ended, in 1977, the Alum Rock program received fewer favorable comments. The critics did not focus so much on the project itself in their criticisms, but on the limitations that accompanied the program (Kirkpatrick, 1990). The low participation rate emerged as one such limitation (Kirkpatrick, 1990). Several critics question whether the Alum Rock project constitutes a true test of the voucher idea.

Milwaukee

The Milwaukee school choice program received a great deal of publicity because it was it was well organized and enjoyed a high level of support within the Milwaukee metropolitan area. It is the nation's oldest consistently operating voucher program (Figlio & Page, 2003). For the past dozen years, it has generally included slightly over 100 private schools, but the number of participants has steadily increased from small numbers in the early 1990s to over 10,000 in the early 2000s and to over 20,000 currently (Van Dunk & Dickman, 2003;

National School Boards Association, 2013). Supporters of the program targeted youth of low socioeconomic status in the city, which helped galvanize a large degree of support. Helping the unfortunate is a major priority among a wide spectrum of American society and given that this was the initiative's chief emphasis, this helped ensure broad support. The intractable nature of the gap in academic outcomes that exists between students of certain races of color and white students as well as those of low versus high socioeconomic status has been of considerable concern to educators and the American public (Rippeyoung, 2009; Roscigno, 1998). Ronald Roach (2001, p. 377) recently asserted that "in the academic and think tank world, pondering achievement gap remedies takes center stage."

The Milwaukee program enjoyed a great deal of area support not only because of the altruistic aims of the program, but also because various individuals and groups that often do not operate together chose to work in harmony (Van Dunk & Dickman, 2003). Van Dunk & Dickman (2003, p. 12) assert, "School vouchers in Milwaukee were supported by an odd coalition of conservatives and liberals."

Although a myriad of individuals supported the Milwaukee school choice initiative, the benefits of the program were rather slow to accrue in a measurable way (Van Dunk & Dickman, 2003; Witte, Wolf, Dean, & Carlson, 2011). The Milwaukee choice program was passed by the Wisconsin legislature in 1990 and initially included only public schools (Van Dunk & Dickman, 2003). It was not until 1998 and 1999 that the voucher program expanded to include religious schools (Van Dunk & Dickman, 2003). The program added faith-based schools, in part because the early data on the efficacy of the Milwaukee program was inconclusive at best (Figlio & Page, 2003; Witte, Wolf, Dean, & Carlson, 2011) With the perspectives of individuals like Coleman, Hoffer, and Bryk in mind, the thinking by many was that the addition of faith-based schools would infuse some life into the program (Jeynes, 1999, 2002a). In early assessments of the effects of school choice programs, voucher students did no better than public school students (Greene et al., 1996; Walberg, 2007; Witte, Wolf, Dean, & Carlson, 2011). However, studies by Greene, Witte, and others indicated that the voucher students began to outperform their counterparts in public schools, especially after the first year in the voucher program (Greene et al., 1996; Witte, Wolf, Dean, & Carlson, 2011). A number of social scientists attributed this to the fact that the first year was a time of transition for the voucher students because they were attending a new school (Greene et al., 1996; Walberg, 2007; Witte, Wolf, Dean, & Carlson, 2011). Research studies on the effects of the voucher schools indicated that once one controlled for socioeconomic status, race, and gender, low-income students who went to the voucher schools outperformed those who attended traditional public schools (Greene et al., 1996; Walberg, 2007; Witte, Wolf, Dean, & Carlson, 2011). These later studies with sophisticated controls indicated that the longer students remained in the Milwaukee voucher schools, the better they tended to do. Nevertheless, it is not particularly clear what the effects of different facets of the Milwaukee program are because among the voucher schools are included both faith-based private schools and independent private schools (Figlio & Page, 2003).

Cleveland

The Cleveland voucher program, much like the Milwaukee one, focuses on children of low socioeconomic status (Viteritti, 2003; Jeynes, 2012a, 2012e). The program in Cleveland could be a model of how voucher schooling could save city and state governments a great of money because the voucher private schools spend at a level per student of only about 58 percent the level of traditional public schools (Viteritti, 2003). In Cleveland, the voucher that students participating in the choice program receive as about 50 percent of the private school tuition (Viteritti, 2003). Cleveland and Milwaukee both target low-income children as those most likely to participate in choice. In contrast, Florida defines those in need by their past educational experiences, that is, those in public schools they believe are in greater need than those who have attended faith-based schools (Figlio & Page, 2003; Viteritti, 2003).

Other Programs

A variety of other voucher and privately funded school choice programs have been initiated in such places as Dayton, Indianapolis, San Antonio, the District of Columbia, Florida, and Charlotte (Howell, Wolf, Peterson & Campbell, 2006; Jeynes & Beuttler, 2012; Peterson, Howell, Wolfe & Campbell, 2003). School choice scholarships were offered in a number of these cities. For example, "the School Choice Scholarships (SCSF) in New York City offered

1,300 scholarships with up to $1,400 annually toward tuition at a private school for at least three years" (Howell, Wolf, Peterson & Campbell, 2006, p. 185). There is clearly a demand for school choice. In New York City alone, Peterson and colleagues report that there were 20,000 applicants. In Dayton, the scholarships covered half of the private school tuition (Howell, Wolf, Peterson & Campbell, 2006; Peterson, Howell, Wolfe & Campbell, 2003). In Dayton, over 32,000 students met the eligibility requirements, and about 3,000 of these students applied for the voucher program (Peterson, Howell, Wolfe & Campbell, 2003).

In Washington, DC, the school choice program was initiated in 1993, paid for about 60 percent of the tuition, and focused on students below the poverty line (Howell, Wolf, Peterson & Campbell, 2006; Peterson, Howell, Wolfe & Campbell, 2003). The overwhelming majority of the students served were either African American or Latino (Howell, Wolf, Peterson & Campbell, 2006). Within two years, students of color in these schools were scoring at much higher levels than their counterparts in public schools to the degree that the racial achievement gap was reduced by a third (Howell, Wolf, Peterson & Campbell, 2006; Peterson, Howell, Wolfe & Campbell, 2003). Due to its success, the program was expanded and changed in January 2004 when President George W. Bush signed into law the District of Columbia School Choice Incentive Act, which made it a true federally funded private school voucher program. It was the first *federally funded* voucher program in the United States (Wolf et al., 2011).

Students who switched from public to private schools tend to have improved their performance on academic measures and fared better than their counterparts in public schools (Peterson, Howell, Wolfe & Campbell, 2003). Peterson and colleagues (2003) note that in the cases of New York, Dayton, and Washington, DC, combined, "African American students who switched from public to private schools" had reading and math combined scores of 3.9 points higher than their counterparts the first year after transferring, and 6.3 and 6.6 points higher after the second and third years, respectively. Jay Greene studied a private voucher program in Charlotte, North Carolina, and found that scholarship lottery winners outperformed losers by 6 percentage points after one year (Walberg, 2007, p. 39). Hoxby (2006) has found that students in voucher schools outperform their counterparts in public schools.

Voucher Defeats and Victories at the Voting Booth

The news that scores of students who utilize vouchers are up has spread to some extent and is giving the school choice movement some momentum that it did not possess in the 1980s and 1990s (Peterson, Howell, Wolfe, & Campbell, 2003). Peterson and colleagues (2003, pp. 124) also note, "Most studies have found that families who use vouchers to attend an area private school are much more satisfied with their schooling than are families who remain in public schools."

School Choice Overseas

Charles Glenn (2003, p. 173) makes an interesting observation when he asserts, "Virtually every nation in the world allows parents to send their children to a school other than those operated by public authorities; reportedly there are more private schools in China under its Communist regime than in the United States." Glenn (p. 174) continues by stating, "While the debate in the United States is over vouchers, most countries don't consider them necessary and provide funding directly to private schools, paying teacher salaries or giving a general subsidy." Further buttressing Glenn's perspective, Plank and Sykes (2003, pp. vii-viii) aver, "In most parts of the world, governments are moving steadily and often boldly to increase choice and competition in the educational system."

In Europe in particular, there are two concurrent ironies: (1) Western Europe, which in the Cold War was the center of democracy, is becoming increasingly socialistic and secularized. In contrast, eastern Europe, which was once the bastion of Communism, is experiencing Christian revival (Jeynes, 2012d). Faith Church in Budapest, Hungary, is now the third largest church in the world, with a membership of 120,000 (http://innovationlab.leadnet.org/warren). The Ukraine, formerly part of the Soviet Union, has three of the largest churches in the world, including one of 30,000 and two of somewhat smaller size (http://innovationlab.leadnet.org/warren). (2) In western Europe, while the number of Christians has been in decline, the influx of young eastern European immigrants is causing the number of faith-based schools to rise (Dronkers & Robert, 2004). These realities are affecting the spread of faith-based schools in those areas and the openness to school choice.

School Choice in Great Britain

During the 1980s and 1990s, Great Britain followed the same direction as several other industrialized nations and "saw the dramatic reorganization of state-maintained educational systems giving a greater choice of school to families with the explicit aim of encouraging competition among schools" (Walford, 2003, p. 68). Ironically, it was in the midst of fighting Germany's tyranny in 1944 that the stage was established for this degree of autonomy in the 1944 Education Act for England and Wales (Glenn, 1989; Walford, 2003). This edict established the rights of parents to express preference for certain types of schools. In 1988, the Education Reform Act for England and Wales allowed market processes to come to English education (Walford, 1994). In 1993, the act began to encourage the opening of new schools to enhance the supply of schools in order to maximize the choices available to parents. Research indicates that initially, families did not make choices in schooling based on academics so much, but rather they focused on other factors. This same research, however, is indicating that these trends are beginning to change (Carroll & Wolford, 1997).

The main thrust of the school choice program in England and Wales was to increase competition between schools and to encourage parents to make choices between schools. Nevertheless, as Macedo and Wolf (2004, p. 12) point out, in England and Wales, what is in place is a "broadly regulated school choice." After initial cheers among British parents in the 1980s, the prospects for greater parental freedom in the choice of schools appears to be diminishing substantially and may actually be headed in the reverse direction. Harris (2004, p. 117) notes, "The increasing regulation of education in England and Wales has now caught up with the independent schools." While the threat of eventually absorbing faith-based schools into the larger state system remains, a large number of social scientists now believe that the government can accomplish almost the same aims by regulating them (Harris, 2004). They admonish those who are perhaps overly elated about prospects for choice in the United States that this degree of regulation is hardly ideal and could dilute the very qualities that make faith-based schools effective (Glenn, 2000).

To the credit of the British, they do not appear to have the same fear of addressing issues of faith, love, and character that Americans do (Harris, 2004; Jeynes, 2010a). Instead, the British government understands that the Bible is the most published and influential book in the history of humanity and that to be an educated individual, one needs to have a working knowledge of its contents. Moreover, the British believe that teachers should help parents teach children to have qualities such as love, responsibility, and kindness (Harris, 2004; Jeynes, 2009, 2010c). In Great Britain, much like in eastern Europe, it is believed that these virtues need to be taught for people in society to trust one another and thrive (Glenn, 2000; Jeynes, 2010a, 2010c).

School Choice in the Netherlands

The Dutch initiated vouchers in 1917, and 76 percent of the nation's students now attend private schools. Surveys indicate that parents are highly satisfied with the schooling their children are receiving. Some called this initiative the Dutch Peace Treaty (Mouw, 2003). Among many advocates of school choice, the Netherlands is a model because as Macedo and Wolf (2004, p. 9) articulate, in the Netherlands, "School choice is the norm."

The Perspective of Abraham Kuyper

Abraham Kuyper (1837–1920) served as a Calvinist pastor, university professor, member of Parliament, and eventually prime minister of the Netherlands. During this period, he sought to restructure the entire Dutch educational system into a system of school choice. What Kuyper asserted and obtained was constitutional recognition that parents have the right to determine the religious or philosophical direction of their children's education. The Dutch program of school choice reflected this declaration. Kuyper went this direction because many Calvinists and Catholics, in particular, complained that they could not send their children to the public schools without violating their conscience (Glenn, 1989; Jeynes & Naylor, 2007). Kuyper stated that to uphold the fundamental human right to freedom of conscience, the state was obligated to permit parents to choose the religious direction of their child's education, without putting the family at a financial disadvantage (Jeynes & Naylor, 2007). A struggle known as the school struggle ensued, eventually resulting in the recognition that parents possessed the fundamental right to direct their children's education. Equal and complete subsidies were provided to all private schools.

The motto of his Anti-Revolutionary Party on the schools issue was: "Free Schools the norm, State Schools a supplement" (Kuyper, 1890).

To be sure, Kuyper wanted to draw education out from under government control, but he was not a libertarian. He believed that government had a God-given responsibility to oversea quality schooling. Kuyper ideally preferred parents to pay directly for education rather than imposing excessive government taxation (Glenn, 1989; Kuyper, 1890). He believed direct parent payment of tuition imperative to maintain what he called free initiative among parents and the citizenry. But in the real world, he believed that government sustaining schools—in part by taxation—was essentially unavoidable (Kuyper, 1917).

In 1889, the School Law was passed, which for the first time provided a limited federal subsidy to all schools (Kuyper, 1890, 1917). In 1900, Kuyper and other leaders of the free school movement worked out a unified plan (called the Unie Rapport) concerning the schools issue. Essentially, they advocated for a system in which the costs of all schools would be shared by the parents and the national government. It should also be noted that from Kuyper's perspective, national school choice not only did not violate the separation of church and state, but rather was absolutely essential to guarantee the separation of religion and the state (Kuyper, 1890, 1917). Kuyper believed that if the government subsidized only state schools, this would guarantee that state schools would prevail over religious schools and that faith-based schools would eventually face near extinction (Kuyper, 1890, 1917). By funding only state schools with this result, it was basically insisting that people receive their religious instruction from the government (Kuyper, 1890, 1917). State funding to both public and private schools should be equal, in Kuyper's view (1890, 1917). Only in this way could the state avoid privileging certain religious perspectives over others and protect the fundamental human right of freedom of conscience. Nevertheless, with this equal funding in mind, Kuyper opined that all schools, both public and private, should be required to meet certain realistic minimum academic standards.

Kuyper maintained that state regulation and inspection of a school's academic achievements must never be allowed to infringe upon the religious character of its educational program. In fact, he called upon the public to be wary of any such interference because it was a violation of the Dutch constitution (Kuyper, 1890, 1917).

In terms of how the Dutch model, and Kuyper's view specifically, might relate to the American application of school choice, not all embrace this paradigm. That is, there are skeptics.

Among those who see the potential for government entanglement in the affair of religious schools, two issues frequently come to the forefront. First, they argue that government involvement in religious schools in Europe has diluted the religious identity of these schools (Jeynes, 2004a; Jeynes & Naylor, 2007). Second, the trend in the United States is for the government to often stipulate some degree of secularization of religious programs in exchange for government funding.

The Netherlands' commitment to school choice is interesting, especially when in conjunction it is understood that in global comparison achievement tests, the Netherlands consistently ranks as one of the six or eight best school systems in the world (Infoplease, 2003). Naturally, there are likely a number of reasons Dutch children do well in school, but school choice may be a contributing factor.

School Choice in Finland

Finland is one of the nations most dedicated to school choice (West & Ylonen, 2010). Especially, there are a large number of Evangelical Lutheran schools because it is the largest denomination in Finland (West & Ylonen, 2010). Finland is much more dedicated to a fully developed system of choice than is Great Britain (West & Ylonen, 2010). Finland esteems school choice in part because it has a larger percentage of devout religious people than other areas of Scandinavia. This is in part bolstered by religious people immigrating to Finland from the old Soviet Union and other northern eastern European nations who suffered the persecution of Christians by a variety of communist regimes (Goldstein, 2008; West & Ylonen, 2010). Finnish people also have a respect for the important place that religion has in people's lives, and therefore they emphasize the study of the Bible in schools and sometimes study other religious texts as well (Goldstein, 2008; West & Ylonen, 2010). They are not as uncomfortable and intolerant about religious expressions as American educators are, and therefore "Merry Christmas" is a greeting that schoolchildren believe is uplifting and supportive (Goldstein, 2008, p. 1). Finland's commitment to choice is notable especially because in terms of a combination of reading, math, and science achievement in global surveys, Finland ranks as the number one school system in the world (Infoplease, 2003). As in the case of the Netherlands, there are probably several reasons for this performance, but school choice may well play a part.

School Choice in Canada

Canada's version of school choice is somewhat different than what one finds in most countries in that it emphasizes what Macedo and Wolf (2004, p. 16) describe as "Choice, civics, federalism, and results-based accountability." Although the United States and Canada are in close geographical proximity to one another, their attitudes toward school choice are quite distinct (Campbell, 2004). "In Ontario," for example as David Campbell (2004, p. 188) points out, "religious schools already are funded directly with public dollars." Campbell (2004, p. 189) adds, "Canadians do not perceive public funding for private schools as having harmed the preparation of Canadian youth for civic life." It is also notable that although Canada, like the United States, is a land of immigrants, its students far better than American students on international comparison tests (Infoplease, 2003).

School Choice in France

In France, the government's concept of school choice involves competition between Roman Catholic schools and the modern French state (Glenn, 1989; Macedo and Wolf, 2004). Dennis Meuret (2004, p. 238) points out that in the equivalent of the U.S. Constitution in France, there is a "liberty of teaching." In the eyes of the French, this is just part of living in a democracy, and many leaders there do not view private schools as less democratic than public schools. About 65 percent of the French attend public schools, while approximately 20 percent attend private, predominantly Catholic, ones (Glenn, 1989; Meuret, 2004). Meuret (2004, p. 247) shares that "under the current public-private compromise, then, existing private schools are almost fully financed through public money, while it is somewhat difficult but not impossible to create new ones."

Noting these developments in France is particularly important because what happens in this nation often influences what educational developments transpire in other nations (Dronkers, 2004).

School Choice in Germany

Germany views faith-based schools as completing the public system (Macedo and Wolf, 2004). Germany has had a long tradition of a dual system of public and private education, although the focus of the government leaders and educators on one sector or the other has swung in one direction or the other over time (Glenn, 1989; Reuter, 2004). Monastery and church schools started in the 700s and in the 1200s, the government developed public Latin schools (Reuter, 2004). Nevertheless, as Reuters (2004, p. 217) points out, "Traditionally, German public schools were based on clear-cut religious beliefs." As time went on, however, German schools became more secularized and in recent decades, the German people have come to view faith-based schools as supplementing public ones.

School Choice in Oceania and Asia

Japan

Plank and Sykes (2003, p. vii) observe about Japan, "In Japan people have few opportunities to choose schools within the regular school system, but there is a thriving market for 'juku'/'cram schools' and other supplementary educational programs."

New Zealand

In 1989, New Zealand embarked on a program of *public* school choice that is very similar to the charter school program that spread in the United States (Fiske & Ladd, 2003). The New Zealand government called their initiative Tomorrow's Schools and turned all educational institutions into schools of choice (Ramler, 2001). The nation's efforts were limited, however, in two very profound and meaningful ways. First, the program was limited only to public schools and therefore is likely to offer little insight into the potential efficacy of broader programs that would involve faith-based and other private schools (Jeynes, 2002a, 2002c). Second, New Zealand possesses a population of only about 4 million. Therefore, it is questionable how relevant its experiment is to a nation with a population of 80 times that number (Fiske & Ladd, 2003). In addition, 96 percent of New Zealand's students attend public schools (Thrupp, 2007). Therefore, the argument that increased competition from the private sector could enhance overall school achievement is more nebulous and less certain because a significant increase in private school enrollment would likely have to take place to make this a reality.

There are certain situations in which the New Zealand government allows struggling faith-based schools to integrate into the state system, if these schools are viewed as being of "special character" (Gordon & Whitty, 1997; Zehavi, 2009). Nevertheless, these cases are quite rare (Gordon & Whitty, 1997; Zehavi, 2009).

In spite of the fact that New Zealand's system of public school choice has received a considerable amount of international attention, the results have actually been less than impressive. There does seem to be evidence that the government paid less attention to schools in areas with high percentages of low-income families and nonwhite students (Carpenter, 2012). Moreover, the test comparisons been choice and nonchoice students have been inconclusive (Carpenter, 2012).

Australia

Australia supported the idea of funding private schools well before most other nations (Angus, 2003). Australia initiated this effort beginning in the 1970s. In many respects, the history of K-12 education in Australia, at least in terms of the presence of the private and public sectors, paralleled that of the United States. Angus (2003, p. 112) notes, "A dual system of public and private schooling was set in place soon after the European settlement in 1788." The government's conviction in support of a dual system of a strong private and public sector endured throughout the remainder of the 1700s. That changed in the late 1800s when the government decided it would favor public schooling (Angus, 2003). As a result of this change in orientation, the public sector of schooling grew substantially during the next 80 or so years, while the percentage of students attending faith-based and independent private schools contracted substantially (Angus, 2003).

As the second half of the twentieth century emerged, it became clear that a large percentage of disadvantaged parents desired to send their children to faith-based and independent private schools. The Australian government, especially under Prime Minister Gough Whitlam, began to realize that seeking to help children by their degree of need rather than whether they attended a public or private sector school was of the greatest importance (Angus, 2003). Under Whitlam, the government decided to more seriously try to financially help students attend school. Given that so many of these students desired to attend religious schools, "the effect of the Whitlam government's intervention was to energize the private sector" (Angus, 2003, p. 114). Enrollment at existing religious schools rose as a result of the government's actions, and new ones opened as well.

Australia's students, like those in Finland and the Netherlands, perform among the six or eight highest among the nations tested on international comparison tests (Infoplease, 2003).

School Choice in Other Western Europe Nations

Sweden

"In 1993 the Swedish government required all local education authorities to fund schools of choice at a per student expenditure level of 85 percent the per student cost of traditional public schools" (Walberg, 2007, p. 51). Walberg adds, "Sweden formed a national agency responsible for approving new independent schools. Swedish students are able to choose any public or participating school, including those governed and operated by for-profit firms" (p. 51).

The main challenge for the Swedes in encouraging school choice has been to stimulate school development, parental choice, and higher levels of academic achievement and yet encourage equity (Daun, 2003, p. 92). Sweden remains a more homogeneous society than most other nations in western Europe, and yet the challenges of concurrently addressing issues of quality and equity are as apparent here as in many other European Union nations (Daun, 2003).

Belgium

In Belgium, like the Netherlands, as David Plank and Gary Sykes (2003, p. vii) state, "Students have for a century been able to take state funding to the school of their choice, including religious schools." In other words, as Macedo and Wolf (2004, p. 15) note,

Belgium emphasizes "pluralistic policies and pluralistic schools." Belgium's trek into a school choice paradigm may have been facilitated by the fact that "in 1830 Belgium became an independent unitary and centralized state" (De Groop, 2004). In other words, Belgium is a rather young entity. When foreigners hear of the nation's lines of royalty or the Belgian film star Audrey Hepburn—who was named the third most influential film star in history—the sophistication of royalty and Hepburn seem to indicate a long history. But the nation is actually quite young. Between 1970 and 1993, the 1831 constitution was reformed to develop a federal system that established school choice (De Groop, 2004; Glenn, 1989).

School choice is particularly fitting for Belgium because there are a large number of Flemish people in the country, who tend to be Roman Catholic. Nevertheless, these individuals also believe that citizens who do not share their faith have a right to a public education (De Groop, 2004; Glenn, 1989). Nevertheless, there is a considerable degree of controversy surrounding the Belgian system because as De Groop (2004, p. 175) puts it, "There is a general tendency of governments to extend their involvements in the details of school life."

School Choice in Eastern Europe

The fact that school choice is a major movement in eastern Europe really should not be surprising for two reasons. First, after suffering under communist oppression that resulted in the killing of tens of millions of civilians, the hunger for freedom that people in eastern Europe had was immeasurable (Bernstein & Politi, 1996; Glenn, 1995; Rowe, 1994). This includes a longing for freedom of religious expression. The former Soviet bloc nations that included the Soviet Union and satellite nations is now experiencing a revival of Christianity that is beyond anything that this area of the world has experienced in anyone's memory (Curtis, 1994; Holger, 2009; Rowe, 1994). Second, Glenn (2003, p. 174) makes a vital point of which most people are unaware: "Not only is publicly supported school choice the norm in almost all countries with well established systems of public education, but it is also strongly supported by various international covenants that define what respect for human rights requires."

The Czech Republic and Hungary

To be sure, the fall of communism in the late 1980s produced a considerable amount of change across eastern and central Europe. With all the political changes that occurred in the aftermath of these historic events and the media coverage they received, many outside of the former Soviet bloc are not cognizant of the fact that some of the most fundamental changes to take place in eastern and central Europe took place in the education system (Munich, 2003). The Czech Republic quickly inaugurated a school choice voucher system after communism fell in the late 1980s. Under communism, the government developed a reputation for running a dilapidated and inefficient school system. Given that this was the case, when school choice programs began, 50 percent of families signed up their children for private, overwhelmingly religious, schools (Munich, 2003; Walberg, 2007). This percentage has declined to some degree but is still quite high, especially when one considers that since 1995, private schools, which are usually faith based, are funded only at a 60 to 90 percent level to that of state schools (Muinch, 2003).

Given that Hungary maintained a looser form of communism than did the Czech Republic, prior to the fall of communism, there were some faith-based private schools in Hungary even prior to the fall of communism (Munich, 2003). It is also true that faith-based schools may not grow in Hungary and the Czech Republic to the degree that might normally be expected because government schools in both Hungary and the Czech Republic encourage prayer and the study of the Bible in much the way that the United States did before 1962 and 1963. Other nations in eastern Europe such as Romania, Poland, Ukraine, and the Baltic states encourage a high degree of religious freedom in the schools (Bucur & Eklof, 1999; Jeynes, 2012h; Preda, 2009). Therefore, the incentive that some parents might have to send their children to faith-based schools is not as great as it otherwise might be.

Meta-analyses and distinct studies comparing student achievement in various geographical locations indicate that the advantage religious schools hold over their public school counterparts is greater in the United States than in Europe and may be larger in eastern Europe than in eestern Europe (Dronkers, 2004; Jeynes, 2012a).

Russia

Glenn (2003, p. 180) notes, "The Russian education law adopted in 1992 promises public financing for accredited nonpublic schools, but establishes an elaborate process to gain accreditation that it has been compared to a combat course in military training."

Russian people believed that after years of government oppression and an emphasis on loyalty to the dictatorship, rather than on faith and character, Russian pupils had become "hard and selfish" (Rowe, 1994, p. i). Increasingly, parents were referring to these children as "the lost generation" (Rowe, 1994, p. i). Concurrently, these same parents were petitioning Christians and church leaders to "help our children to find values in life" (Rowe, 1994, p. i). As a result, schools throughout Russia and the former Soviet bloc have prayer and Bible reading as an important part of their school day (Daniel, 2006; Curtis, 1994; Rowe, 1994). In particular, Boris Yeltsin believed that Christianity would provide a source of moral strength to the nation, and he ordered countless millions of Bibles to be placed in Russian public schools.

From the Russian perspective, because Christians were most responsible for founding their school and university system before the 1917 Bolshevik Revolution, it was only natural to desire schools to have a religious influence (Daniel, 2006). The vast majority of Russians now understand that they were subject to brainwashing under the leadership of communist regimes under Lenin, Stalin, Khrushchev, and others (Daniel, 2006; Glenn, 1995). Consequently, they are suspicious of too much government control of schooling (Daniel, 2006; Glenn, 1995). As a result, they welcome the participation of Orthodox and prominent Protestant denominations in the "architecture" of both public and private school education (Daniel, 2006). Russians believe that the contribution of Christians in developing school curricula, especially that which involves religious instruction and Christian history, serves as a nice counterbalance to the influence of the government (Daniel, 2006). Therefore, Russian educators do not adhere to the "Christophobia" that often infects American public schools (Daniel, 2006). They believe that a strong church presence in schooling acts as insurance against previous and potential government hegemony both in education and life generally (Daniel, 2006; Rowe, 1994).

The growing openness to school choice in Russia since the fall of communism was greatly helped by Boris Yeltsin (Jeynes, 2012d). Yeltsin (1992) stated that schooling should be a top priority and spoke of "reviving the people's spirituality." Yeltsin believed that Christianity should have a prominent role in strengthening Russia's education system. Consequently, since the fall of communism in the Soviet Union, many Christian schools have been established. One of the most notable is the International Academy of St. Petersburg, a Christian school founded in 1993 (Rowe, 1994).

Following the fall of the Berlin Wall and the Iron Curtain, Christian education and school choice greatly benefited from the perseverance of the Protestant, Catholic, and Orthodox churches during the years of communist oppression (Bingen, 2009). Bingen (2009, p. 56) states that following the communists' seizure of power after World War II, "The Roman Catholic Church became the only large-scale societal organization not to be controlled and organized by the party state in Poland." In Germany, via the organization of churches, especially leading up to the fall of the Berlin Wall, 100,000 believers rallied in the street to protest with lighted candles (Holger, 2009). The church played a major role in dismantling communism in many nations across eastern Europe (Bingen, 2009; Holger, 2009; Preda, 2009).

School Choice in South America

Chile

Chile initiated a very decentralized voucher system. The government was greatly influenced by the thoughts of Milton Friedman, who asserted that education suffered when the operation of the schools became too centralized. As a result, in 1980, Chile's government transferred responsibility for running the schools from the National Ministry of Education to the local municipalities. Moreover, they used vouchers to finance parents who desired to send their children to private schools (Carnog and McEwan, 2003). The government also felt that teacher unions were a hindrance to educational reform. Therefore, they disbanded the teachers unions. No one argues for an actual disbanding of these unions in the United States, but there is a sense among many that these unions are the most powerful force in schooling and that a more equal distribution of power in education would likely be a positive development (Carnog and McEwan, 2003; Moe, 2003).

As a result of the program, there was tremendous growth in enrollment at faith-based private schools and independent private schools (Walberg, 2007). Walberg (2007, p. 53) notes, "Claudio Sapelli found in later research that after controlling for budget differences and for socioeconomic characteristics of students and their peers, students in private subsidized (that is, voucher) schools, outperformed those in public schools." The academic and behavioral edge held by students from private, usually religious, schools became widely known throughout Chile. This fueled an increase in the percentage of Chileans attended private schools from roughly 15 percent in the early 1980s to 33 percent by the early 2000s (Carnog and McEwan, 2003).

Chile arrived at some sobering conclusions about the ultimate results of a public school monopoly, which was a major reason they so completely embraced a school choice program that included private schools. Carnog and McEwan (2003, p. 24) summarized the situation well when they stated that many in Chile "claimed that because public education is a government monopoly it inherently denies consumers free choice in their children's education."

The results of the Chilean voucher programs are very encouraging to school choice proponents in many ways. Indeed, private schools produce student results that are often as strong or stronger than public school outcomes at a lower per student cost (Carnog and McEwan, 2003). Nevertheless, it should be pointed out that contrary to what Chubb and Moe (1990) predicted, the introduction of greater direct competition between the public and private sector has not "raised all ships." That is, there is no evidence of any improvement in student achievement in public schools as a result of the added competition (Carnog and McEwan, 2003).

Columbia

The government in 1991 provided vouchers equaling about half the cost of tuition for students of low socioeconomic status (Walberg, 2007).

Ramifications for the School Choice Debate in the United States

There is a certain irony to the fact that school choice is practiced in foreign nations more than it is in the United States, a nation known as "the land of the free." There is a great deal of data presented in this book that will help in the debate on school choice. Nevertheless, even with the availability of these data, it stands clear both from the lack of school choice research cases, that social scientists presently lack the data to arrive at any definite conclusions on the efficiency of school choice. To be sure, the data presented in this book, along with studies other academics have done, are immensely valuable in giving direction to what this nation might expect under a much broader school program that involved private, especially faith-based, schools. With this in mind, however, to truly know the impact of school choice, school choice programs need to be practiced on a much broader scale and then tested.

It is noteworthy that the Netherlands and Australia, which may have the most developed school choice systems in the world, have two of the top six or eight K-12 school systems in the world, as indicated on comparison tests. Finland, which also practices school choice, ranks number one on these tests (Infoplease, 2003). It is also interesting to note that nations with the highest rate of participation tend to yield the most impressive results.

One can argue that if each state provided adequate transportation and if the government extended choice to include private schools, participation rates would rise. Yet, even if participation did rise, based on rates of people using public school choice in places like Minnesota and Cambridge, Massachusetts, the rates may not rise significantly enough to impact the school system as much as choice supporters think. Participation rates will likely rise with increased competition. The extent of competition that emerges also depends on the degree to which parents choose certain schools in order to avoid particular schools or because they want the best school available. Some social scientists suggest that parents of higher socioeconomic status tend to be more particular about the schools they choose (Nechyba, 2003).

Do these facts mean that school choice carries no value? No, but they do mean that we cannot even begin to view school choice as our education system's salvation until educators find ways to increase participation rates. This is especially crucial in urban areas, where students could probably benefit the most from school reforms.

Chapter 4

Private versus Public Schools:
The Private School Edge

There are few educational debates that are currently attracting more attention than the controversy surrounding school choice. One of the most heated educational questions that has been addressed in political circles concerns whether school choice programs should include vouchers or tax breaks for religious schools. Naturally, part of the arguments used in this debate involves church-state issues and whether government educational policy should address the needs of only public schools. While these debates have some merit, an overriding issue exists. That is, do students that attend religious schools actually perform better academically than students who attend nonreligious schools? If there is no difference in achievement or if religious school students perform poorly, the argument that the inclusion of religious schools in a program of choice would increase standards lacks merit. On the other hand, if students attending religious schools perform better than their counterparts in nonreligious schools, one wonders whether the inclusion of religious schools could increase competition and overall school quality. The answer to this question has ramifications not only concerning school choice, but also in regards to whether public school educators can benefit by examining the religious school model.

Researchers have only rarely specifically examined this question of religious versus nonreligious school achievement. Instead, usually researchers have compared student academic achievement in private versus public schools (Chubb & Moe, 1990; Coleman, Hoffer, & Kilgore, 1982; Bryk, Lee, & Holland, 1993). To the extent that church-state issues rest at the heart of much of the debate surrounding school choice, examining the effects of religious schools on the academic achievement of students appears to be a worthy endeavor. Beyond this, even if one resists the notion of school choice, if these differences in academic achievement exist, then this might indicate there is something that educators from public schools can learn from the way religious schools are run. There are many social scientists who do not favor school choice but who do believe educators can learn from the religious school model (Bryk, Lee, & Holland, 1993; Schmidt, 1988).

Even if differences in academic achievement do emerge, some social scientists have asserted that they are due to differences in socioeconomic status and racial composition (Baker, 1998, 1999; Ball, 2003). To arrive at proper conclusions regarding educational policy, these possible explanations need to be investigated and addressed. Should it be the case that no real differences exist, it would affect the merits of the argument that promoting school choice for religious schools will help improve the American system of education.

Over the last 35 or 40 years, there has been a considerable amount of debate on the effects of private schools on the academic achievement of children (Chubb & Moe, 1990; Coleman, Hoffer, & Kilgore, 1982; Bryk, Lee, & Holland, 1993). Part of this debate has focused on private schools versus public schools in general (Chubb & Moe, 1990; Lamb, 1994). Other aspects of this debate have focused almost solely on Catholic schools (Coleman, Hoffer, & Kilgore, 1982; Bryk, Lee, & Holland, 1993; Morris, 1998). Increasingly, however, social scientists have acknowledged the importance of examining the effects of religious schools, on the whole, on the academic achievement of children (Chubb & Moe, 1990; Gaziel, 1997). There are three primary reasons for this acknowledgment. First, non-Catholic private schools make up an increasing percentage of faith-based schools in the United States (Russo & Rogus, 1998). Second, there are a rising number of different religious groups represented in America. Third, simply comparing the academic achievement of private school students versus public school students tends to give private school students an advantage. This is because the cohort of private school students includes prep school students, who often come from economically advantaged backgrounds.

Social scientists differ about the reasons students from religious schools may outperform students from public schools. Gaziel (1997) asserts that the achievement gap can specifically be attributed to differences in school culture. Some social scientists argue that to the extent to which this is true, faith-based schools do a better job of helping disadvantaged students (Gaziel, 1997; Irvine & Foster, 1996; Morris, 2010). An alternative or supplemental view given by some is that religious schools promote parental involvement more than public schools do (Coleman, 1988; Jeynes, 2010d; Riley, 1996).

Although many researchers now acknowledge that religious schools are associated with higher academic achievement, some question the extent to which this advantage is due to certain positive qualities in the way the schools are run. Some researchers believe that students from Catholic, Protestant, and Jewish schools outperform students in public schools simply because public schools have a high percentage of low-SES and racial minority children (Baker, 1998, 1999; Ball, 2003). They assert that religious schools have a distinct advantage in that they are able to choose which students they want to attend their schools, and this translates into having families with a higher SES (Ball, 2003). Moynihan (1989), however, presents evidence suggesting that the racial distribution of students in Catholic schools is similar to that found in public schools. In addition, some research suggests that religious schools may benefit minority students (Morris, 2010; Neal, 1997). Nevertheless, many social scientists question whether religious schools really help children from low-SES and racial minority backgrounds more than the public schools do (Bracey, 1997; Brunsma, 1998).

The achievement gap that exists between students from Catholic and public schools is substantial enough so that even public school leaders are examining what makes Catholic schools so successful (Hudolin, 1994). The Chicago's public school system, for example, is attempting to model several aspects of the Catholic school system (Hudolin, 1994). Although some factors that contribute to the success of Catholic schools may be difficult to imitate, many social scientists believe that Catholic schools are a useful model for public schools (Bryk, Lee, & Holland, 1993; McEwen, Knipe, & Gallagher, 1997; Morris, 2010). For those who are concerned about what kinds of morals are taught in the public schools, the previous facts may provide some solace (Halstead & Lewicka, 1998).

Although there have been a number of attempts to quantify the differences in academic achievement between students from private and public schools, a large portion of these studies have possessed certain limitations. First, many of these studies did not use nation-wide data sets. Second, many studies that did use nationwide data sets examined the effects of private schools generally or Catholic schools specifically. Third, some of the most convincing studies that have been done are somewhat dated, given that there has been such an increase in the number of children attending religious non-Catholic schools. Fourth, the vast majority of studies on religious schools do not address the specific issue of how students of low-SES or racial minority backgrounds perform in religious schools versus nonreligious schools.

This chapter's study uses the National Education Longitudinal Survey (NELS) for the year 1992 to address four specific questions. First, how do twelfth grade students in religious schools (most of which are Catholic or Protestant) perform academically versus their counterparts in nonreligious schools (public schools, prep schools, and other nonreligious private schools)? Second, what are the effects that emerge when one controls for socioeconomic status (SES)? Third, how do black and Hispanic twelfth grade students in religious schools perform academically versus their counterparts in nonreligious schools? Fourth, how do low-SES (the bottom half) twelfth grade students in religious schools perform academically versus low-SES (the bottom half) twelfth grade students in nonreligious schools?

Methods and Data Sources

The population that this study draws from includes students who participated in the National Education Longitudinal Survey (NELS) for the year 1992. The NELS research project was sponsored by the U.S. Department of Education's National Center for Statistics. National Opinion Research Center (NORC) and NORC subcontractors designed the study. The Educational Testing Service (ETS) designed the achievement tests used in this study.

In 1988, using a "two stage probability design," the researchers selected a nationally representative sample of schools and eighth grade students (U.S. Department of Education, 1992). There were

24,599 students from 1,052 schools who participated in this study. This cohort of students was followed up on in the tenth grade (1990) and again in the twelfth grade (1992). Of the students sampled, 69 percent were white, 13 percent were Hispanic, 11 percent were African American, 6 percent were Asian, and 1 percent were Native American. For each year that income data was taken, the median income level was between $40,000 and $50,000. Among the parents, 26 percent had at least a four-year college degree, and 89 percent had earned a high school diploma. In terms of gender, 50.6 percent of the students were female. Questionnaires regarding a vast array of topics, were given to students, parents, and teachers. Achievement tests in mathematics, reading, science, and social studies (history, civics, and geography) were also given to the students. These tests were "curriculum based cognitive tests that used item overlapping methods to measure" academic achievement (U.S. Department of Education, 1992).

From the NELS questionnaires, religious commitment variables were created to be used in General Linear Model (GLM) regression analysis. Religious school dummy variables were created to indicate whether a student was attending a religious school ("yes" for this dummy variable = 1). All twelfth grade students attending a Catholic, evangelical, or other religious school were included in this category. All students who did not attend a religious school—whether it was a nonreligious private school, a prep school, or a public school—were coded as not attending a religious school.

Academic Achievement Variables

Standardized tests. Standardized test scores were obtained using tests developed by ETS. IRT scores (Item Response Theory scores) were obtained for the Reading Comprehension Test, the Mathematics Comprehension Test, the Social Studies (History/Citizenship/Geography) Comprehension Test, the Science Comprehension Test, and the Test Composite (Reading and Math test results combined).

Left back. This dummy variable measured whether a student had been held back a grade at any time in his or her life.

Basic core. Coded with the value 1 if a twelfth grade student had taken the basic core courses identified by the NAEP (National Association of Educational Progress). This basics program consisted of four years of English courses, three years of social studies courses, three years of science courses, three years of math courses, two years of foreign language courses, and half a year of computer science courses. Students who had not taken the basic core courses were coded with the value 0.

Other Independent Variables

Variables Involving Race

For each variable measuring race (Asian, Hispanic, Black, and Native American), a student was coded with a 1 if he or she was a member of this race and coded with a 0 if he or she was not.

Variables Involving Socioeconomic Status

The socioeconomic status of a child's family was determined "using parent questionnaire data, when available." Five components composed the socioeconomic status variables: (1) father's level of education, (2) mother's level of education, (3) father's occupation, (4) mother's occupation, and (5) family income.

The occupational data were recoded using the Duncan SEI (Socioeconomic Index) scale, which was also used in the High School and Beyond Survey. If any of the components were missing from the parent questionnaire, equivalent or related questions were used from the student questionnaire to determine SES. Three coded SES variables were used.

Gender. Coded with the value 1 for a female. Males were coded with the value 0.

Models

When all the students in the NELS sample were examined, two models were used in analyzing the effects of religious schools: the SES Model and the No-SES Model. Each model possessed variables for gender and race. The SES Model possessed variables for SES, while the No-SES Model did not. The use of these models is important for the following reasons:

- To obtain overall effects for religious schools.
- To use models that are the most commonly used by educational researchers so that the results of this study can be understood in

reference to the work that other researchers have done. If controls are used in an educational study, these are the most common variables used.

Regression analysis was used, using the general linear model, in the analyses.

The primary purpose of this study was to compare the academic achievement of children attending religious schools with the achievement of students who did not fall in this category. Data was collected using the 1992 (twelfth grade) data set.

Results

The results indicate that children attending religious schools achieve at higher levels academically than their counterparts who are not attending religious schools, even after race and gender are controlled for. Table 4.1 shows the effects for twelfth graders attending a religious school, using the No-SES Model. Among the standardized test measures, the effects ranged from .43 standard deviation units for the Test Composite to .29 standard deviation units for the Science test. With the exception of the Science test, all the effects for the standardized tests were about .4 of a standard deviation. For the nonstandardized measures, the effects were .42 for the Basic Core set of courses and −.21 for being the Left Back a Grade variable.

Table 4.2 shows the results for all students in the twelfth grade sample, using the SES Model. The absolute value of the regression coefficients for attending a religious school declined, although all of the regression coefficients for this variable remained statistically significant. Three of the standardized test measures produced regression coefficients of .18. The betas for each of these achievement variables—Reading, Social Studies, and the Test Composite—all maintained the same level of statistical significance, as was evident using the No-SES Model. Among the standardized test measures, the Science test once again had the smallest beta, .07. For the nonstandardized measures, the effects were .31 for the Basic Core set of courses and −.11 for being the Left Back a Grade variable.

The effects for black and Hispanic children attending religious schools was then examined. Table 4.3 shows the effects for black and Hispanic children attending religious schools, controlling for SES and gender. Among the standardized test measures, the effects

Table 4.1 Effects (in standard deviation units) on Academic Achievement for Twelfth Grade (1992) Children Attending a Religious School Versus Children Not Attending a Religious School, Using the No-SES Model ($N = 20{,}706$)

Academic Measure	Reading	Math	Social Studies	Science
Religious school	.39[****]	.40[****]	.41[****]	.29[****]
Asian	.13[***]	.34[****]	.21[****]	.09[*]
Hispanic	−.51[****]	−.58[****]	−.49[****]	−.64[****]
Black	−.70[****]	−.80[****]	−.65[****]	−.91[****]
Native American	−.61[****]	−.65[****]	−.67[****]	−.66[****]
Race missing	−.56[****]	−.56[****]	−.52[****]	−.57[****]
Gender	.29[****]	−.09[****]	−.29[****]	−.29[****]

Academic Measure	Composite	Left Back[a]	Basics[a]
Religious school	.43[****]	−.21[****]	.42[****]
Asian	.25[****]	−.11[***]	.28[****]
Hispanic	−.58[****]	.19[****]	−.12[****]
Black	−.80[****]	.25[****]	−.11[****]
Native American	−.67[****]	.29[****]	−.32[****]
Race missing	−.61[****]	.19[****]	−.11
Gender	.06[***]	−.17[****]	.07[****]

Note: a = Logistic regression analysis was used
[*] $p < .05$
[**] $p < .01$
[***] $p < .001$
[****] $p < .0001$

are generally about .05 of a standard deviation larger than were found when the SES Model was used for all the students in the sample. In other words, the achievement test gap between students from religious and nonreligious schools was somewhat larger for blacks and Hispanics than it was the rest of the student sample made up primarily of white students. All of the effects were at least .2 of a standard deviation, with the exception of the Science test. The largest effect was for the Social Studies test, at .26. The effect for the

Table 4.2 Effects (in standard deviation units) on Academic Achievement for Twelfth Grade (1992) Children Attending a Religious School Versus Children Not Attending a Religious School, Using the SES Model ($N = 20{,}706$)

Academic Measure	Reading	Math	Social Studies	Science
Religious school	.18****	.16****	.18****	.07**
SES quartile 2	.28****	.33****	.32****	.29****
SES quartile 3	.50****	.58****	.53****	.51****
SES quartile 4	.92****	1.08****	.99****	.93****
Asian	.11**	.32****	.19****	.06*
Hispanic	−.25****	−.27****	−.21****	−.37****
Black	−.47****	−.53****	−.41****	−.68****
Native American	−.37****	−.37****	−.42****	−.42****
Race missing	−.39****	−.36****	−.33****	−.40****
Gender	.22****	−.07****	−.14****	−.27****

Academic Measure	Composite	Left Back[a]	Basics[a]
Religious school	.43****	−.11****	.42****
SES quartile 2	.32****	−.28****	.17****
SES quartile 3	.59****	−.40****	.29****
SES quartile 4	1.07****	−.48****	.45****
Asian	.23****	−.11***	.27****
Hispanic	−.28****	.19****	.01
Black	−.54****	.25****	.00
Native American	−.40****	.29****	−.21****
Race missing	−.40****	.19****	−.02
Gender	.08****	−.17****	.07****

Note: a = Logistic regression analysis was used
* $p < .05$
** $p < .01$
*** $p < .001$
**** $p < .0001$

Table 4.3 Effects (in standard deviation units) on Academic Achievement for Twelfth Grade (1992) Black and Hispanic Children Attending a Religious School versus Black and Hispanic Children Not Attending a Religious School, Controlling for Gender and SES (N = 20,706)

Academic Measure	Reading	Math	Social Studies	Science
Religious school	.23**	.21**	.26***	.10
SES quartile 2	.23****	.23****	.24****	.22****
SES quartile 3	.46****	.50****	.46****	.46****
SES quartile 4	.78****	.91****	.81****	.89****
Gender	.15****	−.07****	−.15****	−.29****

Academic Measure	Composite	Left Back[a]	Basics[a]
Religious school	.24****	−.15	.17*
SES quartile 2	.24****	−.27****	.11**
SES quartile 3	.51****	−.39****	.31****
SES quartile 4	.90****	−.44****	.42****
Gender	.03	−.22****	.11**

Note: a = Logistic regression analysis was used
* $p < .05$
** $p < .01$
*** $p < .001$
**** $p < .0001$

Science test was the only standardized test regression coefficient that was not statistically significant. Among the nonstandardized measures, the effect for taking the Basic Core set of courses was statistically significant, but the effect for being Left Back a Grade fell just short of statistical significance. Therefore, black and Hispanic children attending religious schools were more likely than their counterparts in nonreligious schools to take the Basic Core set of courses recommended by the NAEP. In the case of being left back a grade, although the direction of the regression coefficient indicates that black and Hispanic students were less likely to drop out than their counterparts in nonreligious schools, the result was not statistically significant.

Table 4.4 shows the regression coefficients that emerged for low-SES students (the lowest half), when controlling for race and gender. The results show that low-SES students in religious schools, on average, consistently outperformed low-SES students in nonreligious schools. The ranges of absolute values for the regression coefficients are quite similar for both the standardized and nonstandardized measures. The absolute value of the effects range from .37 to .23 for the standardized measures and .37 to .27 for the nonstandardized

Table 4.4 Effects (in standard deviation units) on Academic Achievement for Twelfth Grade (1992) Low-SES Children Attending a Religious School versus Low-SES Children Not Attending a Religious School, Controlling for Race and Gender (N = 20,706)

Academic Measure	Reading	Math	Social Studies	Science
Religious School	.36[****]	.33[****]	.31[****]	.23[****]
Asian	.06	.37[****]	.26[****]	.02
Hispanic	−.29[****]	−.32[****]	−.25[****]	−.43[****]
Black	−.53[****]	−.59[****]	−.46[****]	−.75[****]
Native American	−.40[***]	−.35[***]	−.40[***]	−.49[****]
Race missing	−.38[***]	−.38[***]	−.34[**]	−.44[****]
Gender	.19[****]	−.09[****]	−.14[****]	−.30[****]

Academic Measure	Composite	Left Back[a]	Basics[a]
Religious School	.37[****]	−.27[****]	.37[****]
Asian	.23[****]	−.11[***]	.49[****]
Hispanic	−.33[****]	.10[**]	−.02
Black	−.60[****]	.21[****]	−.02
Native American	−.40[****]	.24[*]	−.17[****]
Race missing	−.40[****]	.10	−.04
Gender	.05[*]	−.24[****]	.08[***]

Note: a = Logistic regression analysis was used
[*] $p < .05$
[**] $p < .01$
[***] $p < .001$
[****] $p < .0001$

measures. The effects for the Test Composite and the Basic Core set of courses were the largest. The effects for being Left Back a Grade and the Science test were the smallest.

Discussion

The results show that twelfth grade students attending religious schools outperform their counterparts attending nonreligious schools. These results hold even when controlling for SES. The results also indicate that black and Hispanic twelfth graders attending religious schools generally do better than their less religious counterparts. Finally, children from low-SES backgrounds attending religious schools also perform better academically than their counterparts attending nonreligious schools. The results support the notion that religious schools benefit children to an extent that significantly surpasses any explanations that can be attributed to racial and socioeconomic factors alone. These results appear to support the beliefs of many researchers that there are certain aspects of the way religious schools are run that explain the achievement gap that exists between religious and nonreligious schools (Bryk, Lee, & Holland, 1993; Gaziel, 1997; Morris, 2010).

The results favoring students attending religious schools holds quite well across the measures of academic achievement. Among the nonstandardized measures, the effects for being Left Back a Grade are weaker than for taking the Basic Core set of courses. This may reflect the high standards that many religious schools maintain. Religious schools generally require students to take a larger array of advanced courses than do most nonreligious schools do (Jeynes, 2012h, 2014). In addition, religious schools are less likely to engage in "social promotion" than most nonreligious schools are (Jeynes, 2002a, 2014). To the extent that these statements are true, one would expect larger differences to emerge between religious and nonreligious schools for taking the Basic Core courses than for being left back a grade. Among the standardized measures, the effects of attending religious schools are weakest for the Science test. Again, upon closer examination, this result probably makes sense. Religious schools generally spend considerably less money per student than nonreligious schools do (Gumbrecht, 2012). The budgets of religious schools are generally tight. Building a strong science curriculum requires spending large sums of money for laboratories, chemicals, biological specimens, and other materials. Of the academic disciplines examined, building a solid science curriculum is probably the most expensive. On average, nonreligious, especially public, schools have more money available to fund the science curriculum than religious schools. It is quite possible that the results of this study reflect this fact. Although Bower (1997) notes that many religious schools "inspire math reasoning," if religious schools lack scientific equipment, this advanced ability to think logically regarding mathematics may not produce as large an advantage in science.

The results of this study support the findings of other research that suggests religious schools may produce considerable benefit for those students who are "nontraditional" students, in various senses of the word. Sander (1996), for example, found that Catholic schools produced the largest academic advantage for non-Catholic students. Jeynes (1999) hypothesizes that nontraditional students in terms of religion, race, or SES may actually benefit more from religious schools than they do students of faith do. Jeynes argues that nontraditional students may enjoy a greater "marginal utility" from attending a religious school than more traditional religious students. In the latter case, he argues, religious students often already possess the values espoused by religious schools. Therefore, to the extent that the religious culture of a school encourages students to achieve at higher academic levels, religious students who have previously experienced this culture would benefit less than their less-religious counterparts. In his research, Jeynes (1999, 2002a, 2003c) has shown that black and Hispanic religious students, as well as religious students in general, academically outperform their less religious counterparts. This adds credence to findings that suggests there is something about the culture of religious schools that manifests itself in the way that they are run, which helps explain why students from religious schools excel academically. This is not to say that SES and the "selectivity" factor do not play a role. It is clear, however, that there is something more at work in religious schools that helps explain why students from religious schools, on average, outperform students from nonreligious schools. Research also indicates that the gap between "advantaged" and/or "high-ability" students and "disadvantaged" or "ability students" is less in religious schools than it is in public schools (Gamoran, 1992; Russo & Rogus, 1998).

Although previous research has established that students attending Catholic schools perform better academically than those attending public schools, this study includes all students attending religious schools and all students attending nonreligious schools (public and private), in order to create broader conclusions regarding the effects of religious education.

Policy Implications

Ultimately, the results of this research have important implications for educational policy in the following ways: (1) assessing whether school choice programs that include private schools should be initiated and (2) determining whether public school educators may have something to learn from certain aspects of how religious schools are run.

Addressing Whether School Choice Programs Should Be Initiated

A primary reason school choice attracts so much attention is the belief that school choice will produce an overall increase in school quality. Milton Friedman (1994) uses this argument in favor of school choice when he states, "Choice produces competition. Competition produces quality." This assertion gains some credence when one examines the results of this study that suggests students in religious schools outperform their counterparts in nonreligious schools.

Although numerous social scientists acknowledge the academic advantage that religious schools enjoy, a significant number of them question whether school choice is an attractive option. The reasons given are as follows. First, opponents of choice question whether such a program would really produce the level of competition that its supporters claim. These opponents contend that for the competition level to increase, there would need to be a large number of students willing to leave their current schools and participate in school choice programs. In reality, although the current evidence is limited, those few places that have school choice programs have low student participation rates. The participation rate in American and British school programs, which includes either public schools alone or both public and private schools, is only about 15 percent (Ball, 2003; Woods, Bagley, & Glatter, 1998).

Second, some educators question whether other types of reform might produce stronger results than a program of school choice. Roseberg (1989, p. 11) states:

If choice is used as a cheap substitute for this more fundamental pursuit, then the prospects of turning around our public school system and dramatically improving the education of our children will be more remote than ever.

Some educators believe that learning from religious schools, reducing class size, and encouraging more parental involvement are more essential reforms than school choice (Jeynes, 2014).

Third, opponents of school choice have concerns about choice's possible influence on equity. Some social scientists believe that school choice will primarily benefit the wealthy. Three central potential equity problems concern these educators. First, impoverished people may not receive sufficient information about the options available to make the best choice (Nicotera, Mendiburo, & Brends, 2011; Stevens, dela Terre, & Johnson, 2011). Second, producing educational markets may not be in the best interests of the public. Some social scientists are concerned that school choice turns parents into "customers," and these customers may choose easy or trendy schools, rather than high-quality schools (Bauch, 2000). Third, transportation concerns are also evident. Numerous poor people might be unable to pay for the transportation they need to attend the school of their choice.

Localities that practice school choice have most successfully responded to the concerns about equity. In fact, in a number of school choice programs, at-risk students make up over half of the participants (Colopy & Tarr, 1994). However, the other two issues may be harder to address.

There is some evidence that students participating in private school choice programs perform better academically than they do in public schools. For example, Greene (1996) and colleagues found that students participating in the Milwaukee voucher program scored higher than they did in public schools and higher than similar Milwaukee children who were not participating in the program. The results of this study support Greene's findings. In this study, children from low-SES backgrounds who attended religious schools outperformed their counterparts attending nonreligious schools. This is a salient result because one of the greatest concerns of educators has been how to reduce the gap between low-SES and high-SES students. The results of this study indicate that this gap is smaller in religious schools than it is in nonreligious schools. To the extent to which this is true, this fact may alleviate or override some of the other concerns just mentioned. For example, one would think that if it becomes widely known that the achievement gap for low-SES and black and Hispanic children is less in religious schools than in nonreligious schools, this fact alone could produce a certain level of competition. If parents of low-SES and black and Hispanic students perceive that their children are more likely to perform well academically, religious schools are more likely to attract more students. This will enhance competition among schools. In addition, to whatever extent religious schools help low-SES and black and Hispanic children more than high-SES and white children, this trend may override any disadvantages that these parents face in terms of access to information about available schools and so forth. It is therefore conceivable that contrary to what many public school educators believe, it may be that low-SES and racial minority families may be among the groups that benefit the most by school choice programs.

Determining Whether Educators in the Public Schools May Have Something to Learn from Religious Schools

A number of social scientists believe it is crucial that public school educators learn from the example set by religious schools. The findings of this study support the views of these social scientists. The results of this study indicate that students in religious schools outperform their counterparts in nonreligious schools on virtually every measure of academic achievement, and in religious schools, the academic gaps that commonly exist between low-SES and high-SES students as well as black and Hispanic versus white students are reduced. Given that these represent some of the primary goals of educators, it is logical that if educators in religious schools have learned to produce these outcomes, they have something to teach the secular educational community. Many public school educators have attempted to reduce these persistent academic gaps for years. If religious educators have already developed a strategy that reduces these gaps, public school educators would be wise to seriously examine the religious school model.

Different theorists have unique explanations about why religious school pupils may outperform nonreligious school pupils. Bryk, Lee, and Holland (1993) opine that religious schools have a more disciplined atmosphere. Other researchers contend that religious schools excel because they emphasize traditional values (Hyde, 1990; Schmidt, 1988). Further analyses need to be done to be able to conclude just what aspects of religious schooling give students from these schools the academic advantages that they enjoy. Based on the research and theorizing that has been completed thus far, there do exist certain definite attempts to imitate religious schools. Researchers should attempt to confirm whether the areas that are being imitated help explain the academic gap between students in religious and nonreligious students and whether these attempts at imitation are working.

The foremost area that public school educators are imitating is the moral education emphasis that religious schools have (Halstead & Lewicka, 1998; Bryk, Lee, & Holland, 1993; McEwen, Knipe, & Gallagher, 1997). Moral education used to be a major part of public school education. However, after state-sanctioned prayer and Bible reading were removed from the public schools in 1962 and 1963, character education ceased to be a major emphasis in many public schools (Haynes, 1999; Miller, 1999). Immediately following 1963, there was an abrupt decrease in most major academic achievement measures and a sudden increase in adolescent crime (U.S. Department of Education, 1999; U.S. Department of Justice, 1993). From 1963 to 1980, average scores on tests such as the Stanford Achievement Test, the California Achievement Test, the Scholastic Achievement Test, and the Iowa Test of Education Development decreased by more than at any time in the history of these tests (Harnischfeger & Wiley, 1975; U.S. Department of Education, 1999). Concurrently, most measures of juvenile crime and delinquent behavior rose 300–700 percent (U.S. Department of Health and Human Services, 1992; U.S. Department of Justice, 1993). Social scientists differ on the extent to which they believe the absence of character education in the public schools contributed to these trends (Brunsma, 1998). However, in the eyes of many educators, character instruction is important in the development of the self-discipline necessary to perform well in school and avoid harmful behavior (Edwards, 2000; Ryan & Bohlin, 1998; Smagorinsky, 2000).

Preserving high scholastic standards is a second area in which social scientists believe public educators can learn from religious schools. Mentzer (1988) points out that religious schools frequently require more homework to be done by the students. Hoffer (1997) and Bryk, Lee, and Holland (1993) note that religious schools encourage students to take college preparation courses more often than is done in public schools. Research evidence suggests that disadvantaged children in particular benefit from this emphasis on high academic standards (Coleman, 1988; Coleman, Hoffer, & Kilgore, 1982; Gaziel, 1997). Social scientists suggest that there may be a myriad of other areas in which religious schools can serve as a model for public schools. For example, Hoffer (1997) and Coleman, Hoffer, and Kilgore (1982) suggest that religious schools are better than public schools at encouraging parental involvement in education. Irvine and Foster (1996) argue that religious schools have a higher degree of racial harmony and that this helps explain why minority children do well in religious schools. Recent research supports the notion that there is a higher degree of racial harmony in religious schools than in nonreligious schools (Jeynes, 2003b).

Although there are many social scientists who believe public educators can learn from religious educators, there are some who believe this is impossible or very difficult. Gaziel (1997) believes that the achievement gap between religious and public schools can be explained by a difference in school culture. To the extent that this is true, it may be difficult for public schools to replicate the results that often emerge in religious schools. Carbonaro (1999) and Hallinan and Kubitschek (1999) have suggested that the religious school culture that includes an emphasis on family values and personal morality plays a large role in explaining why religious school students do so well academically. Given that public school educators may not place an emphasis on these same areas, this limits the degree to which public schools can benefit from the strengths of the religious school system.

While educators are frequently divided over the merits of school choice, there is a growing consensus that public schools can benefit by imitating some of the strengths of the religious school model. Although there may be limitation on just what qualities can be imitated, character education, high academic standards, and parental involvement are areas that can be imitated (Hyde, 1990; Schmidt, 1988).

Although educators often emphasize their differences in opinion rather than their similarities, ultimately, virtually all educators desire the American school system to be the best that it can be. It is for this reason that educators have a special interest in the academic success of religious schools. While debate continues regarding precisely how the presence of religious schools can benefit the American education system, there is no question that the religious school system can make a significant contribution. As educators continue to debate over the next several years, it shall become increasingly clear what its contribution will be. The results of this study suggest that religious education is a healthy part of the schooling system in the United States. It also should encourage researchers to examine more closely specifically why students attending religious schools outperform their counterparts in nonreligious schools. It also supports the notion that including religious schools in a system of school choice conceivably could help the overall quality of the American education system.

The Evidence That Private Schools Are Encouraging Moral Behavior

While it is clear from numerical data and a variety of studies that religious factors in schooling and personal commitment are associated with higher scholastic outcomes, it is also true that they are associated with improved behavioral results (Jeynes, 2006a, 2009, 2010c). The meta-analysis indicated that the religious school advantage over both traditional public schools and charter schools is in the neighborhood of .26 to .28 standard deviation units, without the incorporation of sophisticated controls. That advantage is .34 to .35 standard deviation units when applied to behavior. What is especially interesting is that, as will be even more evident in Chapter 7, there is very little dilution in the behavioral effect sizes when SES and other sophisticated controls are included in the equation. Chapter 7 will also elucidate the results that emerged using more specific behavioral components than were used in Chapter 2.

Why Religious Schools Have an Edge over Public Schools

Although it is apparent that religious schools have an edge over public schools, the question that emerges is about what features of religious schools help to explain these advantages. Social scientists commonly propound three reasons to explain the advantage.

First, they believe that the culture of the religious schools contributes to the faith-based school advantage (Gaziel, 1997). Some social scientists argue that to the extent to which this is true, religious schools do a better job of helping disadvantaged students (Gaziel,

1997; Morris, 2010). In terms of the outward manifestations of this culture, theorists note several differences that can be objectively measured by using the NELS data set. Some social scientists believe that the religious school advantage is due to the school atmosphere (Coleman, 1988; Jeynes, 2001, 2005e; Morris, 2010). Another possibility is that religious schools require students to do more homework (Mentzer, 1988). Other researchers believe that religious schools are less likely to have violence or threats of violence, which can often serve as major distractions for students trying to learn (Hudolin, 1994; Irvine & Foster, 1996). Still other social scientists believe that a higher level of racial harmony exists at religious schools because of the common thread of faith and Christian brotherhood (Irvine & Foster, 1996). Finally, some social scientists believe that religious schools are likely to have modes of discipline that make them more prone to success (Morris, 1994; Sander, 1996).

A second reason, family factors or a broader sense of what Coleman described as "social capital," results from both family-based and community-based sources (Coleman, 1988; Coleman & Hoffer, 1987). Educators, sociologists, and psychologists have been quick to point out that religious people are more likely to remain in intact families, become engaged in their children's education, and provide an upbringing and community that encourage an atmosphere of morality and self-discipline (Jeynes, 2005a, 2006b, 2007b).

Finally, a third possible factor is that religious schools promote Christian, Jewish, or other forms of devotion (Irvine & Foster, 1996; Jeynes, 2003d). This, in turn, yields positive effects. Each of these three factors is explained further in the following sections.

Culture of the School

The first factor to which social scientists point in helping to explain the religious school student advantage is school culture. This study sought to statistically examine many aspects of school culture. First, the study focused on five aspects of school culture: (1) school atmosphere, (2) racial harmony, (3) level of school discipline, (4) school violence, and (5) amount of homework done. The results demonstrate that religious schools outperform nonreligious schools in all of the five school trait categories and in nearly all of the individual questions that make up those categories. Table 4.5 shows the effects of attending a religious school for all the individual questions under

Table 4.5 Effects (in standard deviation units) of Religious Schools versus Nonreligious Schools on the Five School Variables for the Twelfth Grade (1992) (N = 18,726)

	Results Controlling for Gender and Race	Results Controlling for SES, Urban Setting, Gender and Race
School Atmosphere Variables:		
School Spirit	.26****	.30****
Teachers Interested	.30****	.18****
Racial Harmony Variables:		
Friendly	.20****	.13****
Racial Fights	.56****	.57****
Discipline Variables:		
Disruptions	.17****	.11***
Ignore Cheating	.05	.01
Offered Drugs	.13****	.20****
Violence Variables:		
Many Gangs	.54****	.66****
Threaten to Hurt	.10***	.11**
Fights	.06*	.03
Homework	.14****	.05**

Note: *$p < .05$
**$p < .01$
***$p < .001$
****$p < .0001$

each school trait category. In the first column, data are adjusted for SES, race, gender, and whether the school was in an urban setting; in the second column, data are adjusted only for race and gender. All of the differences are listed in standard deviation units, a procedure that is important for effectively comparing different measures because different assessments have different grading units and the scores vary to different degrees. Presenting the results in a standardized form makes it possible to compare the results of different tests more fairly and accurately. The effects for racial harmony and school atmosphere, on average, showed the largest advantage for the religious schools.

When data are adjusted for race and gender but not for SES and for whether the school was in an urban setting, the results were as follows. The regression coefficient for fewer racial/ethnic fights occurring at religious schools was .56. The regression coefficient for students being friendly with other racial groups was .20. The effects for the school atmosphere category were .26 for school spirit and .30 for teachers being interested in the students. Statistical analysis indicated that there was less than a 1 in 10,000 possibility that each of these results emerged by chance or coincidence. The effects for school violence were also noteworthy but varied considerably depending on the question. The effect for whether there were many gangs showed a regression coefficient of .54 for attending a religious school, meaning that there were fewer gangs in religious schools. This result, based on statistical analysis, also had just a 1 in 10,000 possibility of occurring by chance or coincidence The regression was smallest in this category for getting into a physical fight at school: .06. Going to a religious school also meant that students generally did more homework; the regression coefficient in this case was .14. The effects for school discipline were generally the smallest of the five categories. In fact, one of the three questions in this category, whether teachers ignore student cheating, yielded near zero effects. The effects for disruptions that impede learning and drugs offered to the students at school yielded effects of .17 and .13, respectively.

When data were adjusted for SES and for whether a school was in an urban setting in addition to race and gender factors, the results showed a similar pattern, with the regression coefficient rising for whether there were gangs (.66), racial fights (.57), and a school spirit (.30). Some regression coefficients decreased, including whether teachers were interested in students (.18), whether the school was racially friendly (.13), and whether the students did more homework (.05).

When one examines the effects of learning habits on achievement, the results are quite intriguing (see Table 4.6). The results indicate that the three learning habits in which religious students enjoy the greatest advantage over their public school counterparts are the learning habits that are most strongly related to academic achievement. That is, taking harder courses, diligence, and overall work habits were the learning habits in which religious school students enjoyed the largest advantage over public school students.

Table 4.6 Rank Order of Learning Habits in Which Religious School Students Enjoy the Largest Advantage over Public School Students and Learning Habits Most Closely Associated with High Academic Achievement

	Largest Advantage for Religious Students Not Considering SES Factors	Largest Advantage for Religious Students Considering SES Factors	Greatest Influence on Math Achievement Not Considering SES Factors	Greatest Influence on Math Achievement Considering SES Factors	Greatest Influence on Reading Achievement Considering SES Factors
First Largest Effect	Taking harder courses	Diligence	Taking harder courses	Taking harder courses	Taking harder courses
Second Largest Effect	Diligence	Taking harder courses	Diligence	Diligence	Diligence
Third Largest Effect	Work habits	Work habits	Paying attention	Work habits	Work habits
Fourth Largest Effect	Work handed in on time	Work handed in on time	Work habits	Paying attention	Paying attention
Fifth Largest Effect	Paying attention	Paying attention	Less absenteeism	Less absenteeism	Less absenteeism

Family and Social Capital

A second reason that social scientists frequently cite for the faith-based school advantage is the fact that Christian and other religious schools emphasize the role of parental involvement more than is commonly found in public schools (Coleman, 1988; Jeynes, 2003a; Moe, 2006). Research also indicates that highly religious couples are more likely to remain married than are less religious couples and that intact families, on average, have children with considerably higher levels of achievement than do nonintact families (Jeynes, 2002a; Sullivan, 2001). Coleman (1988) and colleagues assert that these two facts enable religious school students to possess, on average, a higher level of social capital than their public school counterparts have. He believes that social capital represents the degree to which certain key members of a society invest their time, energy, wisdom, and knowledge in an individual or institution.

According to Coleman and other social scientists, given that Christian and other religious school students are more likely to have had parents, teachers, churches, and other factors invest in them, they are more likely to excel academically. Religious school students are more likely to have involved parents, caring teachers, and other factors that have shown to be positively associated with high academic outcomes (Coleman & Hoffer, 1987; Jeynes, 2002c). One might ask why religious schools are more likely to be correlated with parental involvement and caring teachers. Coleman avers that religious and public schools have very different orientations that result in religious school students eventually being endowed with higher levels of social capital. He asserts that the orientation of the public schools is one that "sees schools as society's instrument for releasing a child from the blinders imposed by accident of birth into this family or that family. Schools have been designed to open broad horizons to the child, transcending the limitations of the parents." By contrast, the religious school orientation "sees a school as the extension of the family, reinforcing the family's values" (Coleman & Hoffer, 1987, p. 3).

Encourage Religious Commitment

A third factor that social scientists frequently use to help explain the religious school advantage is that Christian, Jewish, and similar schools encourage religious commitment among their students.

Especially since the Supreme Court decisions of 1962 and 1963 removing prayer and Bible reading from the public schools, religious commitment has not been encouraged in public schools (Blanshard, 1963; Jeynes, 2005a, 2013; Kliebard, 1969).

There are a number of reasons religious commitment could have a beneficial impact on academic outcomes that could ultimately reduce the achievement gap. The first of these reasons, and historically probably the most acknowledged, deals with a religious work ethic. This is often referred to as the Protestant work ethic. Recent research, however, indicates that it may extend beyond the Protestant sphere to other religious groups. For example, Novak (1993) and Tropman (2002) have found that Catholics in the United States possess a strong work ethic. Research in the social sciences has consistently indicated the existence of a religious work ethic (Mentzer, 1988; Novak, 1993).

A second reason religious commitment could positively affect school outcomes stems from the finding of some studies that suggest religious people are more likely to have an internal locus of control (Jackson & Coursey, 1988; Shrauger & Silverman, 1971). Educational researchers have found a rather consistent relationship between having an internal locus of control and performing well in school (Garner & Cole, 1986; Johnson, 1992).

A third reason to think that there might be a correlation between religious commitment and scholastic outcomes emerges from the tendency for religious people to eschew behaviors that are often viewed as undisciplined and harmful to educational achievement. A number of studies indicate that religiously committed teens are less likely to become involved in drug and alcohol abuse (Bahr, Hawks, & Wang, 1993; Jeynes, 2002d). Other studies indicate that religiously committed teens are less likely to engage in sexual behavior or become pregnant while they are still teenagers (Beck, Cole, & Hammond, 1991; Holman & Harding, 1996).

Public School Bureaucracy/Governance

The public school system in the United States is so vast that roughly one out of six people abiding in the United States attends public schools. When one considers that only a small fraction of Americans are of school age, this statistic is quite amazing. The results of the meta-analysis suggest that the sheer size of the public school system and bureaucracy may be such that no matter what education paradigm is spawned through that system., the results will be roughly the same. That is, the system is so prodigious and inefficient that substantial change is not possible.

Concluding Remarks

It would seem that the body of research is sufficient to affirm that the religious school advantage is real. The United States would be wise to develop a school choice program that allows those advantages to propel many children to succeed rather than oppose, stifle, or hinder those advantages from being expressed.

Chapter 5

Fairness and Taxation

Early History

The question of whether school taxation is justified and just how much is appropriate goes back to the days of the early Christians. These religious individuals were the first to assert that education should be available to all (Dupuis, 1966; Marrou, 1956). They maintained this conviction because they averred that all people were equal, and therefore all should be educated (Dupuis, 1966; Marrou, 1956). These beliefs were held based on Bible verses such as "There is neither Jew nor Greek, there is neither slave nor free, there is neither male nor female ..." (Holy Bible, Galatians 3:28). The declaration that all people were created equal is a concept Americans now take for granted, but it was revolutionary at the time (Dupuis, 1966; Marrou, 1956). Before the time of Christ, there was a universal belief that leaders of certain types were superior to the general populace (Dupuis, 1966; Marrou, 1956). Government leaders were threatened by this viewpoint and viewed Christianity as inspiring revolt (Dupuis, 1966; Marrou, 1956). As a result, the persecution of Christians followed (Dupuis, 1966; Marrou, 1956). It was this Christian tenet that helps explain why 80 percent of the early Christians were either slaves or women (Dupuis, 1966).

This foundation is important to note for the Western world—and the United States in particular—because with the rise and spread of

Christianity in these areas developed a consensus that all youth were to be educated. The understanding that settlers in the 1600s maintained is that to make this possible, schooling had to be free of charge or nearly gratuitously given (Bailyn, 1960; Cubberley, 1934; Willison, 1945, 1966). With this emphasis in mind, the Puritans established what was called a charity school system in which families paid whatever they could afford to go to school (Eavey, 1964). The Puritans were not the first to advocate this position. Many church leaders, including Martin Luther, had propounded this perspective for centuries (Eavey, 1964; Jones, 1964; Raitt & McGinn, 1987; Randell, 1988). However, the Puritans were clearly the first group to successfully inaugurate a system that would make charity or free schools a widespread practice (Eavey, 1964; Jones, 1964).

Given that the settlers were generally not wealthy, for the vast majority of people, this meant that they paid little or nothing for their children's elementary and secondary school education (Rothstein, 1994; Szasz, 1988). The Puritans extended this grace to Native Americans for their college education so that the tribal young people could attend Harvard for free (Adams, 2005; Lin, 2005; Marshall & Manuel, 1977). The Puritans were committed to educating Native Americans at Harvard. Harvard's charter of 1650 specifically states that the college was committed to "the education of the English and Indian youth of the country" (Wilson, 2005, p. 3). The Puritans understood that unless they made it a priority to offer schooling at little or no cost to the elementary and secondary school pupil, countless thousands of children would go uneducated. They therefore developed the charity school as a low-cost means of instructing these children, with the idea that the upper and upper middle class would financially support these schools (Jones, 1964; Rothstein, 1994). At first, this rubric was limited in practice to the Puritans themselves, but in the aftermath of the Revolutionary War, it became a common paradigm used throughout most of the United States (Cremin, 1980; Jones, 1964). From the period of the 1600s through the first half of these 1800s, these charity schools were almost always private schools that were run based on the generosity of a variety of those relatively well-off citizens and the frugality of those who operated the schools (Jones, 1964; Rothstein, 1994).

In the eyes of those who ran these charity schools from the 1600s until the mid-1800s, taxation was steadfastly to be avoided, if at all possible (Cremin, 1980; Jones, 1964). This is because charging a tax was essentially the same as charging tuition, except that the cost was distributed over one's lifetime rather than simply during a child's schooling years (Eavey, 1964; Jones, 1964). In the eyes of the Puritans, other settlers, and post–Revolutionary War Americans, a society needed to be committed to free or near free education for the good of humanity, and this required frugality, generosity, and the eschewing of taxation if at all possible (Jones, 1964; Rothstein, 1994). Fortunately, frugality was part of the Puritan ethic and when the idea of charity schools spread throughout the country following the Revolutionary War, Joseph Lancaster (a Quaker British man) perfected a highly efficient delivery system for schooling using the charity school paradigm (Bourne, 1870; Cornog, 1998; MacMullen, 1991).

In early American society, there was an understanding that the small number of wealthy people that there were had a responsibility to support other members of society (Jones, 1964; Rothstein, 1994). As a result, wealthy settlers would pay for 20, 50, or 100 pupils (Jones, 1964; Rothstein, 1994). The commitment of the early settlers, and especially the Puritans, to universal education dictated that free education be made available to all American children no matter what their financial conditions were and no matter what the color of their skin was (Carter, 1969; Cremin, 1976). No one benefited more from charity schools than African Americans in the north (Andrews, 1969; Woodson & Wesley, 1962). The financial resources of the wealthy were not as great as their counterparts in Europe, so it was vital that the middle class also contribute to enable poor children to go to school (Jones, 1964). Fortunately, because providing universal education was such a deeply held belief among the Puritans, many middle-class people responded to the need (Jones, 1964).

Both charity schools and public schools arose out of the quest for universal education. Charity schools were gradually converted into public schools in the mid-nineteenth century because people realized that because of the considerable increase in the number of immigrant poor, taxation was necessary to make universal education a reality. The question now, however, is whether school taxes have become so high that they have become onerous to the point at which it is becoming increasingly impossible for the middle class and the poor to afford tuition even for faith-based schools in addition to the arduous level of school and overall taxes that the government demands.

In the days of charity schools, schooling for many was truly free of charge. Nevertheless, as time went on and a constant increase in the number of immigrants coming to the United States continued unabated, the balance between the financial resources of the wealthy and the number of poor fell out of equilibrium. Seemingly, something needed to be done to enable poor children to go to school. Many educators looked to taxes to solve the problem (Mann, 1907; Gatto, 2001). Indeed, taxes might have emerged as part of the solution if the level of federal, state, and local taxation had remained low (Acemoglu & Robinson, 2012). It did not take long, however, for tax rates to balloon so that the option of sending children to a faith-based school, for example, remained an elusive dream to all but the wealthiest Americans (Gilder & Forbes, 2012).

Horace Mann

To be sure, Horace Mann, Henry Barnard, and others who advocated taxation to continue to make schooling accessible to the impoverished did so with good motives. It is clear, for example, from the letters that Horace Mann, the government education leader in Massachusetts, and Henry Barnard, Mann's counterpart in Connecticut, exchanged with each other that both believed they were messengers of God bringing spiritual wisdom, morality, and intellectual development to a broader cross-section of American youth than had ever been the case previously (Mann, 1840). Mann contended that common schools would promote the common good in American education. There were a number of reasons Mann maintained this perspective. He believed that the presence of common schools would level the playing field between the rich and the poor (Mann, 1907). He believed that wealthy individuals had an advantage over the indigent in that they were able to send their children to the best schools. Mann opined that the availability of schooling would make it feasible for the poor to compete more adequately with the rich for the best jobs that were available (Mann, 1907).

Mann claimed that the dream of a common school needed financing (Mann, 1840, 1844; Mann, 1907). He managed to convince the American public that the common school was worthy of taxpayer financing (Mann, 1840, 1844; Mann, 1907). Mann was unapologetic about his insistence on taxation to support schools (Mann, 1840, 1844; Mann, 1907). A large number of Americans resented people like Horace Mann and Henry Barnard because they felt that these men's emphasis on taxation to "feed" government schools was usurping power that rightly belonged in the home (Gatto, 2001; Messerli, 1972). The level of taxation that Mann and Barnard called for was quite moderate by contemporary standards. Nevertheless, even though the motives of these individuals may have been altruistic, even many people at the time discerned that a trend was now in place (Gatto, 2001). They understood that taxes almost never go down over time; they almost always go up (Gilder & Forbes, 2012). Therefore, the new acceptance of school taxation did not bode well for the family and school choice.

The Kalamazoo Court Case

In spite of the growth of public schooling throughout the mid-1800s, by 1872, two-thirds of American high school children still attended private schools (King, 1964). The ratio between students attending public and private high schools changed dramatically with a Michigan State Supreme Court case in 1872 that generally upheld the Kalamazoo, Michigan, case (King, 1964). In that decision, the court upheld public taxation for high schools (King, 1964). This decision made it almost inevitable that the number of public high schools would eventually exceed the number of private high schools. This is because if a person wanted to send his or her child to a private high, school he or she would have to pay for private school tuition and pay taxes for public high schools, as well.

As a result of the Kalamazoo decision, by 1890, there were 2,526 public high schools in the United States with over 200,000 students (King, 1964). In contrast, there were about 1,600 private secondary schools and academics that enrolled about 95,000 students (King, 1964). The growth of public high schools continued in the years that followed. By 1900, there were 6,005 high schools in the United States, and by 1910, that number had increased to over 10,000 (King, 1964).

Evidence of the School Taxation Burden Placed on Families

The Rising Cost of Real Estate Taxes

Even today, most taxes for schools are raised via local property taxes (Gilder & Forbes, 2012; Hoxby, 1997). It is true that localities are increasingly using state taxes to making up an increasing percentage of the revenues brought in for schools (Gilder & Forbes, 2012;

Hoxby, 1997). Nevertheless, revenue from real estate taxes still makes up a large percentage of the money brought in to support public schools (Gilder & Forbes, 2012; Hoxby, 1997). Even though a growing amount of money from state taxes goes to support public schools, concurrently, the percentage of the average American's income that is going toward property taxes continues to steadily increase (Wong, 2011). According to the Tax Foundation (2013), 3.5 percent of the average American's annual income now goes to pay local property taxes. Tax brackets for state income tax vary from about 1 percent in the lowest brackets of income for some states to just under 14 percent for the highest bracket in other states (Tax Foundation, 2013). CNN reported in June 2012 that the U.S. national average for per pupil expenditure is $10,615 (Gumbrecht, 2012). It naturally varies by locale, with the number being $18,667 in Washington, DC, the highest in the country, to $6,064 in Utah, the lowest in the country (Gumbrecht, 2012). This $10,615 figure compares to the average per capita income in the United States of $42,687, or 24.87 percent of the average per capita income. In 1950, the U.S. per capita income was $9,573, and expenditures per pupil were $232, or 2.4 percent of the average per capita income (Nationmaster, 2012; U.S. Department of Education, 2012). Admittedly, household income has risen since 1950 in part because of a greater percentage of women in the workforce (Korkki, 2007). Nevertheless, even when one uses household income, per pupil expenditures have risen five times since 1950, when measured in constant dollars (U.S. Department of Education, 2012).

When examined from one perspective, this surge in per pupil expenditures by the public schools is very encouraging. From this viewpoint, it is hard to argue against increased expenditures on public school students. On the other hand, because nearly all public school revenues are received through taxation in one form or another, it also reflects an increased tax burden for the American people (Acemoglu & Robinson, 2012; U.S. Department of Education, 2012). There is no question that since 1950, the increased tax burden has made it more difficult for parents to send their children to private schools (Gilders & Forbes, 2012; U.S. Department of Education, 2012).

The fact is that the majority of property tax revenue goes to support the public schools, There is another trend that is nearly guaranteed by this fact. That is, state and local governments have every incentive to both allow and encourage property values to increase. In this way, property tax revenue will increase, and politicians will rejoice (Gilders & Forbes, 2012). The increased tax revenue serves a number of purposes. First, naturally, the public schools are more easily funded than if property values remained stable. Second, the large amount of accrued revenue supports other government functions as well (Gilders & Forbes, 2012). Third, the rise in property values enables the government to have the luxury of steadily increasing revenue coming in without engaging in the unpopular task of increasing tax rates. In this way, the citizens of a given state or community are under the impression that their taxes are within reason, yet concurrently the taxes they are paying are consistently climbing. Fourth, the fact that local governments are receiving relatively prodigious amounts in property taxes makes it so that other levels of government bear less of the tax burden for supporting public schools. Fifth, given that people feel good when they feel that public education is being adequately supported, the general populace feels content knowing that teacher salaries are increasing, school facilities are improving, and their property tax rates are likely not increasing.

Whether Private Schools Should Be Included in School Choice Programs

The Concerns of Religious School Educators

Religious educators are concerned about a number of realities facing faith-based schools at this juncture. One of the primary concerns has just been addressed. That is, they are cognizant of the ever-increasing extent to which increased taxation is proving to be an inexorable burden to parents desiring to send their children to faith-based schools (Cavanagh, 2012). They believe that the rate of increase in the tax pressures is so considerable that it almost guarantees that the number of faith-based schools will continue to experience significant decline. A second concern that religious instructors have is that they feel they are at an increasing financial disadvantage to the heavily government-subsidized public schools (Cavanagh, 2012; Walberg, 2007). These teachers and administrators believe there are many areas in which they cannot reasonably compete with the public schools, including teacher salaries, facility quality, accommodations for youth with special needs, and so forth (Cavanagh, 2012; Walberg, 2007). A good number of religious educators wonder whether this situation is at least partially intentional (Cavanagh, 2012; Walberg, 2007). They sometimes wonder whether many politicians and public educators are more concerned about public school pupils than they are about school children as a whole (Jeynes & Beuttler, 2012).

Third, many teachers and administrators of faith, particularly those of the Catholic Church, believe that vouchers and tax credits are the great equalizers in enabling faith-based schools to have any chance of competing with public schools on anything close to a level playing field (Green, 2011). A growing number of these educators believe that without these vouchers or tax credits, faith-based schools and especially those operating in high-poverty areas, are doomed to near extinction (Green, 2011). In fact, President George W. Bush was so concerned about the trend of religious schools closing down in inner-city areas that during his State of the Union address in January 2008, he called for an Education Summit among many of the nation's top educators to discuss advice they had to redress this trend (Jeynes, 2008a, 2008b).

There is no question that the financial concerns expressed by many religious educators are valid, but it is also true that public school leaders have issues on their minds as well.

The Concerns of Public School Educators

While it is true that those who serve in Christian, Jewish, private independent, and other private schools possess certain concerns about the present school system, which they think is heavily skewed in support of public schools, those functioning within the government-based system—whether as teachers, administrators, or politicians—also have concerns. The primary concern these individuals have is that they believe that under a system of school choice, some money that would normally go to the public system would instead remain with individuals (Bartman, 2007; Berliner & Biddle, 1995; Bracey, 1997). Many of these individuals would, in turn, then use that money to send their children to private schools (Berliner & Biddle, 1995; Bracey, 1997). Within this concern rest two overall complaints. First, those in the public sector are concerned that the relative strength of the private schooling sector would increase. Second, they are concerned that impoverished children and ethnic minorities would be hurt most of all by school choice (Bartman, 2007).

Each of these concerns is worthy of addressing. As one would imagine, quite a number of public educators are concerned about school choice programs that include private schools producing a situation in which family money that might have gone to the public schools instead will be used to pay tuition at faith-based and independent private schools (Bartman, 2007; Berliner & Biddle, 1995; Bracey, 1997). There is a sense in which it is understandable why those in the public sector would feel this way. On the other hand, there is a need to get beyond concerns about the relative strength of each sector and focus instead on creating a schooling system in which the welfare of America's children is maximized (Bartman, 2007; Jeynes, 2008c). In other words, too frequently educators focus concerns on their own particular sector (Bartman, 2007; Berliner & Biddle, 1995; Bracey, 1997). Public educators tend to be most concerned with the success of public schools, and faith-based instructors often are most focused on the health of religious schools. There is a sense, however, in which it is wise for people to think more broadly in terms of what is best for all sectors of American schooling. Ultimately, the success of both sectors influence American children, and it is their welfare with which Americans are most concerned (Jeynes, 2014).

The second concern about the possibility of impoverished children and those of color being inadvertently hurt by school choice is much more good-hearted than the rather self-oriented concern about the public sector increasing its power. As has been discussed earlier, school choice advocates have really focused their efforts on meeting the needs of these children, whether the choice programs are in New Hampshire, Cleveland, Milwaukee, Louisiana, Washington, or a host of other localities (Jeynes, 2014). With these programs in place, it might seem that this concern is something of a non sequitur, if the premises are based on objective evidence. Nevertheless, one could argue that it is healthy that such concerns exist because it maximizes the chances that school choice programs will continue to be sensitive to the challenges faced by needy children. Indeed, school choice advocates would argue that few educational initiatives in recent history have been as sensitive to the needs of these children as theirs because they grant access to high-quality schools for these children that otherwise these children would not have (Chubb & Moe, 1990; Walberg, 2007).

The Dilemma of the School Choice Debate: It Is Not about What Is Most Important

Whatever one's view is about the school choice debate, there is a certain degree of irony about the debate. That is, it is really a sad commentary on the degree of polarization in America when the school choice debate usually has more to do with politics, the relative strength of the public and private sectors (especially when the public school sector is already so dominant), teacher unions, and economics than it does with what is in the best interest of the children.

One might ask why it is that only a small segment of the U.S. population has considered school choice, including private schools, as a vehicle for reducing the achievement gap and raising achievement, both of which faith-based schools appear to be successful at doing (Jeynes, 2014). Much of the reason rests in the increasing tension that exists in this country between those in the private and public sectors and the steady growth of the power of the public sector relative to the private sector (Kurtz, 2010). Few would doubt the notion that over the past few decades in particular, a rising tension has emerged between the public and private sectors (Bracey, 1997; Ravitch, 2010). Sadly, one could argue that those in the public sector are most concerned about what is good for them, and those in the private sector are also most cognizant about what is best for those functioning in that sector. This near-sightedness has manifested itself along a number of dimensions: educational, political, and in the economics of alleviating budget deficits (Hagel & Kaminsky, 2008; Harwood & Seib, 2008). Unfortunately, it is very rare to find a public school educator concerned about the health of religious schools. In fact, a plethora of teachers are antagonistic toward Christian schools, for example Decter (1995) and Olasky (1988). Similarly, there is an increased political tension between those in public sector jobs and those in the private sector (Berliner & Biddle, 1995; Ravitch, 2003).

People may maintain a particular stand on school choice, but whatever one's stand happens to be, this tension described here needs to end. The goal of educators should be to do what is best for the children and society at large.

Is the Cost Worth the Benefit?

On the surface, it may seem axiomatic that society would benefit from the activities of religious schools, especially to the extent to which they reach out to the impoverished. As one would expect, the private schools under the most severe pressure are usually religious schools operating in some of the poorest sections of the country, for example, in inner cities and in rural areas (Anitt, 2003; Peterson,

2006; Steinfels, 2003). According to White House estimates, during the 2000–2006 period 1,162 inner-city faith-based schools were closed, and nearly 425,000 students were lost, mostly due to insufficient funding (White House, 2008). By definition, these schools were not founded with the goal of making a profit (Hoffer, 1998; Peterson, 2006). This is not only axiomatic because churches and other religious organizations are nonprofit, but because efforts to educate in these areas are viewed as a divine and altruistic attempt to help those who are less fortunate (Hoffer, 1998; Peterson, 2006).

On the surface, it would seem advantageous to society, the government, and faith-based schools to have religious schools, via school choice, even more involved in helping the poor. To those who are antireligious or antiprivatization, the advantages may not seem that ostensible. The advantages are even less apparent to people of faith because they face the specter of government interference in their daily operations (Glenn, 2000). Therefore, although there are benefits that would accrue to faith-based schools, the costs of government entanglement in the affairs might be great.

Chapter 6

The Politicized Nature of School Choice

Few would question the idea that the debate about school choice has become very politicized. In a sense, this is a real shame because there does exist some real bipartisan consensus on some of the advantages of school choice, but such consensus does not exist regarding the implementation. This chapter highlights some of the reasons this is the case.

Reason 1: Republicans Favor a Broad School Choice Program, and the Democrats Want to Limit Such a Program to Public Schools

Both the Republicans and Democrats have promoted school choice initiatives during the period since 1980; however, they were somewhat different. Both political parties believed school choice would benefit the nation's education system. However, the Democrats under Bill Clinton favored a choice system that was limited to public schools, and Republicans favored extending the choice to include private schools as well (Finn, Manno, & Vanourek, 2001; Kirkpatrick, 1990).

The Republican movement to initiate school choice programs that included private schools grew under Reagan, George H. Bush, and George W. Bush (Kirkpatrick, 1990; Minutaglio, 1999). Although their desire for private school choice has never been adopted except at an experimental level, it remains a major plank of the Republican Party's platform.

Although Reagan supported school choice, the movement really did not gain much momentum until the publication of Chubb and Moe's book *Politics, Markets, and America's Schools* (1990). In their book, Chubb and Moe ask an interesting question: Why is it that America's university system is generally regarded as the best in the world, but our public school system is regarded as below average? Chubb and Moe hypothesize that it is because at the university level, schools in the private and public sector compete against one another, while at the elementary and secondary school level, public schools have a virtual monopoly (Chubb & Moe, 1990). At the university level, institutions like Stanford (private) and UC-Berkeley (public) as well as USC (private) and UCLA (public) compete against one another, and each institution is made better by that competition. However, at the elementary and secondary school level, the school tax burden is substantial enough so that most people feel they cannot afford to send their children to private school (Chubb & Moe, 1990).

Chubb and Moe (1990) assert that to restore American elementary and secondary school education to a high-quality enterprise, private schools must be allowed to compete on more equal footing with public schools. They argue that if the government allows this to transpire, two positive educational effects will occur. First, more American children will attend private school, where they will receive a better education, on average, than they would in a public school. Second, the competition from private schools would compel public schools to become better. Consequently, Chubb and Moe maintain, America's entire elementary and secondary school system would improve.

The way to end the public school monopoly, Chubb and Moe (1990) assert, is to ease parents' financial burden by giving a voucher to each family who sends its children to private school. This voucher would partially compensate for the fact that families pay taxes to support public schools even if their children do not receive their training through public education (Chubb & Moe, 1990; Fernandez & Rogerson, 2003). Other proponents of school choice have recommended that tax breaks, instead of vouchers, be given to parents engaging in choice (Bryk, Lee & Holland, 1993; Fernandez & Rogerson, 2003). One potential advantage of this approach is that it might be easier to adjust the tax break to the income of the family. For example, a given school choice plan would likely give a larger tax break to the poor than to the wealthy. In contrast, one advantage of granting a voucher is that it might be easier to give school choice benefits to those individuals who do not pay any taxes.

Reason 2: School Choice Creates Political Division within Political Parties

One of the primary reasons vouchers are not practiced is because it politically divides, for example, on the Democratic side, African Americans and Latinos favor them, but unions are against them (Jeynes, 2007a; Kerchner, 2006; Moe, 2006).

Teacher unions constitute one of the most formidable forces opposing choice. Since 1965, teacher unions have become perhaps the most powerful force in the country in the determination of educational policy in the United States (Ravitich, 2000; Stern, 2003). In fact, Terry Moe (2006, p. 123) asserts that "teacher unions have more influence on the public schools than any other group in American society." They have been highly instrumental in bringing about higher teacher salaries, a great deal of that increase is reflected in the fact that public school expenditures on individual children have more than doubled in real terms since 1965 (U.S. Department of Education, 2010). With this in mind, however, teachers unions are, as the name implies, designed to operate in the best interests of teachers (Kerchner, 2006; Moe, 2006; Smylie & Miretsky, 2004). They tend to strongly oppose school choice, more days and longer hours for pupils to help them compete in the world marketplace, teacher accountability, and any action that would in any way dilute their power (Kerchner, 2006; Lieberman, 2000; Moe, 2006). Terry Moe (2006, p. 128) adds, "Unions are the primary force restricting pay based on performance, choice, reform, etc."

Of course, teacher unions stand for some causes that are quite justifiable and good (Kerchner, 2006; Smylie & Miretsky, 2004). Virtually all Americans believe that teachers should be paid well. A recent political battle in Chicago over the length of the school day occurred when teachers balked at the idea of longer school days for students to help the youth better compete in the global marketplace (Council for Citizens against Government Waste, 2012). Chicago residents were stunned at the request, however, once they learned that the average Chicago teacher already made about $76,450 a year, while the average Chicago wage earner made $37,000 (Hinz, 2012). This scenario is a reminder that although it is important for a teacher to live well, the primary concern needs to return to what is best for the students. Terry Moe (2006, p. 133) strongly expresses the extent of union power when he states, "They are mostly engaged in the politics of blocking." Charles Kerchner (2006) is a little bit more optimistic, believing that they can be a force for reform. But he also adds, "Let's face it. Teacher unions can be a terrible nuisance" (p. 144).

Although Republican presidents have backed school choice in principle, the implementation of school choice has been limited to isolated efforts in cities like Milwaukee and Cleveland (Greene et al., 1996; Jeynes, 2000a; Peterson et al., 1996). At first, this may seem surprising because one of the groups whose support is important to school choice, African Americans, is generally the most enthusiastic ethnic group when it comes to school choice (Phi Beta Kappa/Gallup Poll, 2002). Not only do polls indicate a high degree of African American support for school choice, but also many African Americans have protested outside the White House, declaring that the federal government was not doing enough to promote school choice (Stolberg, 2008).

The primary reason for the strong African American support is easy to understand. Many African Americans live in dilapidated urban areas where public schools are dens for drug pushers and gangs (Green, 2000; Phi Beta Kappa/Gallup Poll, 2002; Stolberg, 2008). Concurrently, most African American parents cannot afford to send their children to religious and other types of private schools, where gangs and drug pushers are rare (Green, 2000; Jeynes, 2000a; Stolberg, 2008). Many African American parents would love the opportunity to be given a tax break or a voucher so that they could afford to send their children to these private schools. As has already been intimated, a primary reason African Americans want school choice is often more out of a desire to remove their children from baneful influences than it is for scholastic reasons.

It is largely because of support among African Americans that school choice initiatives have been launched in Milwaukee and Cleveland (Figlio & Page, 2003; Greene et al., 1996; Howell & Peterson, 2002). Nevertheless, it is noteworthy than in spite of the support of three Republican presidents in the last quarter-century, school choice has not emerged as a large-scale practice (Jeynes, 2000a). One of the primary reasons for this is because while many Americans would feel comfortable with poor urban and rural

Americans getting a tax break or voucher, most would not feel at ease with the affluent or upper middle class getting such a boon. It is very likely that if school choice is ever implemented on a large scale, tax breaks and vouchers would have to be distributed on a sliding scale. That is, the poor would get a large benefit, the middle class would receive some degree of benefit, and the wealthy would receive no benefit at all. There are some states, such as Florida and Colorado, that allow children who are doing poorly in school and who attend schools that have been designated as failing to use public funds to go to a better performing school, whether it be public, evangelical, Catholic, or other private school (Greene & Winters, 2006). In Florida, Pennsylvania, and Arizona, individuals and corporations can make tax-deductible contributions to fund scholarship-granting programs (Greene & Winters, 2006). Scholarships can be used to cover the cost of private school tuition or tutoring (Greene & Winters, 2006).

Reason 3: Ongoing Divisiveness in Localities where Choice Is Debated

One reality that has a deleterious effect on the prospects for school choice specifically and school reform generally is that there is so much political contentiousness in some of the cities with the largest populations. New York City is a prime example of how politics of a variety of stripes often subjugate the greater good of the people (Jeynes, 2007a, 2010a, 2012c, 2012f). For example, Diane Ravitch's book *The Great School Wars* chronicles the city-wide melee that transpired in 1968 among the city's dogmatic ideologues that had far more to do with stubbornness, territorialism, unionism, and intimidation than it did with what was in the best interests of the city's children (Jeynes, 2004b; Ravitch, 2000). Sol Stern (2003, p. 104) shares regarding Albert Shanker, the city's primary teacher union leader of the time, "... in 1968, Shanker found himself accused of racism because he led his teachers into a bitter strike over the arbitrary dismissal of Jewish teachers by black militants running Brooklyn's Ocean Hill Brownsville community school board." Stern (p. 104) continues by asserting, "The 'limousine liberals' of the time were convinced that uncaring white teachers were responsible for the low academic performance of the minority students. They assumed that learning performance could be improved by empowering the black community to make its own decisions on curriculum and who should teach in the schools. It was a misguided assumption."

Stern is correct in a number of his declarations, but the drama was political on the part of the teachers as well. In fact, the intransigence on both the sides in Ocean Hill Brownsville reached such a level that the entire public school year was almost cancelled and finally started up just before Thanksgiving (Podair, 2002; Ravitch, 2000). To compensate for the lost time, New York City schoolchildren had to endure eight-hour school days and a school year that lasted until mid-July. A lot of this political quagmire emerged because New York City schools were in the largest city and the place that had historically served as a beacon of educational light. New York City was, in many respects, the battlefield of choice for educational clashes related to race, autonomy, and unionism (Carter, 1971; Podair, 2002). Barbara Carter (1971, p. 9) incisively explained the challenge facing New York City urban schools:

> Here was the nub, the heart of the thing—the profound frustration over the failure of the system to improve education in the ghetto.... For all that the system had tried, and it had made many attempts—special serve schools, after-school reading clinics, Head Start centers, tutorial programs—little impact had been made.

Taken together, Stern's and Carter's remarks summarize well the frustration that too frequently becomes infused into educational debates.

This was not the only time New York was the center of quixotic educational debates. School choice advocates in New York were heartened when in the late 1970s and early 1980s the powerful politician Mario Cuomo stated to his Catholic supporters that he was a major supporter of Catholic schools (Stern, 2003). But by the time he ran for governor and held office, he backed only public schools. Cuomo told his Catholic voting base that he favored vouchers, but while he served as governor of New York, he opposed them (Stern, 2003). Thomas Sobol, a fellow Democrat and commissioner of the Board of Regents at the time, was stunned that Cuomo backed down on his promises regarding vouchers (Stern, 2003).

Consequences of the Politicization of School Choice

Consequence 1: Experimentation, but Not Wide Implementation of School Choice

Early assessments of the school choice programs presently in place indicate that children generally do receive a moderate academic benefit from attending a private school instead of a public one, although the first year of attending a different school is often a period of adjustment for the children (Greene et al., 1996). Research also suggests that even when adjusting for socioeconomic status, children attending religious schools outperform children from public schools (Coleman, Hoffer, & Kilgore, 1982; Jeynes, 2002c). However, not all social scientists are convinced that the analyses of school choice programs in Milwaukee and Cleveland offer decisive evidence in favor of these programs (Witte, 1999, 2000; Rouse & Barrow, 2009).

It is difficult to determine the degree to which Republican presidents will pursue the practice of school choice. In the ideal world, it is clearly one of the party's top priorities (Garrett, 2005). However, while many Americans support the poor having school choice, presently, Republicans do not have a majority of Americans backing a broad-based plan. Therefore, instead of initiating extensive school choice programs, Presidents George H. W. Bush and George W. Bush chose to sponsor initiatives to facilitate school choice program implementation at a later time (Howell & Peterson, 2002). For example, George Bush Sr. during his administration called for the establishment of magnet schools across the country (Bush, 1989). He also initiated a $13 million federal government investment to expand experimental educational programs, including school choice (Bush, 1989; Edwards et al., 1989).

Consequence 2: There Is a Lack of Data Related to the Effectiveness of School Choice, and This Dearth of Helpful Information Is Likely to Continue

One of the greatest problems in assessing the effects of school choice abides in the lack of relevant data collected on its impact on children. In addition, almost none of the research has examined the effects of school choice on academic achievement. Gewirtz, Ball, and Bowe (1995) observe, "Most of the empirical research is piecemeal and tends to be very specifically focused" (p. 3). Gewirtz, Ball, and Bowe therefore contend that much of the research on school choice has been "inadequate" (p. 6). To be sure, there are some recent data that indicate school choice *may* positively impact academic achievement (Greene et al., 1996; Peterson et al., 1996; Witte & Thorne, 1996), but overall, the evidence is sparse. There are three reasons one comes to this conclusion. First, the number of studies that social scientists have done measuring the influence of school choice is relatively small. Second, for those studies that have attempted to assess the effects of school choice, it is not clear whether this is in fact what has ultimately been measured. Many studies have focused on how choice affects: (1) the distribution of students among schools (Ball, 2003; Woods, Bagley, & Glatter, 1998) and (2) what parents consider when making their choices (Woods, Bagley, & Glatter, 1998). Third, the dynamics of school choice are complex and difficult to examine (Ball, 2003; Irvine & Foster, 1996). For example, the effects of school choice are going to differ in urban areas, where there will be more choices, versus rural areas, where choices are limited (Ball, 2003). School choice will often differ depending on how schools promote themselves and will have various effects rooted in copious education philosophies (Colopy & Tarr, 1994; Pardey, 1991). Fourth, the school choice debate has become so politicized that it has become hard to disentangle the research of many social scientists from their political views.

Beyond these problems, it is not clear how many of the effects found in favor of choice or nonchoice students are a product of choice and how many result from simply changing schools or from certain students dropping out of a choice program. Greene and colleagues (1996) found that by the third year of participation, children participating in the Milwaukee voucher program, for example, obtained an academic advantage over similar Milwaukee children not participating in the program. Opponents of choice can take solace in the fact that choice did not produce an academic edge for choice students during the first two years of the program. However, the fact that it took over two years for differences to emerge may be explained in large degree by the fact that changing schools is a difficult experience for many children (Jeynes, 2006b; McLanahan & Sandefur, 1994). Nevertheless, supporters of choice have some satisfaction because academic achievement rose by the third year. One can argue that this may partially be a result of children that are struggling in their new schools, often dropping out of the project by the third year to leave only those students who are doing reasonably well as the study's sample. Overall, Greene's study appears to partially support some of the merits of school choice programs that include private schools, but more research needs to be done. Although broad programs of school choice have not yet been implemented, school choice that includes private schools remains one of the chief educational desires of the Republican Party. Nevertheless, school choice also remains a controversial part of the Republican perspective on education.

Attackers of School Choice

People who attack school choice come from a number of different perspectives or a combination of them. There are some, for example, who feel uncomfortable with the private sector being involved in education, just as there are those who feel equally convinced that the government is too inept, biased, and powerful to do the job effectively. Others feel a proclivity toward opposing school choice because they are antireligious and do not like the idea of churches and other places of worship being involved in schooling children. A third reason is that many in the public sector want to protect their dominance in schooling children. Finally, there are some who believe that school choice would discourage diversity (Smith & Meier, 1995)

Those Who Feel Uncomfortable with the Private Sector Being Involved in Education

Some of the concerns that opponents of choice hold regarding equity relate to the privatization issue. In fact, even some people who support public school choice actually oppose private school choice, largely because of equity concerns (Brighouse, 2003). There exists some evidence from other nations that maintain a system of private school choice that the system benefits those that choose but hurts those who do not (Glenn, 1989). Advocates of school choice believe it would benefit education systems because the worst schools close down due to competition (Chubb & Moe, 1990; Walberg, 2007). Yet, this prospect rattles many teachers and school administrations (Jeynes, 2012a, 2014). In all the nations that include private schools in choice programs, public schools still thrive (Glenn, 1989).

On the other hand, some proponents of vouchers and/or tax credits wonder if indeed America has become a nation that is antiprivatization (Glenn, 2000; Moe, 2006). They warn that the American school system borders on a type of "compulsory socialism" (Kirkpatrick, 1990). Even if this statement appears excessive, in recent years, there have been an increasing number of Americans calling for a more socialist form of education and schooling (as noted in Engelhardt, 2013 and Gatto, 2001).

Antireligious Opponents

One of the reasons there remains such a strong sentiment among many that there should be school choice is that there is a belief by many both in and out of the faith community that public school educators are often antireligious and demean people of faith (Jeynes, 1999, 2012e, 2012h). Joseph Viteritti (2003, p. 19) explained the situation well when he stated, "At times public schools have been insensitive or even hostile to the beliefs of devout observers. For many devout observers who regard education as an instrument for instilling faith-based values, a public education is either irrelevant or counterproductive."

Antonin Scalia (1989), a Supreme Court justice, believes that including only nonreligious private schools in a choice program, as some propose, discriminates against religious Americans. The issue of school choice among Catholics and evangelical Christians might not create the intense debate that it does in secular circles, did these religious people perceive that the public schools were more tolerant of religious expression. The problem probably started in 1962 and 1963 when in a series of three Supreme Court cases, prayer and Bible reading were removed from the public schools. In an increasingly pluralistic society, people saw the need for increased religious tolerance. Unfortunately, most religious people and most Americans as a whole do not believe that the Supreme Court decisions encourage religious tolerance; instead, they view the decisions as disallowing religious expression in the schools (Andryszewski, 1997; Blakeman, 2005). Furthermore, most religious people assert that values taught in school are not neutral, as educators claim, but are antireligious in nature (Blakeman, 2005; Decter, 1995; Olasky, 1988). Examples of this are likely already known to the reader and therefore, the specific issues will not be explicated here. Rather, what is important is to realize that this perception by people of faith often contributes to their embrace of school choice (Jeynes, 2000a).

Many people have a growing sense that not only is there an antireligious sentiment in the public schools, but that these public schools are focused more on subjective opinion rather than the facts themselves. This growth of "defactualization" is one of the main reasons an increasing number of people are interested in expanding school choice. Defactualization is a term I developed back in 2002 to describe societies in which facts are either habitually denied or relegated to irrelevance due to an emphasis on subjectivity. Defactualization is quickly becoming one of the greatest crises of modern times. Many Westerners are increasingly denying biological and historical facts. They call life in the womb not life. Laws are being passed in some states that assert that it does not matter what gender you are; what matters is the gender that you say that you are. Regarding historical facts, there is of course some room for differences in interpretation. Nevertheless, history is made up of facts that cannot be denied, be they the Holocaust, Islamic military expansionism in the 700s, or the bombing of Pearl Harbor.

Desiring to Keep Public Schools' Monopoly

It is unfortunate that a myriad of public educators appear to desire an entire or near monopoly for public schools (Perry, 2003). It is ironic that a copious number of Americans view the United Nations as an organization that is considerably to the left of most of the positions taken by the United States. And yet on this particular issue, the United States is far to the left of the official position of the United Nations (Glenn, 2003; Swift, 2003). Adam Swift (2003, p. 7) states it well when he declares, "The UN Declaration of Human Rights states that 'Parents have a prior right to choose the kind of education that shall be given to their children.' The European Commission of Human Rights, which was incorporated into the law in 2000 states that, 'The State shall respect the rights of parents to ensure ... education and teaching in conformity with their own religious and philosophical convictions.' "

The Claim That School Choice Will Discourage Diversity

The idea that opponents of school choice are concerned about this issue is ironic because common sense would appear to dictate that a public school near monopoly would be much more likely to yield this result. Furthermore, as Ravitch (1992) and others point out, the concurrent presence of both a strong private and a strong public sector in schooling encourages diversity. Advocates of school choice claim that without the exercise of liberty inherent in choice, cultural uniformity will result. They accuse liberals of not really desiring pluralism in the schools, but rather the inculcating of their ideology into the minds of children (Gutman, 2003; Kirkpatrick, 1990). If conservatives who support school choice take the defensive on equity issues relating to choice, they clearly march on the offensive on this issue. If liberals who often oppose school choice support pluralism so strongly, why do they not support choice, which would probably increase the nation's pluralism?

Nathan Glazer believes that given the pluralistic nature of our society, the "truly common school, in which all are educated together, simply will not work" (Glazer, 1983). Glazer asserts that a greater variety of schools, public and private, is inevitable (Glazer, 1983). Ellen Goldring echoes some of Glazer's remarks, asserting that parents want the liberty of choosing a school that fits their ideology (Goldring, 1991).

Harry Brighouse (2003) raises concerns about cultural uniformity from another perspective, that is, that of social justice. He asserts that the present U.S. education system cements a culture of underachievement in which the lower class does not enjoy fair access to some of the best schools, which are often in the private sector.

Many historians believe that the United States, historically speaking, follows prominent trends in Europe. That is, trends prevailing in Europe now will eventually pervade the United States. If so, a school choice program leading to less cultural uniformity in our schools looms on the horizon. The Netherlands, for example, encourages a mosaic of schools. These even include denominational public and private schools (Goldring, 1991). Britain also encourages pluralism through school choice (Goldring, 1991).

With all the warnings by America's followers about placing too much power in the hands of the government, there is no question that the relative power of the federal and state governments compared to the private individual is much more vast than it was in 1776 (Johnson, 1997). Aside from the sheer level of taxation, the fact that schooling was overwhelmingly the job of the private sector in the 1700s and 1800s (and at the university level until the end of World War II) helped protect the minds of the young against government attempts to intimidate its people (Johnson, 1997). But we live not only in a time of *a new world order*, but also in one of a *new national order* in which the government dominates most of the major institutions in America. Government leaders claim that they desire pluralism, but their actions often indicate otherwise. American schooling is by many measures more monolithic than ever. Private schooling is such a small part of the educational pie that the government runs the risk, via excessive taxation and other policies, of driving it into irrelevancy. At what point is the government domination of schooling enough? Is it when it runs 92 percent of the schools, 95 percent, or higher? Whatever one's view of school choice might be, the debate should not be politicized to the degree that it is. Schooling is about what is good for the children and society, not what buttresses the power of politicians.

Chapter 7

What Will Be the Effects of School Choice?

Any time a nation considers the implementation of a given educational policy, an overriding question should naturally be whether the American school system will benefit and just what the precise effects will be (Bryk, Lee, & Holland, 1993). Therefore, in this chapter, a number of key questions are addressed.

Will School Choice Improve the American Education System?

The answer to this general question is rather complex. From preceding analyses presented in this book, there is good reason to believe that a broad school choice program that includes private schools would likely lift academic achievement. The extent of that improvement would naturally depend in large part of the number of students attending private schools (Jeynes, 2000a). However, the meta-analysis presented in chapter 2 also indicates that limiting choice to only public schools will be highly unlikely to improve the American education system.

Public School Choice

This author did not possess the perspective just stated before undertaking the meta-analysis in Chapter 2. Before this researcher performed this meta-analysis, his perspective was that the charter school movement was a step in the right direction. It seemed that public charter schools, with greater autonomy than traditional public schools and because they attempt to imitate the strengths of faith-based schools, would yield positive results. However, those are not the results that emerged in this meta-analysis.

It may puzzle some how an academic can change his mind on the basis of a meta-analysis he conducted. To be sure, there are a copious number of theorists who will adamantly maintain their view-point even if every objective measure indicates otherwise. To be a good quantitative social scientist, however, one must possess a certain degree of humility and an open mind. The reason this is the case is that there will almost always be certain findings from a quantitative analysis that surprise the researcher. In such cases, he or she is faced with a choice. Either the numbers change, or the researcher must change. Naturally, the numbers are not going to change, so it is the views of the social scientist that must change.

Admittedly, it is difficult for some people to change when they encounter the truth. Therefore, being a quantitative analyst is not for the faint of heart. A person must dedicate oneself to the pursuit of truth and then be willing to change accordingly when it is found. This is particularly true when undertaking a meta-analysis. It can sometimes be relatively easy to dismiss results that emerge from one study as an aberration from the norm. A meta-analysis, however, involves statistically combining all the quantitative studies that exist on a particular topic and then numerically presenting the results of the said research. Given that a meta-analysis constitutes a summary of the existing body of research, the chances of results being an aberration from the norm are extremely small. Therefore, unless a scientist is willing to change his or her views as a result of conducting the meta-analysis, he or she had best choose a different mode of inquiry.

The results of the meta-analysis, which constitutes a major portion of this book, indicate that students from public charter schools do no better than their counterparts from traditional public schools. These are not the results I expected, nor are they ones for which I hoped. But they are the findings I must help interpret and explain. I am reminded of another theorist who upon reviewing the results of another meta-analysis I conducted remarked, "I don't like some of our results." I simply replied, "Neither do I."

There are academics and educators who defend charter schools, but their arguments tend to be quite weak when the most relevant facts are considered. First, those that advocate public charter schools now almost never claim that public charter schools work. Rather, they say, "Effective public charter schools work" (Barr & Parrett, 1997). But that is a tautological argument. It is much like saying, "Fast American runners are fast." Second, they talk of the fact that about two-thirds of Americans support the existence of public charter schools. With all due respect, this statistic has little meaning unless these schools are also efficacious. Over the centuries, many practices have been popular, even when they were deleterious. For example, segregation was popular in the South for 90 years after the Civil War, but it was not a good practice. Second, student tracking is often a popular practice among both parents and teachers, but it exacerbates the achievement gap between low- and high-performing students. Third, for years, supporters of public charter schools have often tried to "explain away" results of certain studies on charter schools because a number of the most prominent ones did not yield results that were favorable to the charter school movement. Advocates would point to insufficient sample sizes or studies that did not have a nationwide sample to justify their dismissal of the findings. Now, however, a meta-analysis has been undertaken that includes a sample size of well over 1 million students and a number of nationwide studies. The results are now undeniable.

Over the past 20 plus years, American political leaders have put a considerable degree of effort into expanding the number of public charter schools in the United States. It is expected that their number will soon reach 6,000 (Center for Education Reform, 2013). This being the case, it is disappointing that public charter schools are yielding about the same results as traditional public schools. It is clear that this fact has ramifications for both how the U.S. government approaches educational policy and how it initiates school choice programs.

The data presented in Chapter 2 suggest that including private schools in a school choice program could yield positive effects for student achievement. Nevertheless, the extent of those positive effects will depend in part on the percentage of students that decide to attend faith-based schools and independent private schools.

Measuring School Improvement Using More Than Just Academics

Two points should be noted at this juncture. First, improved results in schooling can also be measured in terms of student behavior.

This is particularly noteworthy because many families choose to send their young to faith-based schools in particular out of a desire to see their children's character improve (Jeynes, 2009, 2010c). Second, by attending faith-based schools, students might become more inclined to become religious. Therefore, it might be helpful at this point to also consider the effects of religious commitment on student behavior.

The results presented here are those that emerged in the meta-analysis undertaken by this author employing the same general methods described in Chapter 2 and using the following coding system for religious commitment. A person was coded as high in religious commitment if a given study coded a person as such. Generally speaking, religious commitment was defined as high if a person described himself or herself as religious and if that person attended worship service or Bible study at least once a week (Jeynes, 1999).

The effect sizes for both personal religious commitment and attending religious schools are listed in Tables 7.1 and 7.2. The meta-analytic analyses distinguished between those studies utilizing sophisticated controls, especially for socioeconomic status. The results indicate that effects for personal religious commitment were greatest in absolute value for measures such as marijuana consumption, alcohol consumption, cigarette consumption, and attitudes about premarital intercourse, while the effects for attending a religious school were greatest for academic achievement and whether a student was a member of a gang (see Tables 7.1 and 7.2). The effect sizes for personal religious commitment were about four-tenths of a standard deviation or better for marijuana consumption, alcohol consumption, cigarette consumption, and attitudes about premarital intercourse. The examination of those analyses that utilized sophisticated controls did yield somewhat lower effect sizes, but in every case, the differences were .05 of a standard deviation or less and in every case, the effect size remained four-tenths of a standard deviation or more. In only one of these four cases, attitudes toward premarital intercourse, did the examination of analyses utilizing more sophisticated controls yield a level of statistical significance that was less than for the analyses that did not use sophisticated controls.

All other measures for the effects of personal religious commitment also yielded statistically significant results, but they were a good deal smaller than for the four measures just mentioned, particularly when including only those studies that utilized sophisticated statistical controls, such as those for socioeconomic status. For example, the effect sizes (.16, p < .05 and .14, p < .05) for the relationship between personal religious commitment and cocaine consumption were considerably less than for the other measures of substance abuse. In addition, the effect sizes for becoming an adolescent single parent (.22, p < .01 and .20, p < .01) were smaller than those that emerged for attitudes toward single parenthood (.53, p < .001 and .48, p < .01).

The effect sizes for attending a religious school were larger for academic achievement than were the effect sizes for personal religious commitment. Statistically significant effect sizes also emerged for the relationship between attending religious schools and attitudes about premarital intercourse, being a gang member, and marijuana and cigarette consumption. A statistically significant effect size emerged for alcohol consumption, but only for those studies that did not include sophisticated controls. Statistically significant effect sizes did not emerge for cocaine consumption and being an adolescent single parent. In addition, overall, the effect sizes for attending religious schools tended to be smaller than for personal religious commitment. The one exception was for academic achievement.

The meta-analysis also included running different analyses based on the quality rating of the study, which due to space constraints are not presented here. The quality of the study was generally not related to the overall outcomes.

The results indicate that both personal religious commitment and attending religious schools are associated with constructive behavioral, academic, and attitudinal outcomes. The results show four notable trends. First, most of the dependent variables yielded statistically significant results for both the personal religious commitment and religious school variables. In fact, in the case of the personal religious commitment variable, all the variables yielded statistically significant effects. Second, on the whole, the personal religious commitment variable yielded larger effects sizes than the religious school variables. The one clear exception was the academic achievement variable. This finding may support the assertions of James Coleman (1988), who declares that home factors are more prominent in affecting youth than school factors. Third, regarding substance abuse and premarital sexual behavior, religious variables generally had a larger influence on substances that were less severe than others and attitudes about premarital adolescent intercourse more than its results. This may result from variables other than religious ones that coexist

Table 7.1 The Effects of Personal Religious Commitment and Attending Religious Schools for Measures of Substance Abuse and Premarital Sexual Behavior and Attitudes Using Models both with and without Sophisticated Controls; Included in Parentheses are 95% Confidence Intervals

	Personal Religious Commitment without Sophisticated Controls	Personal Religious Commitment with Sophisticated Controls	Religious Schools without Sophisticated Controls	Religious Schools with Sophisticated Controls
Marijuana Consumption	−.42** (−.70, −.14)	−.40** (−.66, −.14)	−.22* (−.04, −40)	−.20* (−.04, −36)
Alcohol Consumption	−.46*** (−.71, −.21)	−.43*** (−.68, −.18))	−.12* (−.22, −.02)	−.11 (−.21, −.01)
Cocaine Consumption	−.16* (−.28, −04)	−.14* (−.25, −.03)	−.07	−.07
Adolescent Single Parent	−.22** (−.36, −.08)	−.20** (−.34, −.06)	−.06	−.06
Attitudes about Single Parenthood	−.53*** (−.85, −.21)	−.48** (−.78, −.18)	−.23* (−.39, −.07)	−.22* (−.38, −.06)

Note: * p < .05
** p < .01
*** p < .001

Table 7.2 The Effects of Personal Religious Commitment and Attending Religious Schools for Cigarette Consumption, Academic Achievement, and Gang Membership Using Models Both with and without Sophisticated Controls

	Personal Religious Commitment without Sophisticated Controls	Personal Religious Commitment with Sophisticated Controls	Religious Schools without Sophisticated Controls	Religious Schools with Sophisticated Controls
Cigarette Consumption	−.51*** (−.77, −.25)	−.46*** (−.74, −.18)	−.20* (−.34, −.00)	−.18* (−.33, −.03)
Academic Achievement	.16* (.03, .27)	.12* (.02, .22)	.23**** (.15, .31)	.21**** (.13 .29)
Gang Membership	NA	NA	−.67**** (−.99, −.35)	−.66**** (−.95, −.37)

Note: NA = not applicable
* $p < .05$
** $p < .01$
*** $p < .001$
**** $p < .0001$

with religious variables to prevent some behaviors that have the most severe consequences. Fourth, these findings generally emerge from studies that examine religious commitment and religious schools separately. Therefore, one wonders what the effect size patterns would have been if these two religious variables would have been examined simultaneously and what interactions might have been. Further research should examine this issue.

Will Vouchers and Tax Credits Make America's School System More Economically Efficient?

It does appear logical that whatever one might think of a school choice program that includes private schools, a program of this nature will likely improve the nation's economic efficiency. School choice is not only an educational issue, but also as an economic one. The U.S. government has a national debt between $16 and $17 trillion. Nearly all of America's 50 states have faced large budget deficits during much of or all of the 2010–2013 period (Jeynes, 2012h; U.S. Department of Education, 2010). In many states across the country, public education represents nearly 50 percent of a given state's budget. There is no question that schooling is worthy of the attention of the American people. It is, however, also a source of the most astronomical degrees of economic waste. The examples of public school waste are numerous in the form of perks, overpaid administrators, and the purchase of hi-tech equipment that is rarely used (Segal, 2004).

Beyond the issue of economic waste is the clear budgetary inefficiency of public schools. Faith-based private schools operate at roughly 60 percent the cost per student that public schools do. What this translates into is that from the perspective of economic efficiency, the United States is spending almost twice as much per student to produce students who score lower than children attending Christian and Jewish schools typically do. Were it not for the fact that nearly all Americans are used to public school dominance, any fair-minded person would question whether the nation's leaders possess a sufficient degree of common sense.

Such reliance on the government for education is creating a degree of economic stress upon taxpayers and the government that is untenable. In addition, given that—on average—over $10,500 is spent per public school student per year, if tax breaks and vouchers are mild, for example, $3,000 per student, spending per public school student will actually increase with a school choice program.

School choice could potentially extricate the nation from an unbalanced and financially onerous system that the nation cannot afford. This effort would also raise the amount per capita that is spent on public school students and is a win-win situation.

What Effect Will Vouchers and Tax Credits Have on Public Schools?

Advocates of broad school choice programs that include private schools argue that allowing public and private schools to compete against one another will be mutually beneficial because both public and private schools will learn from one other. Consequently, both sectors will improve what they offer students. To whatever extent this competition already exists at the university level, one can see that there is some validity to this view. For example, the presence of private universities, which generally have smaller class sizes than their public counterparts, has caused public universities to lower their classes sizes to better meet the needs of students (Jeynes, 2007a). Similarly, the fact that public universities often offer a wider range of majors has compelled private universities to do the same to become more competitive. One could argue that the same phenomenon would be likely to occur at the K-12 level, were choice programs initiated. It is conceivable that choice could encourage public schools to improve their attempts to reduce the achievement gap (because faith-based schools have narrower gaps), raise academic standards, and emphasize the importance of character education (Roach, 2001; Ryan & Bohlin, 1998). Similarly, choice could cause private schools to have more funding, which would enable them to improve special education (Jeynes & Beuttler, 2012). It is conceivable that both private and public schools could become better under a choice program.

Can Religious Schools Increase Competition, when There Are Many Secular Parents?

To be sure, there are secular private schools, but it is an undeniable fact that most private schools are faith based. Therefore, this is a very reasonable question. The reality of the matter is that the answer to this question is really not known. Naturally, religious people will be amenable to the idea of sending their children to faith-based schools.

It is also true that there will be a variety of other people who respect religious values and want their children to attend a school where morality is valued, even if they themselves are not religious. Moreover, there will be individuals who value the academic standards maintained at faith-based schools and want their children to be challenged intellectually, no matter where they attend. Beyond this, there are a host of factors that might make it more likely for a given youth to attend a faith-based school, including whether his or her friends attend there. What has really not been studied is just what percentage of the population would consider sending their children to a religious school if that option were made available to them. This is clearly a topic worthy of further research

How Parents Choose Certain Schools under Choice Programs

Research on the topic of how parents choose schools for their children under a school choice rubric have divulged some interesting trends that make it clear that the process that parents and children go through to select the right classroom environment is a bit more complex than both adherents and opponents of choice have envisioned (Ball, 2003). There are a number of trends that have emerged in the data that are especially enlightening. First, the process that families go through in selecting elementary and secondary schools is considerably different than the selection process at the college level (Ball, 2003; Piehl, 2012). Most notably, it appears that the academic reputation of an institution is more important at the university level than it is in a K-12 situation. In a real sense, this should not be surprising. Research indicates that where a person attends college is highly related to his or her likelihood of succeeding in life. Fifty percent of the nation's top chief executive officers (CEOs) graduated from the country's top 20 universities, and those who gain admission into *Marquis' Who's Who in the World* or *Marquis' Who's Who in America* are much more likely to be from Harvard, Princeton, and other Ivy League–level universities than other schools, even the better state universities (Hamilton, 2005; Wecker, 2012). Harvard University alone produced 13 percent of the CEOs in the Fortune 500 (Wecker, 2012). Going to a good elementary or secondary school might be helpful, but it is not as crucial as attending a strong college.

Second, parents of elementary or secondary school children are much more concerned that the values taught in these schools are in line with their own than is so at the college level (Jeynes, 2006a; Piehl, 2012). It is important that educators understand that when parents decide to send their children to school they not only consider scholastic outcomes, but they also examine the values that instructors espouse (Jeynes, 2006a; Piehl, 2012). Third, families evaluate the logistics involved in the location of a school even more than they look at the location of a college (Jeynes, 2000a). Other factors they may integrate into their cogitations include where the child's friends attend and how familiar they are with the school (Jeynes, 2000a).

Using Vouchers or Tax Credits

There is some debate among school choice advocates regarding whether vouchers or tax credits are the appropriate vehicle for the practice of school choice. Some prefer vouchers because it they are a more direct benefit, and the payment will not depend on a person's tax bracket. Some also prefer this approach because even those people who do not pay taxes will experience a financial relief sufficient to help their children attend private schools (Moe, 2006; Glenn, 2000). There are other people, however, that note that those who pay no taxes already receive a great deal of help from the government and that using a tax break methodology will give some reward to people who work (Chubb & Moe, 1990). There are valid arguments to be made on both sides of this argument. Whatever one's view of this debate, there are likely to be different practices across the full gamut of states because the essence of the American schooling system is based on a decentralized paradigm.

Conclusion

There is no question that there remain many questions about school choice that remain either unanswered or only partially answered. Nevertheless, it is apparent that two results will likely emerge: (1) a broad system of school choice that includes private schools will likely work better than a more narrow approach that is limited to public schools and (2) the evidence indicates that inaugurating a school choice system will increase the efficiency of American schools. While it would be difficult to argue against these conclusions, there are a host of other unanswered questions worthy of pursuit. And ultimately, this trek toward uncovering truth will only be to the benefit of the American education system.

Chapter 8

Will Religious Schools Lose Their Distinctiveness?

The recent growth of the federal, state, and local governments in the United States has been unparalleled in American history (U.S. Department of Education, 2010). By virtually every measure, this trend has become an undeniable fact. Probably the statistical figures that reflect this fact of which most Americans are aware are the national debt, the federal budget deficit, and the percentage of the gross domestic product (GDP) that is under direct government control (Schiff, 2012). As press time, the national debt is approximately $16 trillion, or about $50,000 for every American individual and $130,000 for every American household (Schiff, 2012). Concurrently, the government controls about 44 percent of GDP, which is more than several European nations that often are categorized as socialist (Schiff, 2012). These figures are not shared to resolve whether the United States is a capitalist or socialist state, especially because this issue rests on a continuum. Nor are these figures designed to address to overall health of the American economy. What these statistics are designed to convey is that the U.S. government is a prodigious institution, and it is understandable that many educators are wary that government involvement in school choice could harm whatever potential school choice has (Glenn, 2000). There are many people of faith who oppose school choice based on this concern (Glenn, 2000). It is a significant enough issue that it must be addressed.

Evidence That School Choice Programs Could Boost Achievement

Via meta-analyses and analysis of nationwide data sets in particular, this book has presented a large degree of evidence that school choice *could* boost academic achievement and improve overall student social and personal behavior. To really resolve the issues surrounding school choice, one needs to jettison whatever personal biases he or she may have and look at the objective facts. The reality is that the evidence is overwhelming that students at faith-based schools achieve at higher levels academically than their public school counterparts, even when adjusted for such variables as SES, parental involvement, and selectivity (Bryk, Lee & Holland, 1993; Moe, 2006). Whatever one's views are about school choice generally, there are certain facts that need to be recognized to have a credible conversation about an issue, and this is one of them. It would be much like a World War II debate with a person who denied Japanese expansionism before the war or denied Pearl Harbor, or who was unaware that the Germans surrendered before the atomic bomb was developed. Whatever other issues might be worthy of disagreement related to World War II, it is hard to have a credible conversation with someone unless these facts are understood. Similarly, it is very understandable why people might have a vast array of opinions about the viability of potential school choice programs. Nevertheless, the academic edge that students at faith-based schools generally have is one of those facts that is essential to understand if a credible conversation is to take place.

Having stated this, the question then becomes whether government involvement in school choice programs might dilute the very academic and behavioral advantages faith-based schools now enjoy. Here again, whatever one's view on school choice might be, the possibility that this might happen is a reality. It is an issue that must be addressed if one is to have a credible conversation about the potential merits and pitfalls of school choice (Glenn, 2000).

Concerns about Government Interference in School Choice Programs

One should not assume that people of faith are unanimously in favor of school choice (Jeynes, 2000a). To be sure, Catholics are generally more supportive of the idea than are evangelical Christians (Glenn, 2000; Jeynes, 2000a). Evangelical Christians are generally more wary of the intentions of big government (Macedo & Wolf, 2004). Nevertheless, even within the Catholic community, there is a great deal of hesitation about fully embracing the common tenets of government-directed school choice programs. One such skeptical Catholic is Joseph O'Keefe from Boston University. O'Keefe acknowledges that school choice is a very popular idea among many Catholics (O'Keefe, 2003). He (p. 201) believes that because there are "inconsistencies between Catholicism and the free-market philosophy that up girds the pro-choice position, vouchers cannot be the solution." O'Keefe's position is rather unique among Catholics. First, the overwhelming majority of Catholics support a voucher program or something akin to the essence of the program (Card, Dooley, & Payne, 2008). Second, unlike the primary concerns of evangelical Christians that involve an ever-expanding and imposing government force, O'Keefe views free market solutions as inconsistent with Catholicism.

O'Keefe's view that free market solutions are inconsistent with Catholicism is rather puzzling for a variety of reasons. First, O'Keefe really does not support his view with Bible references. This being the case, they appear a bit unfounded and self-manufactured. Second, O'Keefe does not overtly offer an alternative approach. Would the alternative be what generally is presented as the primary alternative, that is, communism or socialism? Although O'Keefe should be respected as an academic, what he intimates seems rather extreme. The reality is that Jesus Christ not a spiritual figure and not really a political one (Bunn, 2006; Jackson, 2009). While Christ took a stand against the government oppression that is normally associated with communism and greed, He was careful to point out that He came to offer spiritual salvation and concern for the state of the human heart, rather than to propound political solutions (Bunn, 2006; Jackson, 2009). Perhaps because O'Keefe is not a Bible scholar, he is not cognizant of this fact. Nevertheless, his view is representative of the wide spectrum of views that exist on this topic.

The reality is that currently around the world, the government is by far the most powerful entity in virtually every nation (Peterson & Viarengo, 2011). To the extent that this is the case, one can certainly develop a trenchant argument that almost anything the government touches is going to have the imprints of the government upon it (Peterson & Viarengo, 2011). In fact, Coleman (1988), Peterson, and others argue that "it is the way in which schools are organized that is the problem" (Peterson & Viarengo, 2011, p. 51). To the extent to which this is true, it would seem to be in the interests of faith-based schools to have as little government intervention as possible (Jeynes, 1999, 2003c).

Many social scientists are concerned that too much government interference could dilute the very qualities that make Christian schools so efficacious (Garnett, 2004; Galston, 2004). Coleman (1988) enjoys a lot of support in his thesis that it is the "social capital" of these schools manifested especially in the families and the culture of the schools themselves that enable the students that attend them to thrive (Putnam, 2000). Naturally, efficacy is not merely measured by scholastic outcomes, but also behavioral activities. Mocan and Tekin (2006) studied Catholic students versus their counterparts in public schools and found that the Catholic students showed a much lower propensity to engage in bad and risky behavior. Figlio and Ludwig (2001) found that Catholic students were less likely to be arrested and take hard drugs than those in public schools. These are salient findings, especially when one examines recent research indicating that parents consider the likely behavioral outcomes of their children who attend these schools as much or more than the scholastic ones, in terms of determining where they will send their young to attend school (Jeynes, 1999, 2003c; Stein, Goldring, & Cravens, 2011).

The Possible Diluting of the Religious School Identity in Europe

There are many individuals who in the ideal world would likely support school vouchers or tax breaks for religious schools but warn that the historical and international trend is that a large degree of government influence in religious education dilutes the distinctive nature of these schools (Galston, 2004; Garnett, 2004; Glenn, 2000; Jeynes, 2004b). After all, the primary explicit feature of these schools is that they are, in fact, religious. Moreover, research strongly suggests that the overall success of American religious schools is inextricably connected with their faith (Galston, 2004; Garnett, 2004; Glenn, 2000). To the extent to which this is true, the assertion that school choice could potentially damage the religious character of these schools is worthy of note (Glenn, 2000; Galston, 2004; Garnett, 2004). If true, this issue should concern not only Christians and members of other religions who cherish the values espoused by their private school educators, but anyone who supports American quality education.

Richard Garnett (2004, p. 328) summarizes the situation well when he states, "In my view, a healthy civil society can safely tolerate—indeed, it should welcome and likely depends on—meaningfully religious schools. If the price of school choice were the loss of such schools, it would not be worth even the substantial benefits it promises."

Those concerned with possible negative ramifications of school choice point to the European experience with school choice as indicating the long-term consequences of practicing school choice. Becker and Vink (1994) present sobering evidence about the place of religious faith in some European nations where school choice is practiced versus the United States where it is not. Table 8.1 lists three religious faith indicators in the United States, the Netherlands, and Germany. The results of the Becker and Vink study indicate that Americans have much higher levels of religious faith, as measured by these indicators, than their counterparts in the Netherlands and Germany. Among Americans, 94 percent believe in God compared to 55 percent and 67 percent in the Netherlands and Germany, respectively. Americans are also twice as likely to have attended church in the past week than are Germans and the Dutch. Among the three nationalities examined, Americans are the most likely to belong to a church. One would think that more Dutch would express faith in God given that, according to Glenn (1989), only one-third of children in the Netherlands attend public schools. Glenn (2000, p. 139) observes, "Although many social agencies and more than two-thirds of schools continue to have a religious identity, there is considerable evidence that this has been 'hollowed out' by decades of dependence upon the government as well as growing secularization." The German and Dutch data referred to here are fairly typical for European nations where school choice in practiced. In France, for example, one-third of French students spend at least a portion of their education in religious schools, but church attendance and belief in God are at lower levels than one currently finds in the United States. According to Glenn, the government's involvement in religious education is partially to blame for these European trends. Glenn (2000, p. 139) avers, "[A]s organizations become more oriented toward government, they become even more estranged from the religious rank and file."

Table 8.1	Percentage of People Who Answered Affirmatively when Asked the Following Questions Dealing with Religious Faith

	Do you believe in God?	Do you belong to a church?	Did you attend church in the last week?
United States	94%	93%	34%
Netherlands	55%	44%	16%
Germany	67%	89%	15%

The data presented by Becker and Vine (1994) and Glenn (1989, 2000) are intriguing. There are two assertions that arise out of their presentation of various facts. First, these social scientists argue—quite reasonably—that increased government involvement in private education probably watered down some of the religious dynamics previously present in the schools. This first assertion appears logical. However, the second claim emerges out of a correlation rather than out of any proven direction of causality. That is, they suggest that the low levels of the three measures of religious faith are indicative of the extent that government intervention has reduced the religious identity of church-sponsored schools. This may or may not be the case. Glenn acknowledges that secularization is partially responsible for these trends. It is conceivable that government entanglement with religious schools is responsible, in part, for a decline the religious distinctiveness of these schools. Furthermore, it is possible that the deterioration in the religious nature of these schools contributed to the decline in faith among those European nations practicing school choice. However, one can also argue that without the presence of religious schools, the spiritual terrain in Europe might have changed even more dramatically. Therefore, the second assertion is considerably weaker than the first.

There are other trends in France that make one think government involvement in private education could dilute the religious distinctiveness of many of these schools. As European societies have become more secular, many people have argued that governments have decreasingly regarded parental rights. George Jacque Danton, a French politician, stated, "Children belong to the Republic more than they do to their parents" (Glenn, 1989, p. 11). Although many leaders would disagree with Danton, to the extent that some political leaders possess this attitude, government entanglement in private education might reduce the religious identity of Catholic and evangelical schools (Glenn, 2000).

Whether one agrees with the second claim or not, the statistics presented by Glenn (1989, 2000), Becker and Vine (1994), and others do depict a likely scenario of the kind of changes that Americans might expect should school choice be employed on a broad scale in this country. That is, it is likely that school choice would produce a higher percentage of students attending religious schools. However, religious schools probably would frequently experience some dilution of their religious nature. To the extent that this would ultimately be the result, religious people who are concerned about this issue would do well to assess the cost of this trade-off. To the extent that most people of faith want more students attending religious schools rather than less, they would certainly welcome the likely increase in enrollment. However, to the extent that evangelical and Catholic schools, for example, are successful because of their religious character, each religious school might make less of an impact than would otherwise be the case. Ultimately, this could impact the both the educational and religious environment of the country.

Naturally, the extent to which believers are willing to engage in this trade-off depends on the extent the trade-off exists and whether they are necessary. For example, religious educators would probably be more likely to embrace school choice to the extent that the reduction in religious identity will be marginal compared to the increase in Catholic and evangelical school enrollment. It is also true that if these educators are convinced that we can learn from some of the mistakes made in Europe that led to some degree of forfeiture of religious identity among religious schools, this also might reduce some people's aversion to school choice.

One helpful way to assess the extent to which dilution of impact and identity has occurred in Europe is to address this issue via conducting a meta-analysis. Therefore, the next section of this chapter is designed to undertake this task.

Comparing Faith-Based Schools versus Public Schools in the United States and Overseas (Especially Europe)

Methods

In this project, I searched every major database (Psych Info, ERIC, Sociological Abstracts, Wilson Periodicals, and so forth) to find studies examining the effects of religious schools on the educational (academic and behavioral) outcomes of children from grades K-12. I also searched journal articles on religious schools to find additional research articles that addressed this issue. I obtained a total of 124 studies that addressed the relationship under study and found 54 studies that had a sufficient degree of quantitative data to include in the meta-analysis examining the overall effects of religious schools on achievement and 30 that address the effects of religious commitment on personal behavior. The total number of subjects included in these studies was well over 500,000. The 84 studies were then placed in categories, depending on whether they examined religious schools or religious commitment and whether the study took place in the United States or overseas. In this project, a statistical analysis was done to determine the overall effects of religious schools obtained for each study, as well as the specific academically related outcomes that attending religious schools affected. These specific academic outcomes include grade point average (GPA), achievement test outcomes (often identified by specific subject), teacher ratings, and other behavioral outcomes related to school. Two statistical measures were used to reduce sampling and publication bias.

Results

The results indicate that the "religious advantage" is larger for American schools than it is for schools of other nations, which in this case were almost entirely European schools. Table 8.2 lists the effect sizes when overall educational outcomes, achievement test results, grades, and other measures (usually teacher ratings) were examined. Statistically significant differences between the United States and overseas (not from the United States) emerged for all the academic outcomes examined. For the overall educational outcomes measure, the effect size for American schools was .20 ($p < .01$), and for European and other area schools it was .13 ($p > .05$). The difference between these two outcomes was statistically significant at the .05 level of probability. In the case of achievement tests, the effect size for the American schools was .20 ($p < .01$), and for European and other schools it was .05 ($p > .05$). These differences were also statistically significant. Among the academic measures for the American schools, the largest regression coefficient emerged for other measures, .24 ($p < .0001$) and the smallest one for grades, .11 ($p < .05$).

Table 8.2   Effect Sizes of Religious Schools by Area of the World for Different Academic Outcomes

	Overall Educational Outcomes	Achievement Tests	Grades	Other Measures
United States	.20[**][a]	.20[**][a]	.11[*][a]	.24[****][a]
	(.07, .33)	(.07, .33)	(.01, .21)	(.13, .35)
Europe and Other Areas	.13[a]	.05[a]	−.07[a]	.14[a]

Note: a = Effect sizes are statistically significant from the corresponding regression coefficient for the other geographical area under this category

[*]$p < .05$
[**]$p < .01$
[***]$p < .001$
[****]$p < .0001$

The regression coefficients for the European and other schools were also largest for other measures and smallest for grades, but neither of these results was statistically significant.

In contrast, in results not shown here, the effects for religious commitment were statistically significant for American, overseas, and European Christians.

Discussion

The results indicate that for all four measures of academic achievement, the religious school advantage over public schools was greater in the United States than it was in other nations, mostly Europe. However, for religious commitment for the four measures of academic achievement or school-related behavioral measures, the religious advantage over less-religious students was larger for American religious people for only one of the four measures. There are a number of possible explanations for this pattern of results. Two are especially interesting. First, the influence of religious schools may vary more by continent than religious commitment. Second, the differences reflected in the school numbers may reflect differences in the public schools of these nations as much as or more than any distinctions among religious schools.

In terms of the first possible explanation—that religious schools may vary more internationally than religious commitment—research by Glenn (1989) and others (Jeynes, 2002a; Monsina & Sopher, 1997) indicates that the structure and functioning of religious schools does vary considerably across nations. The operation of religious schools within the same denomination or sect may vary according to the extent of government and regulation, laws, culture, and educational philosophy (Glenn, 1989). Religious commitment within the same denomination or sect, on the other hand, certainly varies by culture. However, it is less likely to be influenced by all these other factors (Cochran, 1993; Cochran & Akers, 1989). For this reason, it is conceivable and even logical that the effects of religious schools may vary more in their influence than religious commitment.

The second possible explanation is that the differences reflected in the school numbers may reflect differences in the public schools of these nations as much as or more than any distinctions among religious schools. That is, the gap between religious and public schools may be larger in the United States than it is in other nations, mostly Europe, because public schools in the United States are of an especially low quality. One should remember that American public schools were considered by many educators in the middle part of the twentieth century to be the world's best public elementary and secondary school system (Jeynes, 2012c; Ravitch, 2000). However, many educators believe that by the early 1960s, the American public school system had gone into a protracted decline, which was reflected in consistently retreating nationwide test scores between 1963 and 1980 (Jeynes, 2003c). International test scores support the notion that American public school students have fallen further behind their European counterparts in most measures of achievement (Leestma & Walberg 1992; Lynn, 1988; Stevenson & Stigler, 1992). Given that this is the case, it is quite possible that the wider rift between religious and public school student achievement could be due as much as or more to the inadequacies of the American public school system when contrasted to overseas systems than it does the effectiveness of American religious schools when compared to their European and other international counterparts. Perhaps the safest position to take on this issue is to assert that the larger spread between religious and public schools in the United States may be partially due to the effectiveness of American religious schools and partially due to problems within American public schools. European schools, for example, are often more tolerant of people of faith than are their American counterparts (Harris, 2004). James Hartwick (2007), who was the first to thoroughly examine teachers' faith in American public schools, notes that many of them feel restricted.

Limitations of the Meta-Analytic Approach

The meta-analytic technique has a high degree of utility in ascertaining a sense of what the overall research literature states on a particular area of study. This is one of the major reasons social scientists read meta-analyses so frequently. However, it should be noted that the results of meta-analyses should be taken in the following context. The major limitation of the meta-analysis is that the researcher is totally reliant on the studies that have been done previously. One can only address the questions that have been asked by researchers and cannot fully manipulate the variables in the same way as if he or she were conducting an original study.

The Government's Desire for More Secular Religious Institutions

The second major point made by those concerned about government intrusion is that when it comes to funding, the American government desires more secular religious institutions. Marvin Olasky, of the University of Texas, is one of the foremost proponents of this perspective. He declares that when the government works hand in hand with religious institutions, the government has so many strings attached to its promises to fund that it secularizes the religious institution or outreach. Olasky (1992, p. 149) states, "How were these programs really different from government programs? ... The general result was that many religious programs had effectively been secularized." However, lest one be tempted to demonize government funding, Glenn (2000, p. 42) warns, "It would be too simple to equate public funding with government interference." Research by Monsina and Sopher (1997) indicates that the degree to which an organization becomes less religiously oriented may have more to do with a change of norms within the religious organization itself rather than increased government regulations.

Although current debate rages about the relative degree of responsibility for the secularization of religious organizations that deal with the government, there are certain instances of government interference that are undeniable. For example, in 1980, Mayor Koch of New York City issued Executive Order 50, which made it mandatory for city-funded organizations not to discriminate on the basis of several factors, including sexual orientation. In March 1984 when the Salvation Army objected to guidelines about hiring homosexuals, the city threatened to cancel $4 million of childcare contracts. To the relief of the Salvation Army, in 1985, the New York Court of Appeals ruled that Mayor Koch had acted inappropriately and that such a law could be passed only by the City Council (Glenn, 2000).

It is ironic that the Salvation Army was the subject of the sexual orientation discrimination case because those who are skeptical about government intrusion often point to the Salvation Army as a prime example of how a religious organization can compromise its religious purpose by working closely with the government (Olasky, 1992). Statistics indicate that during the same time that the Salvation Army's social services grew exponentially in the twentieth century, their church membership was flat. Some claim that this means it is difficult for a religious organization to expand its relationship with the government and fulfill its religious mission at the same time.

A number of social scientists have pointed out that technically, it is not so much the government funding that leads to a compromising of religious values by churches and related organizations, but the government regulations that accompany the funding. An incident that took place in Braintree, Massachusetts, is important to note in this regard. In the early 1980s, a public school superintendent wrote to a church to ask if the teachers in a private school were certified. This was rather an aggressive move by the superintendent, particularly because private schools were not required to have certified teachers. After the church leaders responded, the superintendent asked for a list of the curriculum used at all the school's grade levels. The superintendent added that state officials would soon be visiting the school to ensure that the submitted information was correct. The church took the case to court, and in *Braintree Baptist Temple et al. v. Holbrook Public Schools et al.* (1984), it did prevail. However, the series of events reminded many religious educators of what could easily happen if the government were to become more involved in the intricate workings of private education (Glenn, 2000).

Bicknese (1999) undertook a thorough investigation of the drug programs available at Teen Challenge. Teen Challenge is a religious outreach program, connected to the Assemblies of God denomination, that specializes in helping drug addicts, gang members, and alcoholics. One of the issues Bicknese thoroughly examined was the government's attempts to regulate Teen Challenge. Teen Challenge gained nationwide attention, particular among government agencies, when it yielded success rates of 95.3 percent for individuals overcoming heroin addiction and 87.5 percent for people overcoming marijuana addiction. Bicknese notes that by comparison, a sample of graduates from public service hospitals had only 26 percent that remained off illegal drugs.

In 1995, the Texas Commission decided that Teen Challenge in San Antonio needed "to be licensed in order to meet licensing requirements" (Glenn, 2000, p. 69). The Texas government declared that Teen Challenge needed to adopt "a rehabilitation approach consistent with the secular methods and assumptions that represent the professional norm" (Glenn, 2000, p. 69). Nevertheless, the leaders of Teen Challenge believe that it is the religious nature of the organization that contributes so much to its success. This incident with Teen Challenge in Texas supports the assertion made by Justice Stewart (*Abington Township School District v. Schempp*, 1963, p. 313) in the Supreme Court case banning the use of the Bible in the opening exercises of school. He argued that the government claim of neutrality was false and that the government was instead supporting "the establishment of a religion of secularism . . ."

The long-term examples of government involvement in religious education and social activities are such that one has basis on which to be concerned about the ultimate ramifications of this involvement. The Milwaukee school voucher program is already seeing evidence of this fact. Now that efforts to scuttle the program have failed in the courts, Glenn (2000, p. 115) states that "the public education establishment sought to choke it to death with regulation." Proponents of choice are learning quickly that managing with government involvement in private education is no easy task.

Even beyond the examples of involvement in religious activities, there is a mixed tendency for the government (at any level) to become more intrusive when there is government funding. Two of the major spheres of government funding are bilingual education and race-related issues such as integration and affirmative action. Regarding the topic of bilingual education, although various levels of government provide funding for bilingual education, there is considerable variation in the degree to which the government interferes with the bilingual education programs that are incorporated. The federal government generally provides a considerable degree of flexibility in how bilingual education is taught (Whitten, 1986). The extent of state government mandates varies considerably by state (Glenn, 2000). Those states with the highest levels of federal funding and of second-language minority groups tend to have the strictest rules regarding how bilingual education is taught (Center for Equal Opportunity, 1998).

The government has also provided funding to encourage racial equality, especially related to integration and affirmative action (Glenn, 2000). Government funding in these spheres has led to heightened government involvement (Glenn, 2000). The government regularly threatens to cut off funds if certain standards are not met. In other sectors, government financial support tends to lead to government involvement or intrusion to the extent there is direct government support. Overall, the more direct the federal funding, the higher the level of government involvement or intrusion. For example, there is often a higher level of government involvement with direct government aid than when the government gave tax breaks (Glenn, 2000; Jeynes, 2007a).

One way the government can secularize religious schools is to make a plethora of regulations that will force faith-based schools to succumb to secular regulations (Hess, 2006). Frederick Hess contends that excessive government regulations already stifle American schools, and burdening faith-based schools with government red tape will only exacerbate the problem.

The Rise of Charter Schools Is Likely to Reduce the Number of Private Religious Schools

There is a growing body of evidence that the rise in the number of charter schools is reducing the number of private religious schools (Toma, Zimmer & Jones, 2006). Apparently, weighed down with onerous rates of taxation an increasing number of parents are concluding that they can no longer afford to send their children to private schools and many of these are opting for charter schools instead (Toma, Zimmer, & Jones, 2006). Largely as a result of this trend, American private school enrollment is at a 55-year low (U.S Department of Education, 2012). This is an unfortunate trend because as Chubb (2006, p. 21) declares: "The prospects of substantial improvement in public education without substantial changes in the education system are not good."

How Should One Approach School Choice?

The evidence presented in this text suggests that one should address government involvement in school choice with caution. First, the potential for a dilution of religious identity clearly exists (Macedo & Wolf, 2004). Macedo and Wolf (2004) admonish individuals and society at large to be careful about embracing school choice too hastily. They warn that although many European nations possess a system of school choice, it is at the price of an unwieldy degree of regulation. Nevertheless, Macedo and Wolf (2004) point out that European nations tend to be much more socialistic than the United States, and most of them have a history of monarchy. Consequently, they tend to be much more comfortable with a strong central government than Americans are. In contrast, most people in the United States feel that the parents should be the primary source of their children's instruction and guidance (Calvert, 2012). To the extent to which this is true, the religious community should proceed with wisdom to ensure that this does not happen. Religious educators need to work to make certain that government neutrality is really just that and does not involve the establishing of secularism. Kuyper (1890) warned of this possibility and encouraged the religious community to be vigilant. Other social scientists have consistently warned of this possibility since that time. There is a general consensus among the religious educational community that part of the academic and moral success of evangelical and Catholic schools rests in their religious identity. Therefore, there are many reasons to argue that religious identity is worth preserving, even beyond purely religious grounds.

Second, the means by which funds are distributed are also important. Funds should be disseminated in such a way that decision making about the quantity and distribution of the funds is done by parents, not the government. The money should be made available in such a way that the government is reminded that it is the parents' money that is being used, not the government's revenue. Kuyper, for example, believed that the financial power of the parents to choose should be maximized in order for school choice to be effective. Contemporary research suggests that Kuyper is correct.

Therefore, using tax breaks, rather than school vouchers, might be a preferable means of providing funding (although vouchers might be provided for those who do not pay taxes).

Third, religious schools need to be proactive in maintaining their faith-based goals, character, and mission. Kuyper (1890) believed that this was quite possible and that the church would be faithful to accomplish these tasks. Contemporary researchers on this issue probably emphasize this third point more than Kuyper did. This appears to be a product of seeing the effects of many decades of government intervention in religious education in Europe and certain aspects of government intrusion in the United States. To the degree that it is a change in the nature of religious institutions that is partially responsible for the decline in the spirituality of these institutions, churches and other religious organizations need to take greater responsibility for upholding the religious foundations and principles on which they were founded.

Conclusion

Some proponents of school choice are enthusiastic about choice to the degree that they are likely overoptimistic about its prospects. And indeed, if properly done, school choice initiatives have vast potential. Nevertheless, one would be imprudent if he or she did not also espy the possibility that government entanglement with religious schools could also emaciate the core sources of strength that faith-based schools provide. This statement is not intended to paint the government as some nefarious institution that must be eschewed at all costs. Rather, it is intended to build on the biblical principle of "counting the cost." That is, there is strength and wisdom in anticipating both the advantages and disadvantages of important actions.

Chapter 9

School Choice: Hope for Inner-City Children and Children of Color

School choice may offer the greatest benefit for the youth in greatest need, that is, children residing in the inner city and children of color. There appears to be a recognition of this fact among many families from these backgrounds (Irvine & Foster, 1996; Stolberg, 2008). They understand that they often do not gain access to the best schools for their children, that the middle class and upper class obtain It is therefore no surprise that African Americans and Latinos are the ethnic groups most supportive of school choice (Kirkpatrick, 1990; Phi Beta Kappa/Gallup Poll, 2002). As Stolberg (2008) points out, many African Americans view obtaining greater school choice as part of the civil rights movement. Stolberg asserts that African Americans want greater access to the nation's best schools, and many of these are private schools. The title of Stolberg's book is *Race, School, and Hope: African Americans and School Choice after Brown*. The title epitomizes the degree to which many African Americans view this as a civil rights issue.

There is no question that school choice proponents have especially emphasized the needs of children of color, especially African Americans and Latinos, and low-SES youth, in inaugurating and continuing their school choice plans (Stolberg, 2008; Walberg, 2007; White House, 2008). One of the reasons is because one of the virtues that Americans cherish most is equality, and school choice advocates see school choice as a potential means of reducing the achievement gap that exists by both race and socioeconomic status (Stolberg, 2008; Walberg, 2007). As Ronald Roach (2001, p. 377) notes, "In the academic and think tank world, pondering achievement gap remedies takes center stage." As it is, many children of color and low-SES children attend public charter schools to experience some of the benefits of choice. However, as the meta-analysis presented in Chapter 2 indicates, while public charter schools may give parents and students a greater sense of autonomy, students attending public charters really do no better academically and behaviorally than those attending traditional public schools.

Problems in the Inner City

Americans have become very aware that inner-city areas face a unique combination of problems. Educators and sociologists bemoan the fact that one of the principle problems these areas face is that a large percentage of the people who live there want to leave (Royster, 2010; Zylstra, 2009). Consequently, what happens is that when circumstances improve for a given family, they depart from the area. When this happens, some of the best community examples of upward mobility and experiencing the American dream are no longer present to serve as models to the children growing up there (Royster, 2010; Zylstra, 2009). The problems faced by children in the inner city are not unique to that environment, but the confluence of factors such as inadequate parental support, single-parent families, high crime rates, inadequate neighborhood revenue, and school bureaucracy are more likely to occur in the inner city than in other locales (Royster, 2010; Zylstra, 2009). As a result, whatever socioeconomic or ethnic achievement gap might exist in somewhat better circumstances is exacerbated (Royster, 2010; Zylstra, 2009). That being the case, if school choice via greater access to faith-based and private independent schools can alleviate the achievement gap, this is a major positive factor in favor of at least more broadly experimenting with school choice.

School Choice and the Achievement Gap

After five decades of trying to reduce the achievement gap and—to everyone's chagrin—encountering repeated failure, researchers are beginning to ask a question (Jeynes, 1999, 2002b, 2003c). That is, could it be that this nation's failure to bridge the achievement could rests in its insular insistence on limiting the number of options utilized to bring about progress (Jeynes, 2010a)? Could it be that educators typically limit the range of options to something less than the full gamut because they consider options available only in the public sector? To the degree that this might be so, social scientists should at least examine the possibility that a school choice rubric that includes private schools could provide at least some of the solutions (Bryk, Lee, & Holland, 1993).

Analyses of the Socioeconomic Achievement Gap

Statistical analyses of the NELS data set and a meta-analysis indicate that a school choice program that includes faith-based schools may indeed reduce the achievement gap.

Two sets of analyses were completed to examine the achievement gap between low-SES and higher-SES students. The first involved comparing low-SES religious school and public school students via SES quartiles in the NELS. The second involved a meta-analysis of the existing studies that compared the academic outcomes of low-SES students attending religious schools to those of low-SES students in public schools. The analysis was based on a literature search in 25 databases in which more than 60 studies were found that examined the relationship between religious schools and academic outcomes. Of these, 13 specifically examined the effects of low-SES students attending religious schools on academic outcomes; those 13 studies are synthesized in this report. Measures of academic achievement included both standardized and nonstandardized measures.

Analysis of the NELS Data Set

The results of the NELS data set analysis indicate that (1) children in the lowest SES quartile who attend religious schools achieve at higher levels than do children in the lowest SES quartile who attend public schools and (2) children in the lowest SES quartile benefit from attending religious schools more than students in the other SES quartiles. Low-SES students attending religious schools outperformed their counterparts in public schools on both standardized and nonstandardized measures. Among the standardized tests, the religious school students' scores varied from 7.8 percent higher for the

Test Composite to 5.4 percent higher for the Science test. The religious school advantage was even greater for the nonstandardized Basic Core measure (8.2 percent higher).

The results listed in Table 9.1 show how the religious school advantage differs by SES quartile in the student sample. For all the academic achievement measures examined, students from the lowest SES quartile showed the greatest academic benefit, as measured by percentage gain from attending religious schools compared to their counterparts in public schools. This advantage was greater than that experienced by students in the other three socioeconomic quartiles. The increase for students in the lowest quartile was 3.0 percent higher than the increase for students in the highest quartile for the Test Composite and Basic Core classes and was at least 2.0 percent higher in every academic category. The religious school advantage was inversely related to the student's socioeconomic quartile. For all measures, students from the lowest SES quartile benefited the most from attending religious schools, followed by the second lowest quartile, and so on. The high-SES quartile students benefited the least from attending religious schools.

Meta-Analysis

The meta-analysis indicated that low-SES students benefit more than moderate-SES and high-SES students do from attending religious

Table 9.1 Effects (in percentage score increases) on the Academic Achievement of Twelfth Grade Children by SES Quartile (NELS Dataset: $N = 20{,}706$)

	Lowest SES Quartile	2nd Lowest SES Quartile	2nd Highest SES Quartile	Highest SES Quartile
Reading Achievement	7.6%	6.8%	5.8%	5.2%
Math Achievement	7.0%	6.2%	5.6%	5.0%
Social Studies Achievement	6.8%	5.8%	5.2%	4.6%
Science Achievement	5.4%	4.0%	3.4%	3.2%
Test Composite	7.8%	6.6%	5.4%	4.8%
Left Back	5.8%	5.0%	4.4%	3.8%
Basic Core	8.2%	6.6%	5.8%	5.2%

Table 9.2   Meta-Analysis Advantage for Low-SES Children Attending Religious Schools versus Their Counterparts in Public Schools by Level of Schooling

	Combined Standardized and Nonstandardized Results	Standardized Results	Nonstandardized Results
All Levels of Schooling Combined	5.1%	5.3%	4.8%
High School Level	5.4%	5.7%	5.0%
Middle School Level	5.2%	5.2%	5.2%
Elementary School Level	3.1%	3.1%	NA

Note: NA = Not applicable

schools. These results held across all the standardized and nonstandardized measures. The difference in the advantage was largest for the Basic Core set of courses (2.7 percent) and least for Math test and being left back a grade (1.7 percent). These differences are similar to those found by using the NELS data set. As indicated in Table 9.2, the meta-analysis showed an advantage of 5.1 percent in favor of low-SES students attending religious schools over their counterparts in public schools. The religious school student advantage was somewhat higher for standardized tests (5.3 percent) than for nonstandardized measures (4.8 percent). This trend also held at the high school level, where the religious school advantages for standardized tests and nonstandardized measures were 5.7 percent and 5.0 percent, respectively. At the middle school level, this pattern did not hold. In this case, the religious school advantages were both 5.2 percent. Another pattern that emerged was that the effect sizes for overall achievement for middle school (5.2 percent) and high school (5.4 percent) were greater than for elementary school (3.1 percent).

These results suggest that the advantage for attending religious schools is greater at higher grades, that is, at the middle school and high school levels. One might interpret these findings as indicating that religious schools do a particularly good job of aiding high school and middle school students. However, another possible explanation is that—at least for the students who begin attending religious schools at a young age—the larger effect sizes may simply be a reflection of giving sufficient time for the religious school advantage to be manifested.

Analyses of the Racial Achievement Gap

When we examine the racial achievement gap, the effects of religious schools are similar to the pattern found for SES. Table 9.3 indicates that the standardized test scores of African American and Latino students varied from 8.3 percent higher than those of their public school counterparts for Math, Social Studies, and Test Composite to 6.0 percent higher for Science. When SES and gender were controlled for, the standardized test scores of African American and Latino students varied from 5.2 percent higher than their public school counterparts for the Social Studies test to 2.0 percent higher for the Science test.

Table 9.3   Effects (in percentage score increases) on the Academic Achievement of Twelfth Grade Children by Race (NELS Dataset: N = 20,706)

	Considering SES and Gender		Not Considering SES and Gender	
	African American and Latino	White	African American and Latino	White
Reading Achievement	8.2%	6.0%	4.6%	3.4%
Math Achievement	8.3%	6.0%	4.2%	3.0%
Social Studies Achievement	8.3%	5.8%	5.2%	3.4%
Science Achievement	6.0%	4.2%	2.0%	1.2%
Test Composite	8.3%	6.0%	4.8%	3.8%
Left Back	5.1%	3.7%	3.0%	2.0%
Basic Core	8.3%	6.5%	3.4%	3.0%

For all the academic measures, whether SES was controlled for or not, African American and Latino students benefited more than whites did from attending religious schools. For the standardized tests, African American and Latino students gained 2.5 percent more than white students for the Social Studies test and 1.8 percent more for the Science test. When SES was controlled for, African American and Latino students gained 1.8 percent more than white students for the Social Studies test and 0.8 percent more for the Science test.

Religious Commitment and Family Factors and the Gap

Faith-based schools naturally emphasize religion and family. Therefore, it is also instructive to use the NELS data set to examine how the combination of religious commitment and coming from a two-parent intact family are associated with the achievement gap. Table 9.4 indicates that when the data are adjusted for SES and gender, black and Hispanic adolescents who are religious and from intact families do just as well academically as white students. In Table 9.4, the academic indicator favors African American and Latino students if the result is listed as a positive number and favors white students if it is a negative number. One can see that once one controls for SES and gender, the achievement gap essentially evaporates for all the standardized test measures except in Science. Moreover, religious African American and Latino students from intact families are actually less likely to be left back a grade and are more likely to take the Basic Core set of courses, as prescribed by the NAEP, than are white students. Even if one does not factor in SES (see the last column of Table 9.4), the achievement gap is quite small when religious African American and Latino students from intact families are compared with white students.

Summary of Thoughts on the Achievement Gap

The results of this study support the argument that attending religious schools is associated with higher levels of academic achievement among low-SES students and students of color. The studies from which this meta-analysis drew generally took into consideration gender, race, and various other factors, including parental involvement and the extent to which a school's program was demanding. One intriguing finding is that the effect sizes tended to be smaller

Table 9.4 Effects (in standard deviation units) on Academic Achievement for Twelfth Grade (1992) Black and Hispanic Children who were Highly Religious and Came from an Intact Family versus White Children, Using the SES Model (N = 24,599)

Academic Measure	Achievement Gap Controlling for Gender and SES	Achievement Gap Controlling for Gender but Not SES
STANDARDIZED MEASURES		
Math	0.4%	−0.8%
Reading	−0.4%	−1.5%
Science	−2.4%	−3.6%
Social Studies	0.0%	−1.5%
Composite	0.0%	−1.3%
OTHER MEASURES		
Left Back[a]	2.0%	1.1%
Basic Core[a]	6.2%	5.6%

Note: a = Logistic regression

for the meta-analysis than for the analysis examining the NELS data set. One of the primary reasons for this difference is that a number of the studies that were included in the meta-analysis controlled for variables such as parental involvement and the extent to which the school had a demanding curriculum, which a number of researchers assert are some of the very reasons students at religious schools perform better than their counterparts in public schools (Coleman, 1988; Coleman & Hoffer, 1987). These findings concerning the reduction and even elimination of the achievement gap are especially noteworthy when we consider that schools have been inundated with programs that have had only marginal success in reducing the gap (Green, 2001; Haycock, 2001).

The results of this research have vital implications for educational policy in assessing whether school choice programs that include private schools should be initiated.

A Barrier to an Open Mind to School Choice: The Tension between the Public and Private Sector

One might ask why it is that only a small segment of the U.S. population has considered school choice, including private schools, as a vehicle for reducing the achievement gap. Much of the reason rests in the increasing tension that exists in this country between those in the private and public sectors and the steady growth in the power of the public sector relative to the private sector (Epple & Romano, 2003; Kurtz, 2010; Skarica, 2011). To open minds to the possibility that school choice programs involving private schools could help alleviate the racial and socioeconomic achievement gaps, it is advisable to understand the present ramifications of this tension, how these tensions arose, and how the growing relative power of the public sector, especially the public school sector, is influencing the debate (Jeynes, 2008a, 2008b; Kurtz, 2010; Skarica, 2011).

Few would doubt the notion that over the past few decades in particular, a rising tension has emerged between the public and private sectors (Bracey, 1997; Epple & Romano, 2003; Jeynes, 2000a; Ravitch, 2010). Sadly, one could argue that those in the public sector are most concerned about what is good for themselves, and those in the private sector are also most cognizant about what is best for those functioning in their own sector. This nearsightedness has manifested itself along a number of dimensions: educational, political, and economical related to alleviating budget deficits (Hagel & Kaminsky 2008; Harwood & Seib, 2008). Unfortunately, it is very rare to find a public school educator concerned about the health of religious schools. In fact, a plethora of teachers are antagonistic toward Christian schools, for example, Decter (1995) and Olasky (1988). Similarly, there is increased political tension between those in public sector jobs and those in the private sector (Ravitch, 2003; Weir, 2007).

From 1900 until the early 1960s, Americans understood that workers who served in the private sector made more income for similar work in the public sector (Morgan & Morgan, 2008; Nagel, 2002; Peterson, 2006). In the minds of most, this reality was readily accepted, especially because the United States was a thriving capitalist country (Nagel, 2002; Peterson, 2006). However, although civilians in the private sector earned more money, it was also understood that those in the public sector enjoyed more security (Nagel, 2002; Peterson, 2006). Government workers, for example, were more likely to have a job for life (Nagel, 2002; Peterson, 2006). Over the past 45 years, however, the federal government has been increasing in power relative to the private sector (Morgan & Morgan, 2008; Nagel, 2002; Peterson, 2006). Presently, government workers not only have more secure positions of employment than their private sector counterparts, but they also now usually make more money (Morgan & Morgan, 2008; Nagel, 2002; Peterson, 2006; U.S. Department of Education, 2010). The U.S. government sector has become dominant and now makes up about 44 percent of American GDP (Kurtz, 2010; Skarica, 2011). This is particularly amazing because this percentage exceeds that found in Great Britain and Germany, which are typically regarded as demo-socialist states (Kurtz, 2010; Skarica, 2011).

The growing hegemony of the U.S. government is no more apparent than in the American elementary and secondary school system, where three realities are ostensible: (1) public school teachers not only generally have a job security that well exceeds that experienced by private school teachers, but they also make far higher salaries (Gross, 1999; Wallace & Graves, 1995). In 2008–2009, the average public school teacher made $54,319 per year, while the average private school teacher earned about 70 percent of that (National Education Association, 2010; U.S. Department of Education, 2011). Second, the public school sector has a near monopoly on the enrollment of elementary and secondary school pupils (Peterson, 2006). Approximately 90 percent of American youth attend public schools (Bracey, 1997; Chubb & Moe, 1990; Peterson, 2006). Third, public school taxation of constituents has risen substantially over the past half-century and has put private schools at such a disadvantage that many of them have been forced to close and others face the dire prospect of closure (Chubb & Moe, 1990; Jeynes, 2007a; Peterson, 2006).

The growing strength of the public sector and the dominance of public schools have yielded two realities. First, those in the public schools tend to limit solutions to educational challenges to the public sector, with private religious schools being almost entirely overlooked as potential partners in crafting solutions to problems such as the achievement gap. Second, the increasing relative power of the public schools through taxation is producing a financial chokehold on myriad religious private schools (Jeynes, 2008a, 2008b). Ironically, with this eventuation, American society may be truncating one of its best hopes of reducing the achievement gap.

As one would only expect, the private schools under the most severe pressure are usually religious schools operating in some of the poorest sections of the country, for example, inner cities and rural areas (Anitt, 2003; Peterson, 2006; Steinfels, 2003). According to White House estimates, during the 2000–2006 period, 1,162 inner-city faith-based schools were closed, and nearly 425,000 students were lost, mostly due to insufficient funding (White House, 2008). By definition, these schools were not founded with the goal of making a profit (Hoffer, 1998; Peterson, 2006). This is axiomatic not only because churches and other religious organizations are nonprofit, but because efforts to school in these areas are viewed as divine and altruistic attempts to help those who are less fortunate (Hoffer, 1998; Jeynes, 2002a, 2003c, 2006a; Peterson, 2006).

The White House Summit and the Reduction of the Achievement Gap in Faith-Based Schools

The problem of the closure of faith-based schools in inner cities and other urban areas has been ostensible enough so that when he was president, George W. Bush called for a White House summit to address this problem (Jeynes, 2008a, 2008b). In this summit, President Bush and the nation's leading researchers and political and economic thinkers converged to speak about the need for faith-based schools in the inner city (Jeynes, 2008a, 2008b). Many remarkable findings emerged out of the White House summit that significantly enlighten the dialogue today regarding the place that faith-based schools have in the education of children of color. Probably the most publicized result of the White House summit surrounded evidence indicating that faith-based schools reduce the achievement gap by approximately 25 percent or more, even when one adjusts for socioeconomic status (Jeynes, 2008a). And indeed, via the examination of nationwide data sets and meta-analysis, it is now apparent that African American and Latino children who attend faith-based schools perform higher academically than their counterparts in public schools (Bryk, Lee, & Holland, 1993; Hoffer, 1998; Jeynes, 1999, 2002a, 2003c, 2010a). Moreover, the achievement gap between African American students and Latinos on the one hand and white

students on the other does tend to be on average about 25 percent narrower in faith-based schools than in public schools (Jeynes, 1999,
2002a, 2003c). What this means is that the advantage of going to
faith-based schools is greater for African American and Latino students
than it is for white students (Jeynes, 1999, 2002a, 2003c).

The results of nationwide data sets and meta-analyses also indicate
that the socioeconomic achievement gap is about 25 percent narrower at faith-based schools than in public schools (Jeynes, 1999,
2003c, 2010a). In fact, the data indicate that religious private schools
benefit the lowest SES quartile of students the most, the second lowest quartile of these youth the second most, and the highest quartile
of students the least (Jeynes, 2002a, 2003c, 2008a).

There is little question that the set of results for both the racial
and socioeconomic achievement gap appear to be the ideal for the
alleviating this social challenge known as the achievement gap. That
is, it appears that one of the most accessible means of narrowing the
achievement gap will not require billions of dollars of additional
government funding; rather, it will take facilitating schools of faith
to do what they already do quite well. Nevertheless, one should point
out that it would be unwise to assume that these results apply to all
the most prominent expressions of schools of faith. Nearly all the
schools of faith in the United States are Christian (U.S. Department
of Education, 2010). Therefore, nearly all the schools available in
the data set were Christian.

The meta-analytic research on the achievement gap indicates that
the extent to which religious schools bridge the various educational
gap is quite consistent across the type of gap and the scholastic measure (Jeynes, 1999, 2002a, 2003c). For example, schools of faith
reduce the socioeconomic educational gap by approximately the same
degree that they reduce the gap that exists by race. In addition,
degree of gap reduction is very similar in size across academic subjects. All of the reductions are statistically significant. Numerically
speaking, there was a slight tendency for the reduction in the achievement gap to be smaller for science, somewhat under 25 percent, but
this difference in reduction was not statistically significantly smaller
than for the other academic measures (Jeynes, 1999, 2002a, 2003c).
There was also a slight tendency for the narrowing of the achievement gap to be greater for nonstandardized measures such as grade
retention and grade point average than for standardized tests scores,

but once again, this difference was not statistically significant (Jeynes, 1999, 2002a, 2003c).

The results indicate, then, that attending faith-based schools narrows the achievement gap across every academic subject and measure (Jeynes, 1999, 2002a, 2003c). This fact adds credence to the idea that the influence of faith-based schools on the achievement gap is both broad and significant (Dunham & Wilson, 2007; Portfeli et al., 2009; Rippeyoung, 2009; Slavin & Madden, 2006; Stevens, Olivarez, & Hamman, 2006).

Other Important Issues

Targeted versus Universal Choice

The issues that face children of color and low-SES children are such that they raise the debate of whether the United States should practice targeted choice that focuses on these children alone or whether universal choice, in which all children benefit, should be practiced. This debate is certainly a worthy one. Advocates of both approaches speak using much the same terminology as each other. They use words like "equality" and "access" to make their cases (Stolberg, 2008; Walberg, 2007). This debate addresses some important questions, such as, What is true equality? Is equality making sure that society accommodates some of the least fortunate, or does it involve giving everyone the same opportunity? The reality is that one could make a good argument for either one of these perspectives.

Whatever one's view on whether a targeted or universal school choice program is most appropriate, individuals should be aware that there is a risk to harping on this debate too long. Sometimes what results from a tedious debate is inaction, so nothing is done. To the extent that the United States has not yet resolved this debate, the most rational solution might be to begin with targeted choice and if it works, there can be a conversation about universal choice.

Do Americans Prefer Diverse Schools over Homogeneous Schools?

Few would doubt the notion that Americans prefer a diverse school system over a homogeneous one. In fact, the United States' education system was founded as a very decentralized system largely with this notion in mind. The number of complaints by academics, educators, and the general public are countless about the increased standardization and centralization in American schools is noteworthy (Jeynes, 2006a). The percentage of American K-12 school students that attend private schools has been dwindling and is now down to well below 10 percent, the lowest in American history (U.S. Department of Education, 2012). The increased standardization of American public schools is undeniable, and many are concerned (Jeynes, 2006a).

The U.S. government is becoming increasingly puissant not only in education, but also in almost every avenue, including regulations and surveillance (Decker & Triplett, 2012). To whatever extent most people view these trends as problematic, they are likely to become worse as children are increasingly raised in a school system that is no longer pluralistic, but is dominated by government mandates (Decker & Triplett, 2012). Some may view the warnings of increased socialism as mere hyperbole, but one only has to look at economic and educational statistics referred to earlier in this book to understand that whether these fears are realized, the warnings are certainly understandable given recent trends. Horace Mann and many others believed that reform begins with emphasizing children, and it would seem that the best hope for a free society is for children to have access to a pluralistic school system. Many countries around the world appear to recognize that, but currently the United States does not. Low-SES children and those of color are likely to be hurt the most by this nation's trend toward a more homogeneous and standardized school system.

Chapter 10

What Does This Mean for School Choice, and Where Does School Choice Go from Here?

Whatever, one's background, for the good of the country, one should be concerned about the success of all schools in the United States. If one finds that he or she is concerned only with the public sector or only with the private sector, this contributes to national divisiveness and gridlock (Hagel & Kaminsky, 2008; Harwood & Seib, 2008; Peterson, 2006). When this is the case, people are no longer merely part of the solution, they are also part of the problem. It is, of course, only normal that various people should prefer either public or private schools, but to simply not care whether one or the other sector does well or not is to wish ill on America's children, and this is a problem indeed. To the extent that it is evident that schools of faith help reduce the achievement gap, if one really cares about children of color more than one's petty biases, he or she should want to encourage the presence of faith-based schools on the educational landscape.

Unfortunately, the presence of Catholic, evangelical, and other schools in inner cities is quickly fading (Anitt, 2003; Peterson, 2006; Steinfels, 2003; Wells, 2002). Most of this development is a product of financial realities (Anitt, 2003; Peterson, 2006; Steinfels, 2003; Wells, 2002). As the number of tax dollars and bond issues to support public schools has increased, faith-based schools have increasingly found themselves at a competitive disadvantage (Cookson, 1994; Peterson, 2006; Wells, 2002).

To understand this historical process, one should examine the trends of the past 200, 100, and especially the last 50 years. Before 1840, the overwhelming majority of elementary and secondary schools were private (Gatto, 2001; Messerli, 1972). Horace Mann emerged as the father of the common schools in 1837, although his school rubric was not fully embraced until after the Civil War (Gatto, 2001; Jeynes, 2007a; Messerli, 1972). Even by 1874, about two-thirds of the students attending high school attended privately run ones, nearly all of which were Christian schools (King, 1964). All of that changed dramatically when the supreme court of Michigan ruled in a case best known simply as the Kalamazoo case that states had the right to tax people to support public high schools even if the family never sent anyone to the public schools (King, 1964). This decision forever changed the balance of power between public and private schools Within 20 years of this decision, instead of being outnumbered two to one in enrollment, public schools surged to a 70 percent to 30 percent advantage (King, 1964).

In many respects, the Kalamazoo decision of 1874 had precisely the opposite effect on secondary schooling that *Dartmouth v. Woodward* (1819) had on college and graduate training (Fribourg, 1965; Horowitz, 1987; King, 1964). The *Dartmouth v. Woodward* case emerged after three major Ivy League colleges were taken over by their state governments in three states. New Hampshire took over Dartmouth, New York took over what is now called Columbia, and Pennsylvania did the same to Penn (Fribourg, 1965; Horowitz, 1987). Because these states concluded they could not inaugurate a college that could possibly complete against these Ivy League institutions, they decided that the only action they could take to assert their control was to take over each of these institutions (Fribourg, 1965; Horowitz, 1987).

As one might imagine, the colleges that were the objects of these takeovers were not particularly pleased. They were aghast that these state governments could confiscate all their property buildings and supplies when all of these were privately funded, built, and supplied (Fribourg, 1965; Horowitz, 1987). Was the government's action not an act of socialism or worse? Dartmouth naturally won the case, and each of the state governments returned the property, buildings, and supplies that they had confiscated earlier. But the message of the Dartmouth case was clear: private universities have the right to exist.

The vast majority of educational historians regard *Dartmouth v. Woodward* as the most important Supreme Court case of the 1800s that involved education (Fribourg, 1965; Horowitz, 1987; Johnson, 1997). The reason historians view the case so highly is because it forced state and private universities to compete against one another, rather than have states take over private colleges (Fribourg, 1965; Horowitz, 1987; Johnson, 1997). What resulted from this decision was good old-fashioned competition. A healthy private sector was allowed to continue to flourish, and a solid public sector in college education was encouraged to develop as well. With this competition in place, what began to emerge was the greatest system of colleges and universities in the world (Fribourg, 1965; Horowitz, 1987; Johnson, 1997).

If one examines the ratings of universities by England, China, Germany, and *U.S. News & World Report* each year, the conclusion is clear. American universities dominate the world's top 25 (Jeynes, 2007a; U.S. News & World Report, 2013). Admittedly, if one examines the list of top American universities ranked by *U.S. News & World Report* each year, private universities dominate the top 20. The Ivy League universities, of course, are there. Harvard and Princeton usually top the list, with Yale not too far behind (U.S. News & World Report, 2013). In the east, in addition to the Ivy League, one has MIT; in the South, Duke and Vanderbilt; in the Midwest, the University of Chicago and Northwestern; and in the West, Stanford and Cal. Tech (CIT) (U.S. News & World Report, 2013). But even though these top private universities do still dominate, once one reaches the rank of 20, between 20 and 40, the best of the state universities begin to appear: UC-Berkeley, University of Michigan, University of North Carolina, University of Virginia, UCLA, University of Wisconsin, and so on (U.S. News & World Report, 2013).

In addition, the Dartmouth case allowed certain key rivalries to develop between public and private universities that nearly all historians agree have made each of the rival schools better (Fribourg, 1965; Horowitz, 1987; Jeynes, 2008b; Johnson, 1997). Some of these rivalries include USC versus UCLA, Notre Dame versus the University of Michigan, Stanford versus UC-Berkeley, and Duke versus the University of North Carolina (Fribourg, 1965; Horowitz, 1987; Johnson, 1997). The competition of the state versus the private sector has caused public universities to lower class sizes to better compete, private universities to expand course offerings, private universities to offer more scholarships, and state universities to upgrade their facilities (Fribourg, 1965; Horowitz, 1987; Jeynes, 2007a; Johnson, 1997).

With all the advantages that accrued from the Dartmouth case due to increased competition, it is unfortunate that the Kalamazoo case yielded the reverse effects. It in essence handed over to the public schools such a prodigious economic advantage that the public sphere enjoys a near monopoly on elementary and secondary school education (Chubb & Moe, 1990; Peterson, 2006).

That is not to state that the Kalamazoo case was totally wrong. One can certainly state objectively and fairly that all citizens should give something to public schools because everyone benefits by their existence (King, 1964; Peterson, 2006). That is, their presence raises the education level of doctors, car mechanics, and so forth, which everyone uses as a part of the life. Almost no one argues that some should pay nothing to support public schools. The question arises, however, whether it is really fair for families that never use public schools to pay the same level of support as family that heavily utilizes those schools. Most fair-minded people would say, "No."

The answer that one gives to this last question appears all the more important because since the 1950s, the various levels of government in the United States have pumped an unprecedented amount of tax and bond money into public education (Chubb & Moe, 1990; Peterson, 2006; U.S. Department of Education, 2010). The amount spent per pupil on public elementary and secondary school education during this time has soared roughly 120 percent in real terms (U.S. Department of Education, 2010). These increased expenditures clearly reveal a commitment to education on the part of various levels of the U.S. government (U.S. Department of Education, 2010). However, these actions have had what some would call an unintended consequence, although others would say it is an intended consequence. That is, local, state, and federal taxes combined have surged so high that because of (1) this increased tax burden and (2) the prodigious financial advantages that public schools have built up, many educators are wondering out loud whether faith-based schools can really survive (Anitt, 2003; Steinfels, 2003).

One can argue the tax burden that Americans bear to support public schools and the benefits that these schools have procured over the years are so enormous, that it has had the effect of running myriad faith-based schools out of business and out of the public square

(Anitt, 2003; Chubb & Moe, 1990; Peterson, 2006; Steinfels, 2003). And there is no end in sight. Sadly, but predictably, the first faith-based schools to close their doors have been in some of the poorest and most needy areas in the country (Anitt, 2003; Chubb & Moe, 1990; Peterson, 2006; Steinfels, 2003).

Adam Swift (2003, p. ix) makes a very good point when he states, "Many parents have little choice. They can't afford to go to private ..." schools. Swift (p. 1) adds, "I blame the government." Swift's remarks are a bit more indelible when one notes that Swift was a self-admitted anti–private sector advocate and asserts that he changed his mind once he became a parent.

These developments are more unfortunate still when one considers that some of the greatest increase in government elementary and secondary school spending occurred between 1963 and 1980 (U.S. Department of Education, 2010). And yet during that same period, average SAT scores plummeted for 17 consecutive years (Jeynes, 2002b; U.S. Department of Education, 2010). Somehow one wonders whether the money was spent the right way. The contrast could not be clearer between a healthy college and university system in which competition levels are at all-time highs and an elementary and secondary school system in which competition is at an all-time low (Chubb & Moe, 1990; Peterson, 2006; U.S. News & World Report, 2013).

One can argue that at least at the elementary and secondary school level, American educators have become too focused on the distinction between the public and private sector, instead of viewing schooling more holistically as really a single organism (Jeynes, 2012h). Increasingly, some educators are wondering whether this nation's policies have, in essence, either allowed or caused faith-based schooling to begin to die in some of the most needy areas of the country (Anitt, 2003; Chubb & Moe, 1990; Jeynes, 2014; Peterson, 2006; Steinfels, 2003). But as one witnesses the nation's achievement gaps remaining ominously high, and perhaps even beginning to increase again, and the nation's public school students struggling more than they did decades ago, the data may cause one to reassess the situation. Could it be that this nation's lack of encouragement for faith-based education is contributing to the failure of some of America's most needy children? Could it be that the health of the public school system is at least to some degree dependent on the health of faith-based schools? The possibility that the answers to these questions is "yes" leads one to consider the potential that a well thought out school choice program would have to offer.

The Potential of School Choice

Individual people may generally favor the private sector or the public sector when it comes to their preferences in schools, politics, employment, and so forth. When it comes to America's disadvantaged children and helping them overcome the achievement gap, what this chapter is interested in is data and evidence. The evidence is strong that youth in faith-based schools make greater progress toward reducing the achievement gap than their counterparts in public schools (Bryk, Lee, & Holland, 1993; Jeynes, 2010b; Keith & Page, 1985). If these youth are religious and from two biological–parent families, the gap may even evaporate (Jeynes, 1999, 2002a, 2003c). With this in mind, it would seem unwise to argue that access to faith-based education should decrease. Beyond this, it is hard to argue that education offered to children of color and low-SES students should decrease, and that includes the presence of faith-based schools. Education in these most needy areas should be on the increase rather than be in a free fall (Jeynes, 1999, 2000b, 2002a, 2003c). The data encourage the research and school community to care about the children affected by private school closings.

Suggested Developments Based on the Research

Given the relationship that exists between private religious schools and a reduction in the achievement gap, it would seem logical and reasonable for the following developments to occur.

First, educators ought to care for children beyond their schooling sphere. That is, public educators should both welcome and hope for the success of faith-based schools. They should not view Christian and other religious school teachers as competitors and certainly not adversaries (Jeynes, 2012h). Rather, they should view those in the faith-based realm as colleagues and "comrades" who love children and are seeking to improve their lives. Concurrently, faith-based educators should possess the same attitudes toward public school instructors.

One can argue that it is particularly important for public educators to have a constructive attitude toward private religious school educators because the size of the state elementary and secondary school sector dwarfs the size of the private religious school sector by nearly 10 to one (U.S. Department of Education, 2010). Those in the government and public sector have the power to debilitate and nearly eliminate faith-based schools. The reverse is not so. Therefore, it is especially vital that those in the public sector have some sense of appreciation for those in faith-based schools.

In addition, the trend over the past 150 years has been for the state sector to increase substantially in size and power, and for the private sector to recede in power (U.S. Department of Education, 2010). For example, in 1874, high school students attending private schools actually outnumbered high school students attending public schools by approximately two to one (King, 1964). However, the advent and increased incidence of taxation in the late 1800s and until and including the present time have played a major role in causing the prodigious shift in the enrollment distribution among public and private schools (Chubb & Moe, 1990; Peterson, 2006). The reality is that if a large number of public school educators continue to disparage the contributions of faith-based schools, there is an increased risk that faith-based schools will continue to decline in number (Berliner & Biddle, 1995). This issue is of particular concern because religious schools are decreasing in number at the highest rate in the localities in which they are likely needed the most (White House, 2008).

Second, the government and public school educators should value faith-based schools for their unique contribution to American education rather than demonstrate intolerance toward these schools by disparaging their efforts. The government and others in the public sector ought to appreciate the fact that faith-based schools have a unique role to play in the American education system. There are certain specific roles played by religious schools that enhance the instructional landscape. There is plenteous evidence that children of color benefit from attending faith-based schools even more than white students attending them (Jeynes, 1999, 2002a, 2003c). Consequently—and not surprisingly—the achievement gap tends to be narrower at religious schools than it is at public schools. This fact should not arouse jealousy on the part of public school educators, but rather should foster appreciation for these schools and some degree of satisfaction that the scholastic achievements of children of color are being maximized. When a set of schools successfully reduces the achievement gap, this should be the cause of celebration, whether those schools are private or public. And yet, the reality is that most leaders and educators in American are not celebrating these achievements. Instead, these accomplishments are causing public schools to become jealous and quickly flee to a defensive posture of trying to defend why it is they are unable to produce commensurate results. This state of affairs, however, is truly unfortunate because if children are doing better in school than they would do otherwise, this is a cause for great joy.

If society at large viewed American education as a single entity designed to help children, it would support sending more children of color to private schools as a means of reducing the achievement gap. In maintaining such a perspective, public school leaders no longer view faith-based schools as adroit competitors, but as partners engaged in the same goal of schooling children (Jeynes, 2012h). To whatever extent Christian schools usually do a better job than public schools of encouraging children of color to reach their full potential, American society should embrace these schools for their strengths and seek to utilize these advantages to help Americans accomplish more in education, not less (Peterson, 2006). If a certain educational sector provides succor to youth who seek to attain at higher levels of scholastic performance, this fact should be appreciated, honored, and utilized.

Third, public schools can learn from the practices of private religious institutions, especially with regard to reducing the achievement gap. If certain sectors of society are fulfilling their goals well, why not present these schools—be they public or private—as examples to emulate to strengthen all demonstrations of education rather than one? It is sensible to think that schools would benefit if they could personally learn from the best schools and educators in the world, rather than merely a small slice of public schools. Clearly, just as there are practices in which private schools can learn from public schools, such as special education, public school teachers can learn a great deal from faith-based instructors, as well. American education will benefit and grow in potency when people realize that faith-based teachers understand certain principles that can potentially benefit schools all across the country. Granted, not every single successful practice that faith-based teachers undertake can be duplicated in the public sphere, but it is also not true that every single ameliorative practice by private school teachers is irrelevant to public school education. There is a copious degree of benefit that faith-based schools can bring to American public schools at large.

Fourth, the findings of this meta-analysis and other similar research presented in this book indicate the U.S. government at all levels should probably pursue educational policy much more prudently and frugally than has traditionally been the case. Until recently, for many decades, the U.S. was a very prosperous nation. The government has so much money, it could spend billions of dollars on a variety of projects, hoping that they would work. Unfortunately, the government often inaugurated policies without fully testing them to see if they worked. For example, beginning in 1993, President Bill Clinton became convinced that encouraging the growth of charter schools was the best way to produce the added competition he believed was necessary to increase overall achievement in the public schools. There is no question that President Clinton possessed the best of intentions, but rather than run some pilot studies or test run his hypothesis in certain cities, he proceeded to tell governors all throughout the country to adopt an educational strategy that fostered major growth in the number of public charter schools in each state. President Clinton is not the first president to spend billions of taxpayer dollars on a program with unproven utility, and he certainly will not be the last. But now that the U.S. economy is no longer of the "superpower" status that it once was, it seems especially wise to learn the lesson that it is best to test something first to avoid having to realize that too often billions of dollars are spent on programs with questionable merit.

Fifth, the results of the meta-analysis and the other findings of this book indicate that for school choice to be effective, political leaders and social scientists should consider other options. In almost every measure that was examined, across a wide array of academic outputs, social behavior measures, and work habits, public charter school students showed no differences from their traditional public school counterparts. This suggests that the sponsor of the school system being analyzed was the paramount factor that determined the overall student trajectory across the numerous specific indicators utilized rather than whether the school was regulated more by the government at the state level or at both the state and local level.

The preceding finding is especially noteworthy when one considers that over the centuries, a copious number of the world's leading thinkers have concluded that a weak, corrupt, or otherwise imperfect leadership will produce inadequate results no matter what the governmental context. Moreover, many of these thinkers have been convinced that a particular style of government will tend to possess the same overriding strengths and weaknesses, even if limited change is attempted. The reality is, therefore, that charter schools, even though they are given some degree of increased autonomy, are still run by the same ruling authorities that maintain the traditional public schools. In retrospect, it is understandable why the results for public charter schools and traditional public schools were roughly the same.

The reader should note that I do not interpret these results to mean that one should close the doors of the charter schools. Nevertheless, to whatever extent charter schools involve vast amounts of overhead costs, funded by the tax dollars of many hardworking Americans, it does not seem like a wise investment. Due to these overhead costs and other financial responsibilities associated with opening a new school, it really does not seem sensible to add further weight to the already burdened debt-ridden state governments that fund these efforts. Why send billions of dollars to get the same results?

Final Thoughts

In 1990, Chubb and Moe—in their seminal book *Politics, Markets, and America's Schools*—asked a penetrating rhetorical question: Why is it that the Unites States has what is internationally considered the best university system in the world and yet has a public K-12 education program that falls well short of mediocre? They posited that the difference was that among private and public universities there is an immense amount of competition, while at the K-12 level, the public schools enjoy a virtual monopoly. Yes, it is true that according *U.S. News & World Report*, all of the nation's top 20 universities are private. Equally true is the fact that Harvard, Princeton, Yale, Chicago, Columbia, and others are private universities that represent the cream of the crop. Nevertheless, beyond this, there are rivalries between private and public universities that make each pair better institutions. Among the most notable are USC versus UCLA, Duke versus North Carolina, and Notre Dame versus Michigan. There is an endless array of others. According to Chubb and Moe, these rivalries yield great benefits to the American university system. Moreover, they agree that such competition is absolutely essential if the American K-12 education system is to reach its fullest potential.

In the view of Chubb and Moe, limiting competition only to the public sector is insufficient. In fact, it is debatable whether the addition of public charter schools has increased or decreased competition. If one views competition in a cursory sense, it may appear that competition has increased because the percentage of the total school population that attends traditional public schools has decreased by almost 1 percent. However, if one examines the ratio of students attending public schools to those attending private schools, that ratio has actually increased from nine to one to the present 11 or 12 to one. The reality is that public charter schools have taken their students from both the private sector and traditional public schools. The result is that the government-run system has even more of monopoly than it did before. To whatever extent monopolies tend to hinder growth in achievement, the rise of public charter schools may impede the improvement of educational outcomes.

The fact that SAT scores have resumed the infamous decline of the 1963–1980 period is not a good sign. Naturally, one cannot and should not conclude that the drop in test scores is mostly due to a lack of competition in the U.S. schooling system. Nevertheless, to whatever extent that public charter schools represent the most salient education reform initiative of recent years, the test score trend does raise some red flags that a lack of competition may be a contributing factor. The fact that SAT scores are depressed should also cause concern because in 1995, the Educational Testing Service renormed the SAT to essentially add points to average scores in an attempt to stem the plethora of complaints that emerged during the 1963–1994 period about the decline in American schools. Consequently, SAT scores are actually a good deal lower than they appear, well below the levels of test results prior to 1963.

Whether Chubb and Moe are right that competition is the key to the high quality of the American university system, there are other reasons to think that the steady near extinction of the U.S. faith-based private school network is not a good development. The reality is that on average, youth perform better in faith-based schools, even when controlling for socioeconomic status, race, selectivity, and parental involvement. Recent research also indicates that faith-based schools do a better job at reducing the achievement gap than do public schools. Meta-analytic research indicates that the achievement gap is 25 percent narrower in faith-based schools than it is in public schools. Yet because of the lack of funding of these faith-based schools, thousands of them are closing down where they are needed the most, the inner city. The reality is that over the decades, the tax burden that the American government has imposed on taxpayers has increased at a considerable rate so that in some states, half of tax revenues go to support the public schools.

The conclusions I share in this book are based on the numbers. This is why these recommendations are balanced. The reality is that the numbers do not offer compelling evidence to totally embrace school choice. Charter schools, on average, offer no better results than public schools. For the good of America's children, educational policy should be guided by the evidence. School choice appears to offer real overall potential if low-cost private schools are included, which especially means faith-based schools. With this is mind, the data suggest applying school choice programs first via widespread experimentation to see if they really help children. European choice programs also indicate that school choice programs should be implemented carefully so that the federal government does not overwhelm the private sector school sphere so that the faith-based core of religious schools is compromised. Doing this requires wisdom, foresight, and what I would term forward-thinking caution. Within this context, school choice appears to offer real promise, especially to those children who need it the most.

References

Abington Township School District v. Schempp, 374, US 222, 313.

Acemoglu, D., & Robinson, J. (2012). *Why nations fail: The origins of power, prosperity, and poverty*. New York: Crown Business.

Alexander, K. L., & Pallas, A. M. (1985). School, sector, and cognitive performance: When is a little is a little? *Sociology of Education, 58*(2), 115–128.

Alexander, K. L., & Pallas, A. M. (1983). Private schools and public policy: New evidence on cognitive achievement. *Sociology of Education, 56*(4), 170–182.

Andrews, C. C. (1969). *The history of the New York African free schools*. New York: Negro Universities Press.

Andryszewski, T. (1997). *School prayer: History of the debate*. Springfield: Enslow.

Angus, M. (2003). School choice policies and their impact on public education in Australia. In Plank, D. & Sykes, G. (Eds.), *Choosing choice: School choice in international perspective*. (pp. 112-142). New York: Teachers College Press.

Anitt, P. (2003). *Religion in America since 1945: A history*. New York: Columbia University Press.

Bahr, S. J., Hawks, R. D., & Wang, G. (1993). Family and religious influences on adolescent substance abuse. *Youth and Society, 24*, 443–465.

Bailyn, B. (1960). *Education in the forming of American society*. Chapel Hill: University of North Carolina Press.

Baird, L. (1983). *Predicting predictability: The influence of student and institutional characteristics on the prediction of grades*. New York: College Entrance Examination Board.

Baker, D. P. (1998). The "eliting" of the common American Catholic school and the national education crisis. *Phi Delta Kappan, 80*(1), 16–23.

Baker, D. P. (1999). It's not about the failure of Catholic schools: It's about demographic transformations. *Phi Delta Kappan, 79*(8), 6–12.

Ball, S. J. (2003). *Class strategies and the education market: The middle classes and social advantage.* London: Routledge.

Barbanel, J. (1992). Is school choice a real choice? *New York Times,* November 16.

Barfield, R. (2002). *Real-life homeschooling.* New York: Fireside.

Barnett, W. D. (2011). A comparative analysis of the academic outcomes of Ohio public K-8 Charter schools and their comparison district. *Dissertation Abstracts International, 71*(10-A). Toledo: University of Toledo.

Barr, J. M., Sadvnik, A. R., & Visconti, L. (2006). Charter schools and urban education improvement: A comparison of Newark's District and charter schools. *Urban Review: Issues & Ideas in Public Education, 38*(4), 291–311.

Barr, R. D., & Parrett, W. (1997). *How to create alternative, magnet, and charter schools that work.* Bloomington, IN: Solution Tree.

Bartman, D. L. (2007). Caring for the children we share. *Perspective, 33*(10), 49.

Bauch, P.A. (2000). Do school markets serve the public interest? More lessons from England. *Educational Administration Quarterly, 36*(2), 309–323.

Bauernfeind, R. H., & Blumenfeld, W. S. (1963). A comparison of achievement test scores of public-school and Catholic-school pupils. *Educational and Psychological Measurement, 23*(2), 331–336.

BBC. (2010). University ranking dominated by US, with Harvard at top. www.bbc.co.uknews/education-11317176.

Beck, S. H., Cole, B. S., & Hammond, J. A. (1991). Religious heritage and premarital sex: Evidence from a national sample of adults. *Journal for the Scientific Study of Religion, 30*, 173–180.

Becker, J. W., & Vink, R. (1994). Secularisatie in Nederland, 1966–1991: De verandering van opvattingen en enkle gedragin. Rijswijk, Netherlands. Sociaal en Culturrel Planbureau.

Beltz, H. (1980). A study of the academic achievement and religious effectiveness of Seventh-Day Adventist education. Unpublished doctoral dissertation. Oklahoma State University: Stillwater, OK.

Bennett, N. (2009). Measurement of academic improvement by historic Arizona charter schools and comparisons to ethnically similar nearby traditional public schools. *Dissertation Abstracts International, 69*(8-A). Minneapolis, MN: Capella University.

Berends, B., Goldring, E., Stein, M., & Cravens, X. (2010). Instructional conditions in charter schools and students' mathematics achievement gains. *American Journal of Education, 116*(3), 303–336.

Berends, M., Cannata, M., & Goldring, E. B. (2011). School choice debates, research, and context. In M. Berends, M. Cannata, & E. B. Goldring (Eds.), *School choice and school improvement* (pp. 3–15). Cambridge, MA: Harvard University Press.

Berliner, D. C., & Biddle, B. (1995). *The manufactured crisis and how our schools create mediocrity and failure*. New York: St. Martin's.

Berliner, D. C., & Biddle, B. J. (1995). *Manufactured crisis: Myths, frauds, & attacks on America's public schools*. Reading, MA: Addison-Wesley.

Bernstein, C., & Politi, M. (1996). *His holiness: John Paul II and the hidden history of our time*. New York: Doubleday.

Bettinger, E. P. (2005). The effect of charter schools on charter school students and public schools. *Economics of Education Review*, *24*, 133–147.

Bicknese, A. T. (1999). The Teen Challenge drug treatment program in competitive perspective. Unpublished doctoral dissertation at Northwestern University. DAI 60-06, p. 2203.

Bifulco, R., & Ladd, H. F. (2005). Results from the Tar Heel State. Older students did better in regular public schools student achievement: Evidence from North Carolina. *Education Next*, *1*(1), 50–90.

Bifulco, R., & Ladd, H. F. (2006). The impacts of charter schools on student achievement: Evidence from North Carolina. *Education Finance & Policy*, *1*(1), 50–90.

Bingen, D. (2009). The Catholic church's contribution Democratic change in Poland. In H. Von Klauskoschorke (Ed.), *Falling walls: The year 1989/90 as a turning point in the history of world Christianity* (pp.43–56). Wiesbaden, Germany: Harrassowitz Verlag.

Blakeman, J. C. (2005). *The Bible in the park: Religious expression, public forums, and federal district courts*. Akron, OH: University of Akron Press.

Blanshard, P. (1963). *Religion and the schools*. Boston: Beacon.

Bobbe, D. (1933). *DeWitt Clinton*. New York: Minton, Balch & Company.

Bodenhausen, J. (1989). Do public and private schools differ in the performance of their students on advanced placement tests? Paper presented at the Annual Conference of the American Educational Research Association, San Francisco.

Booker, K., Gilpatric, S., Gronberg, T. J., & Jansen, D. W. (2007). The impact of charter school attendance on student performance. *Journal of Public Economics*, *91*(5/6), 849–876.

Bourne, W. O. (1870). *History of the Public School Society*. New York: Wood.

Bower, B. (1997). Religious schools inspire math reasoning. *Science News*, *151*, 53.

Boyer, E. (1995). *The Basic School*. Princeton, NJ: Carnegie Foundation.

Bracey, G. (1997). *Setting the record straight*. Alexandria, VA: Association for Supervision & Curriculum Development.

Braun, H., Jenkins, F., & Grigg, W. (2006). A closer look at charter schools using hierarchical linear modeling. NCES 2006-460. Washington DC: National Center for Education Statistics. ERIC Document #ED493062.

Bridges, D. (1994). Parents: Customers or partners. In D. Bridges & T. McLaughlin (Eds.), *Education and the Market Place* (pp. 65–79). London: Falmer.

Brighouse, H. (2003). *School choice and social justice*. New York: Oxford University Press.

Brunsma, D. L. (1998). Effects of school uniforms on attendance, behavior problems, substance use, and academic achievement. *Journal of Educational Research, 92*(1), 53–62.

Brutsaert, H. (1998). Home and school influences on academic performance: State and Catholic elementary schools in Belgium compared. *Educational Review, 50*(1), 37–43.

Bryk, A., Lee, V., & Holland, P. (1993). *Catholic schools and the common good*. Cambridge, MA: Harvard University Press.

Bryk, A. S., & Thum, P. M. (1989). The effects of high school organization on dropping out: An exploratory investigation. *American Educational Research Association, 26*(3), 353–383.

Bryk, A., Lee, V., & Holland, P. (1993). *Catholic schools and the common good*. Cambridge, MA: Harvard University Press.

Buckingham, J. (2011). *School funding, choice, and equity*. St. Leonards, Australia: Center for Independent Studies (Australia).

Buddin, R., & Zimmer, R. (*2005*). Student achievement in charter schools: A complex picture. *Journal of Policy Analysis & Management, 24*(2), 351–371.

Bunn, I. (2006). *444 surprising quotes about Jesus: A treasury of inspiring thoughts and classic quotations*. Minneapolis: Bethany House.

Bucur, M., & Eklof, B. (1999). Russia and Eastern Europe. In R. F. Arnove & C. A. Torres (Eds.), *Comparative education: The dialectic of the global and the local* (pp. 371–392). London: Rowan & Littlefield.

Bush, G. (1989). *Building a better America*. Washington, DC: Government Printing Office.

Bush, T., Coleman, M., & Glover, D. (1993). *Managing autonomous schools*. London: Paul Chapman.

Calvert, K. (2012). Protestant education in early America: A brief history. In W. Jeynes & D. Robinson (Eds.), *The international handbook of Protestant education* (pp. 65–76). London: Springer.

Campbell, D. (2006). School choice and school cohesion. In P. E. Peterson (Ed.), *Choice and competition in American education* (pp. 206–218). Lanham, MD: Rowan & Littlefield.

Campbell, D. E. (2004). Regulating school choice in Belgium's Flemish community. In P. J. Wolf & S. Macedo (Eds.), *Educating citizens:*

International perspectives on civic values and school choice (pp. 187–219). Washington DC: Brookings Institute Press.

Carbonara, W. J. (1999). Opening the debate on closure and school outcomes: Comment on Morgan and Sorensen. *American Sociological Review, 64*(5), 682–686.

Card, D. E., Dooley, D., & Payne, A. (2008). *School competition and efficiency with publicly funded Catholic schools*. Cambridge, MA: National Bureau of Economic Research.

Carnog, M., & McEwan, P. J. (2003). In D. Plank & G. Sykes (Eds.), *Choosing choice: School choice in international perspective* (pp. 45–67). New York: Teachers College Press.

Carpenter, D. (2012). What if school choice in New Zealand included private schools? In W. Jeynes & D. Robinson (Eds.), *The international handbook of Protestant education* (pp. 461–480). London: Springer.

Carpenter, D. M., & Medina, P. M. (2011). Exploring the competitive effects of charter schools. *International Journal of Educational Reform, 20*(1), 33–56.

Carpenter, P. (1985). Type of school and academic achievement. *Australian and New Zealand Journal of Sociology, 21*(2), 219–236.

Carroll, S., & Wolford, G. (1997). Parents' responses to the school quasi-market. *Research Papers in Education, 12*(1), 3–26.

Carter, B. (1971). *Pickets, parents, and power: The story behind the New York City teacher's strike*. New York: Citation Press.

Carter, J. G. (1826). *Essays upon popular education, containing a particular examination of the schools of Massachusetts, and an outline of an institution for the education of teachers*. Boston: Bowles & Dearborn.

Carter, J. G. (1969). *Letters on the free schools of New England.* New York: Arno.

Cavanagh, S. (2012). Private-school-choice backers keen on tax credits. *Education Week, 31*(35), 21–25.

Center for Education Reform. (2011). Charter School Connection. www.edreform.com/?s=Charter+Connection. Retrieved on August 13, 2013.

Center for Education Reform. (2013). Charter Connection. http://www.edreform.com/. Retrieved August 5, 2013.

Center for Equal Opportunity. (1998). Federal control out of control: The office for civil rights' hidden policies on bilingual education. *CEO policy brief.* Washington, DC: Center for Equal Opportunity.

Chubb, J. E., & Moe, T. M. (1990). *Politics, markets, and America's schools.* Washington, DC: Brookings Institute.

Chubb, J. F. (2006). The private can be public. In P. E. Peterson (Ed.), *Choice and competition in American education* (pp. 13–22). Lanham, MD: Rowan & Littlefield.

Cochran, J. K., & Akers, R. L. (1989). Beyond hellfire: An exploration of the variable effects of religiosity on adolescent marijuana and alcohol use. *Journal of Research in Crime and Delinquency, 26*, 198–225.

Cochran, J. K. (1993). The variable effects of religiosity and denomination on adolescent self-reported alcohol use by beverage type. *Journal of Drug Issues, 23*, 479–491.

Cohen, J. (1988). *Statistical power analysis for the behavioral sciences*. 2nd ed. Hillsdale, NJ: Lawrence Erlbaum Associates.

Coleman, J. (1988). Social capital in the creation of human capital. *American Journal of Sociology, 94*, S95–S120.

Coleman, J., Hoffer, T., & Kilgore, S. (1981). *Public and private schools*. Chicago: National Opinion Research Center.

Coleman, J., Hoffer, T., & Kilgore, S. (1982). *High school achievement: Public, Catholic, and private schools compared*. New York: Basic Books.

Coleman, J. S. (1988). "Social capital" and schools: One reason for higher private school achievement. *Education Digest, 53*, 6–9.

Coleman, J. S., & Hoffer, T. (1987). *Public and private high schools: The impact of communities*. New York: Basic Books.

Colopy, K. W., & Tarr, H. C. (1994). *Minnesota's public school options*. Washington D. C.: Policy Studies Associates.

Cookson, P. W. (1994). *School choice: The struggle for the soul of American*. New Haven: Yale University Press.

Coons, S. (1997). Catholic schools serving disadvantaged students. *Future of Children, 7*(3), 140–144.

Cooper, B. S., & Gargan, A. (1996). Private, religious schooling in the United States. Emerging trends and issues. *Journal of Research on Christian Education, 5*(2), 157–178.

Cornog, E. (1998). *The birth of empire: DeWitt Clinton & the American experience, 1769–1828*. New York: Oxford University Press.

Corten, R., & Dronkers, J. (2006). School achievement of pupils from the lower Strata in public, private government-dependent and private government-independent schools: A cross national test of the Coleman-Hoffer thesis. *Educational Research & Evaluation, 12*(2), 179–208.

Coulson, A. J. (1999). *Market education: The unknown history*. New Brunswick, NJ: Transaction Publishers.

Council for Citizens Against Government Waste(2012). Chicago teacher strike highlights importance of public pension reform. 10 September.

Counts, G. (1932). *Dare we build a new social order?* New York: John Day.

Cremin, L. (1980). *American Education: The national experience, 1783–1876*. New York: Harper & Row.

Cremin, L. A. (1976). *Traditions of American education*. New York: Basic Books.

Cubberley, E. (1920). *The history of education*. Boston: Houghton Mifflin.

Cubberley, E., ed. (1934). *Readings in public education in the United States: A collection of sources and readings to illustrate the history of educational practice and progress in the United States*. Cambridge, MA: Riverside Press.

Cullen, J. B., & Rivkin, C. G. (2003). In C. M. Hoxby (Ed.), *The economics of school Choice* (pp. 67–106). Chicago: University of Chicago Press.

Curran, F. X. (1954). *The churches and the schools*. Chicago: Loyola University Press.

Curtis, G. E. (Ed.). (1994). *Poland: A country study*. Washington DC: Library of Congress.

Daniel, W. L. (2006). *The orthodox church and civil society in Russia*. College Station: Texas A&M University Press.

Daun, H. (2003). Market forces and decentralization in Sweden: Impetus for school development or threat to comprehensiveness and equity. In Plank, D., & Sykes, G. (Eds.), *Choosing choice: School choice in international perspective*. (45–67). New York: Teachers College Press.

Davis-Kean, P. E. (2005). The influence of parent education and family income on child achievement: The indirect role of parent expectations and the home environment. *Journal of Family Psychology, 19*(2), 294–304.

De Groop, J. (2004). Regulating school choice in Belgium's Flemish community. In P. J. Wolf & S. Macedo (Eds.), *Educating citizens: International Perspectives on civic values and school choice* (pp. 157–186). Washington, DC: Brookings Institute Press.

Decker, B. M., & Triplett, W. C. (2012). *Bowing to Beijing*. Washington, DC: Regnery.

Decter, M. (1995). A Jew in anti-Christian America. *First Things, 56*, 25–31.

Delgado-Gaitan, C. (2004). *Involving Latino families in schools: Raising student achievement through home-school partnerships*. Thousand Oaks, CA: Sage.

DeLuca, B. M., & Hinshaw, S. (2006). Comparing academic achievement in charter schools and public schools: The role of money. *Journal of Educational Research & Policy Studies, 6*(1), 67–90.

Dewey, J. (1902). *The child and the curriculum*. Chicago: University of Chicago Press.

Dewey, J. (1910). *The influence of Darwin on philosophy*. New York: Holt.

Dewey, J. (1915). *The school and society*. Chicago: University of Chicago Press.

Dewey, J. (1920). *Reconstruction in philosophy*. New York: Holt.

Dewey, J. (1990). *The school and society/the child and the curriculum*. Chicago: University of Chicago Press.

Dickey, J. S. (1954). *Eleazar Wheelock, 1711–1779, Daniel Webster, 1782–1852, and their pioneer Dartmouth College*. New York: Newcomen Society in North America.

Diem, A., & Walter, S. C. (2011). *Who is afraid of school choice?* Munich: Center for Economic Studies.

Doerr, E. (1996). *The case against school vouchers*. Buffalo, NY: Prometheus.

Donkers, J., & Avram, S. (2010). A cross-national analysis of the relations of school choice and effectiveness differences between private-dependent and public schools. *Educational Research & Evaluation, 16*(2), 151–175.

Dronkers, J. & Robert, P. (2004, August). The effectiveness of public and private schools from a comparative perspective. Paper presented at the American Sociological Association in San Francisco, CA.

Dunham, R., & Wilson, G. (2007). Race, within-family social capital and school drop out: An analysis of whites, blacks, Hispanics, and Asians. *Sociological Spectrum, 27*(2), 207–224.

Dunn, J. (1955). *Retreat from learning*. New York: David McKay.

Dupuis, A. M. (1966). *Philosophy of education in historical perspective*. Chicago: Rand McNally.

Eavey, C. B. (1964). *History of Christian education*. Chicago: Moody Press.

Eberts, R. W., & Hollenbeck, K. M. (2001). An examination of student achievement in Michigan charter schools. Upjohn Institute staff working paper. Detroit: Upjohn Corporation. ED 457166.

Eberts, R. W., & Hollenbeck, K. M. (2006). An examination of student achievement in Michigan charter schools. In T. Gronberg & D. W. Jansen (Eds.), *Improving school accountability: Check-ups or choice* (pp. 103–130). Amsterdam: Elsevier.

Edwards, C. H. (2000). The moral dimensions of teaching and classroom discipline. *American Secondary Education, 28*(3), 20–25.

Edwards, C., Hawley, J., Hayes, L., & Turner, C. (1989). *Federal funding priorities under the Bush administration*. Arlington, VA: Government Information Services.

Egan, K. (2002). *Getting it wrong from the beginning*. New Haven, CT: Yale University Press.

Engelhardt, C. (2013). *Education reform: Confronting the secular ideal*. Charlotte, NC: Information Age Press.

Epple, D., & Romano, R. (2003). Neighborhood schools, choice, and the distribution of educational benefits. In C. M. Hoxby (Ed.), *The economics of school choice* (pp. 227–286). Chicago: University of Chicago Press.

Estep, W. R. (1990). *Revolution within the revolution*. Grand Rapids, MI: Errdmanns.

Etzioni, A. (1964). *Social change: Sources, patterns & consequences*. New York: Basic Books.

Fass-Holmes, B. et al. (1996). Evaluation of the Charter School of San Diego, 1994–1995. Assessment Research & Reporting Team #7B.

Fernandez, R., & Rogerson, R. (2003). School vouchers as a redistributive device: Analysis of three alternative systems. In C. M. Hoxby (Ed.), *The economics of school choice* (pp. 49–64). Chicago: University of Chicago Press.

Figlio, D. N., & Page, M. E. (2003). Can school choice and school accountability successfully coexist? In C. M. Hoxby (Ed.), *The economics of school choice* (pp. 49–64). Chicago: University of Chicago Press.

Figlio, D. N., & Ludwig, J. (2001). *Sex, drugs, and Catholic schools: Private schooling and adolescent behavior.* Working paper No. 30. National Center for the Study of the Privatization of Education.

Finn, C., Manno, B. V., & Vanourek, G. (2001). *Charter schools in action: Renewing public education.* Princeton, NJ: Princeton University Press.

Fiske, E. B., & Ladd, H. F. (2003). School choice in New Zealand: A cautionary tale. In D. Plank & G. Sykes (Eds.), *Choosing choice: School choice in international perspective* (pp. 45–67). New York: Teachers College Press.

Fitzgerald, J. (2000). Colorado charter schools evaluation study, 1998–1999: The characteristics and student performance records of Colorado Charter Schools. ERIC Document #ED 443196.

Fitzgerald, M. L. et al. (1991). Should school choice be included in federal education reform? *Congressional Digest, 70,* 298–313.

Fliegel, S., & MacGuire, J. (1994). *Miracle in East Harlem: The fight for school choice in public education.* New York: Times Books.

Fribourg, M. G. (1965). *The Supreme Court in American history.* Philadelphia: Macrae.

Friedman, M. (1994). Commentary on the *Nightly Business Report.* August 2.

Fry, E. (1998). An open letter to United States President Clinton. *Reading Teacher, 51*(5), 366–370.

Gallup. (2011). Religion most important to blacks, women, and older Americans. New York: Gallup. (www.gallup.com). Retrieved July 29, 2013.

Galston, W. (2004). In P. J. Wolf & S. Macedo (Eds.), *Educating citizens: International perspectives on civic values and school choice* (pp. 315–323). Washington, DC: Brookings Institute Press.

Gamoran, A. (1992). The variable effects of high school tracking. *American Sociological Review, 57*(6), 812–828.

Gangel, K. O., & Benson, W. S. (1983). *Christian education: Its history and philosophy.* Chicago: Moody.

Garcia, D. R., Barber, R., & Molnar, A. (2009). Profiting from public education: Education management organizations and student achievement. *Teachers College Record, 111*(5), 1352–1379.

Garnett, R. (2004). In P. J. Wolf & S. Macedo (Eds.), *Educating citizens: International perspectives on civic values and school choice* (pp. 324–338). Washington, DC: Brookings Institute Press.

Garrett, M. (2005). *The enduring revolution.* New York: Crown Forum.

Gatto, J. T. (2001). *The underground history of American schooling.* New York: Oxford Village Press.

Gaziel, H. H. (1997). Impact of school culture on effectiveness of secondary schools with disadvantaged students. *Journal of Educational Research*, *90*(5), 310–318.

Gewirtz, S., Ball, S., & Bowe, R. (1995). *Markets, choice, and equity in education*. Buckingham, UK: Open University.

Gibbons, S., & Silva, O. (2006). Competition and accessibility in school markets: Empirical analysis using boundary discontinuities. In T. Gronberg & D. W. Jansen(Eds.), *Improving school accountability: Check-ups or choice* (pp. 157–184). Amsterdam: Elsevier.

Gilder, G., & Forbes, S. (2012). *Wealth and poverty: A new edition for the twenty-first century*. Washington, DC: Regnery.

Glass, G. V., McGaw, B., & Smith, M. L. (1981). *Meta-analysis in social research*. Beverly Hills: Sage.

Glazer, N. (1983). The future under tuition tax credits. In T. James & H. Levin (Eds.), *Public dollars for private schools: The case of tuition tax credits* (pp. 87–100). Philadelphia: Temple University Press.

Gleason, P., Clark, M., & Tuttle, C. C. (2011). The evaluation of charter schools impact: Final report, NCEE 2010-4029. ED 510573.

Glenn, C. L. (1989). *Choice of schools in six nations*. Washington, DC: U.S. Department of Education.

Glenn, C. L. (1995). *Educational freedom in Eastern Europe*. Washington, DC: Cato Institute.

Glenn, C. L. (2000). *The ambiguous embrace*. Princeton, NJ: Princeton University Press.

Glenn, C. L. (2003). Protecting and limiting school distinctiveness: How much of each? In A. Wolfe (Ed.), *School choice: The moral debate* (pp. 173–194). Princeton, NJ: Princeton University Press.

Glenn, C. L. (2011). *Contrasting models of state and school*. New York: Continuum.

Goldberger, A. S., & Cain, G. G. (1982). The causal analysis of cognitive outcomes of the Coleman, Hoffer, and Kilgore report. *Sociology of Education*, *55*(2/3), 103–122.

Goldring, E. B. (1991). Parents motives for choosing a privatized public school system: An Israeli example. *Educational Policy*, *5*, 412–426.

Goldstein, D. (2008). No education silver bullet. *American Prospect*. December 18.

Gordon, L., & Whitty, G. (1997). Giving the "hidden hand" a helping hand? The rhetoric and reality of neoliberal education reform in England and New Zealand. *Comparative Education*, *33*(3), 453–467.

Graetz, B. (1990). Private schools and educational attainment: Cohort and generational effects. *Australian Journal of Education*, *34*(2), 174–191.

Grant, V. T. (2005). The economics of school choice. *Journal of Education*, *186* (2), 1–8.

Green, M. (2000). Jesse Jackson's education amendment: Don't drink the water. *New Visions Commentary*. Washington, DC: National Center for Public Policy Research.

Green, P. (2011). African Americans in urban Catholic schools: Faith, leadership, and persistence in pursuit of educational opportunity. *Urban Review, 43*(3), 436–464.

Green, S. R. (2001). Closing the achievement gap: Lessons learned and challenges ahead. *Teaching and Change, 8*, 215–224.

Greene, J. P., & Winters, M. A. (2006). The effect of residential school choice on public high school graduation rates. *Peabody Journal of Education, 81*(1), 203–216.

Greene, J. P., Peterson, P. E., Du, J., Boeger, L., & Frazier, C. L. (1996). The effectiveness of school choice in Milwaukee: A secondary analysis of data from the programs of evaluation. Paper presented at the annual meeting of the American Political Science Association, San Francisco. August 30.

Gronberg, T. J., & Jansen, D. W. (2006). Editor's introduction. In T. J. Gronberg & D. W. Jansen (Eds.), *Improving school accountability: Check-ups or choice* (pp. ix–xiii). Amsterdam: Elsevier.

Gross, M. L. (1999). *The conspiracy of ignorance: The failure of American public schools*. New York: HarperCollins.

Gumbrecht, J. (2012). Schools of thought. Atlanta, GA: CNN. http://schoolsofthought.blogs.cnn.com/2012/06/21/which-places-spent-most-per-student-on-education/. Retrieved August 12, 2013.

Gutman, A. (2003). Assessing arguments for school choice: Pluralism, parental rights, or educational results? In A. Wolfe (Ed.), *School choice: The moral debate* (pp. 126–148). Princeton, NJ: Princeton University Press.

Hagel, C., & Kaminsky, P. (2008). *America: Our next chapter; Tough questions, straight answers*. San Francisco: HarperLuxe.

Hallinan, M. T., & Kubitschek, W. N. (1999). Conceptualizing and measuring school and social networks: Comment on Morgan and Sorensen. *American Sociological Review, 64*(5), 687–693.

Halstead, J. M., & Lewicka, K. (1998). Should homosexuality be taught as an acceptable alternative lifestyle? A Muslim perspective. *Cambridge Journal of Education, 28*(1), 49–64.

Hamilton, W. L. (2005). Who are you? Why are you here? *New York Times, 155*(53397), 1–6.

Hanushek, E. A., & Rivkin, S. G. (2003). Does public school competition Affect teacher quality? In C. M. Hoxby (Ed.), *The economics of school Choice* (pp. 23–47). Chicago: University of Chicago Press.

Harnischfeger, A., & Wiley, D. (1975). *Achievement test score decline: Do we need to worry?* Chicago: Camrel.

Harris, N. (2004). Regulation, choice, and basic values in education in England and Wales: A legal perspective. In P. J. Wolf & S. Macedo (Eds.), *Educating citizens: International perspectives on civic values and school choice* (pp. 91–130). Washington, DC: Brookings Institute Press.

Hartwick, J. (2007). The religious and prayer lives of public school teachers. In W. Jeynes & E. Martinez (Eds.), *Christianity, education & modern society* (129–162). Charlotte, NC: Information Age Press.

Harvard Poll. (2007). Americans continue to support school vouchers, Harvard poll shows. www.nje3.org. Retrieved on August 23, 2013.

Harwood, J., & Seib, G. F. (2008). *Pennsylvania Avenue: Profiles in backroom power*. New York: Random House.

Hatcher, R. (1994). Market relationships and the management of teachers. *British Journal of Sociology of Education, 15*, 41–62.

Haycock, K. (2001). Closing the achievement gap. *Educational Leadership, 58*(6), 6–11.

Haynes, C. (1999). Religion in the public schools. *School Administrator, 56*(1), 6–10.

Haynes, C. C., Chaltain, S. E., Ferguson, J. E., Hudson, D. L., & Thomas, O. (2003). *The First Amendment in schools*. Nashville: First Amendment Center.

Hedges, L. (1981). Distribution theory for Glass's estimator of effect size and related estimators. *Journal of Educational Statistics, 6*, 107–128.

Hedges, L. V., & Vevea, J. L. (1998). Fixed and random effects models in meta-analysis. *Psychological Method, 3*, 486–504.

Hess, F. M. (2006). Regulations do more harm than good. In P. E. Peterson (Ed.), *Choice and competition in American education* (pp. 33–42). Lanham, MD: Rowan & Littlefield.

Hill, P. T. (2005). Doing school choice right. *American Journal of Education, 111*(2), 141.

Hinz, G. (2012). Today's story problem is on teacher pay. *Crain's Chicago Business, 35*(15), 2.

Hoffer, T. B. (1997). High school graduation requirements: Effects on dropping out and student achievement. *Teachers College Record, 98*(4), 584–607.

Hoffer, T. B. (1998). Social background and achievement in public and Catholic high schools. *Social Psychology of Education, 2*(1), 7–23.

Hoffer, T., Greeley, A. M., & Coleman, J. S. (1985). Achievement growth in public and Catholic schools. *Sociology of Education, 58*(2), 74–97.

Hoffer, T., Greeley, A. M., & Coleman, J. S. (1987). Catholic High School effects on achievement Growth. In E. H. Haertel, T. James, & H. Levin (Eds.), *Comparing public and private schools* (pp. 67–88). New York: Falmer.

Holger, J. (2009). Continuity and transformation: The churches in Eastern Europe and the end of Communist rule. In H. Von Klauskoschorke (Ed.), *Falling walls: The year 1989/90 as a turning point in the history of world Christianity* (pp.77–87). Wiesbaden, Germany: Harrassowitz Verlag.

Holman, T. B., & Harding, J. R. (1996). The teaching of nonmarital sexual abstinence and members' sexual attitudes and behaviors: The case of the Latter-Day Saints. *Review of Religious Research, 38,* 51–60.

Holmes, G. M., DeSimone, J., & Rupp, N. G. (2006). Does school choice increase school quality? Evidence from North Carolina charter schools. In T. Gronberg & D. W. Jansen (Eds.), *Improving school accountability: Check-ups or choice* (pp. 131–155). Amsterdam: Elsevier.

Holmes, S. (2001). *God of grace and God of glory: An account of the theology of Jonathan Edwards.* Grand Rapids, MI: Eerdmanns.

Holt, M. (2000). *Not yet "free at last": The unfinished business of the civil rights movement; Our battle for school choice.* Oakland: ICS Press.

Horowitz, H. L. (1987). *Campus life: Undergraduate cultures from the end of the eighteenth century to the present.* New York: Knopf.

Howell, W. G., & Peterson, P.E. (2002). *The education gap: Vouchers and urban schools.* Washington, DC: Brookings Institute.

Howell, W. G., Wolf, P. J., Peterson, P.E., & Campbell, D. E. (2006). The impact of vouchers on student performance. In P. E. Peterson (Ed.), *Choice and competition in American education* (pp. 183–193). Lanham, MD: Rowan & Littlefield.

Hoxby, C. M. (1997). *Local property tax-based funding of public schools.* Palatine, IL: Heartland Institute.

Hoxby, C. M. (2003a). Introduction. In C. M. Hoxby (Ed.), *The economics of school Choice* (pp. 1–22). Chicago: University of Chicago Press.

Hoxby, C. M. (2003b). School choice and school productivity: Could school choice be the tide that lifts all boats? In C. M. Hoxby (Ed.), *The economics of school Choice* (pp. 287–341). Chicago: University of Chicago Press.

Hoxby, C. M. (2004). *A straightforward comparison of charter schools and regular public schools in the United States.* Cambridge, MA: Harvard University Press.

Hoxby, C. M. (2006). Do charters and vouchers push public schools to improve? In P. E. Peterson (Ed.), *Choice and competition in American education* (pp. 194–205). Lanham, MD: Rowan & Littlefield. http://innovationlab.leadnet.org/warren. Retrieved of July 18, 2013.

Hudolin, G. J. (1994). Lessons from Catholic schools: Promoting quality in Chicago's public schools. *Educational Forum, 58*(3), 282–288.

Hutson, J. H. (2008). *Religion & the new republic.* Lanham, MD: Rowan & Littlefield.

Hyde, K. E. (1990). *Religion in childhood and adolescence: A comprehensive review of the research*. Birmingham, AL: Religious Education Press.

Imberman, S. A. (2011a). Achievement and behavior in charter schools: Drawing a more complex picture. *Review of Economics and Statistics*, *93*(2), 416–435.

Imberman, S. A. (2011b). The effect of charter schools on achievement and behavior of public school students. *Journal of Public Economics*, *95*(7/8), 850–863.

Infoplease. (2003). International comparison of math, reading, and science skills among 15-year-olds. Boston: Infoplease. www.infoplease.com. Retrieved on August 26, 2013.

Ireland, J. (2005). Teaching about worldviews and values. *Journal of Christian Education*, *48*(3), 59–60.

Irvine, J. J., & Foster, M. (1996). *Growing up African American in Catholic Schools*. New York: Teachers College.

Jackson, G. P. (2009). *The suicide of black-American culture: A spiritual remedy for the self-destructive elements in black-American culture*. Mustang, OK: Tate.

Jackson, L. E., & Coursey, R. D. (1988). The relationship between God control and internal locus of control to intrinsic religious motivation, coping, and purpose in life. *Journal for the Scientific Study of Religion*, *27*(3), 399–410.

Jay, J. (1891). In H. E. Johnson, *The correspondence and private papers of John Jay, 1782–1793*. New York: n.p.

Jefferson, T. (1779). Proclamation appointing a Day of Thanksgiving Prayer, November 11, 1779. *Papers of Jefferson*, vol. 3, pp. 177–179.

Jefferson, T. (1784). Report of the Committee of Revisors by the General Assembly of Virginia in 1776. Richmond, VA: Dixon & Holt, pp. 59–60.

Jefferson, T. (1805/2001). Second inaugural address. *The inaugural addresses of Thomas Jefferson, 1801 and 1805*. Columbia: University of Missouri Press.

Jeynes, W., & Beuttler, F. (2012). What public and private schools can learn from one another. *Peabody Journal of Education*, *87*(3), 265–304.

Jeynes, W., & Littell, S. (2000). A meta-analysis of studies examining the effect of whole language instruction on the literacy of low-SES students. *Elementary School Journal*, *101*(1), 21–33.

Jeynes, W., & Naylor, W. (2007). School choice, Kuyper, and the potential of government intrusion into religious education. *Religion & Education*, *34*(1), 76–97.

Jeynes, W. (1999). The effects of religious commitment on the academic achievement of black and Hispanic children. *Urban Education*, *34*, 458–479.

Jeynes, W. (2000a). Assessing school choice: A balanced perspective. *Cambridge Journal of Education, 30*(2), 223–241.

Jeynes, W. (2001). Religious commitment and adolescent behavior. *Journal of Interdisciplinary Studies, 23*(1/2), 31–50.

Jeynes, W. (2002a). A meta-analysis of the effects of attending religious schools and religiosity on black and Hispanic academic achievement. *Education & Urban Society, 35*(1), 27–49.

Jeynes, W. (2002b). *Divorce, family structure, and the academic success of children.* Binghamton, NY: Haworth.

Jeynes, W. (2002c). Educational policy and the effects of attending a religious school on the academic achievement of children. *Educational Policy, 16*(3), 406–424.

Jeynes, W. (2002d). The relationship between the consumption of various drugs by adolescents and their academic achievement. *American Journal of Drug and Alcohol Abuse, 28*(1), 1–21.

Jeynes, W. (2002e). Why religious schools positively impact the academic achievement of children. *International Journal of Education and Religion, 3*(1), 16–32.

Jeynes, W. (2003a). A meta-analysis: The effects of parental involvement on minority children's academic achievement. *Education & Urban Society, 35*(2), 202–218.

Jeynes, W. (2003c). *Religion, education, and academic success.* Greenwich, CT: Information Age Press.

Jeynes, W. (2003d). The effects of the religious commitment of twelfth graders living in non-intact families on their academic achievement. *Marriage and Family Review, 35*(1/2), 77–97.

Jeynes, W. (2004a). Comparing the influence of religion on education in the United States and overseas: A meta-analysis. *Religion & Education, 31*(2), 1–15.

Jeynes, W. (2004b). Immigration in the United States and the golden age of education: Was Ravitch right? *Educational Studies, 35*(3), 248–270.

Jeynes, W. (2005a). A meta-analysis of the relation of parental involvement to urban elementary school student academic achievement. *Urban Education, 40*(3), 237–269.

Jeynes, W. (2005b). A meta-analysis: Parental involvement and secondary student educational outcomes. *Evaluation Exchange of the Harvard Family Research Project, 10*(4), 6.

Jeynes, W. (2005c). The relationship between urban students attending religious revival services and academic and social outcomes. *Education & Urban Society, 38*(1), 3–20.

Jeynes, W. (2006a). Standardized tests and the true meaning of kindergarten and preschool. *Teachers College Record, 108*(10), 1937–1959.

Jeynes, W. (2006b). The impact of parental remarriage on children: A meta-analysis. *Marriage and Family Review, 40*(4), 75–102.

Jeynes, W. (2007a). *American educational history: School, society and the common good*. Thousand Oaks, CA: Sage.

Jeynes, W. (2007b). The relationship between parental involvement and urban secondary school student academic achievement: A meta-analysis. *Urban Education, 42*(1), 82–110.

Jeynes, W. (2008a). *Preserving a critical national asset*. Washington DC: White House, pp. 78–79, 109.

Jeynes, W. (2008b). The academic contributions of faith-based schools. Speech given at the White House Conference on inner-city children and faith-based schools in Washington DC, in April.

Jeynes, W. (2008c). What we should and should not learn from the Japanese and other East Asian education systems? *Educational Policy, 22*(6), 900–927.

Jeynes, W. (2009). The relationship between Bible literacy and academic achievement and school behavior. *Education & Urban Society, 41*(4), 419–436.

Jeynes, W. (2010a). *A call for character education and prayer in the schools*. Westport, CT: Praeger.

Jeynes, W. (2010b). Religiosity, religious schools, and their relationship with the achievement gap: A research synthesis and meta-analysis. *Journal of Negro Education, 79*(3), 263–279.

Jeynes, W. (2010c). The relationship between Bible literacy and academic and behavioral outcomes in urban areas: A meta-analysis. *Education & Urban Society, 42*(5), 522–544.

Jeynes, W. (2010d). The salience of the subtle aspects of parental involvement and encouraging that involvement: Implications for school-based programs. *Teachers College Record, 112*(3), 747–774.

Jeynes, W. (2011). Help families by fostering parental involvement. *Phi Delta Kappan, 93*(3), 38–39.

Jeynes, W. (2012a). A meta-analysis on the effects and contributions of public, public charter, and religious schools on student outcomes. *Peabody Journal of Education, 87*(3), 265–304.

Jeynes, W. (2012b). A meta-analysis of the efficacy of different types of parental involvement programs for urban students. *Urban Education, 47*(4), 706–742.

Jeynes, W. (2012c). Character instruction in Protestant education throughout history. In W. Jeynes & D. Robinson (Eds.), *The international handbook of Protestant education* (pp. 3–24). London: Springer.

Jeynes, W. (2012d). Protestant education in Russia and the former Soviet Union and the Eastern Bloc. In W. Jeynes & D. Robinson (Eds.),

The international handbook of Protestant education (pp. 275–294). London: Springer.

Jeynes, W. (2012e). Reaching out to make a difference. *Phi Delta Kappan, 93*(6), 80.

Jeynes, W. (2012f). The removal of character education from the public schools and America's moral decline since 1963. In W. Jeynes & D. Robinson (Eds.), *The international handbook of Protestant education* (pp. 25–49). London: Springer.

Jeynes, W. (2012g). The rise of home schooling as a modern educational phenomenon in Protestant education. In W. Jeynes & D. Robinson (Eds.), *The international handbook of Protestant education* (pp. 77–92). London: Springer.

Jeynes, W. (2012h). What public and private schools can learn from each other. *Peabody Journal of Education, 87*(3), 263–264.

Jeynes, W. (2013). Religious education (Protestant). In A. L. Runehow & L. Oviedo (Eds.), *The encyclopedia of sciences and religions* (pp. 2019–2025). New York: Springer.

Jeynes, W. (2014). School choice and the achievement gap. *Education & Urban Society, 46*(2), 163–180.

Johnson, K. A. (1999). *Comparing math scores of black students in D.C.'s public and Catholic schools*. Washington DC: Heritage Foundation.

Johnson, P. (1997). *A history of the American people*. New York: Harper Collins.

Johnson, S. (1992). Extra-school factors in achievement, attainment, and aspiration among junior and senior high school-age African American youth. *Journal of Negro Education, 61*(1), 99–119.

Jones, M. G. (1964). *The charity school movement: A study of eighteenth-century Puritanism in action*. Cambridge: Cambridge Books.

Kamienski, A. (2011). Competition: Charter and public elementary schools in Chicago. *Journal of School Choice, 5*(2), 161–181.

Kay, P., & Fitzgerald, M. (1997). Parents + teachers + action research = real involvement. *Teaching Exceptional Children, 30*(1), 8–14.

Keith, T. Z., & Page, E. B. (1985). Do Catholic schools improve minority student achievement? *American Educational Research Journal, 22*(3), 337–349.

Kerchner, C. T. (2006). Reform, unionism is here. In P. E. Peterson (Ed.), *Choice and competition in American education* (pp. 136–145). Lanham, MD: Rowan & Littlefield.

King, E. A. (1964). *Shaping of the American high school*. New York: Harper & Row.

Kirkpatrick, D. W. (1990). *Choice in schooling*. Chicago: Loyola University Press.

Kliebard, H. M. (1969). *Religion and education in America*. Scranton, PA: International Textbook Company.

Korkki, P. (2007). The count. *New York Times, 157*(54104), 2–3.

Kurtz, S. (2010). *Radical and chief: Barack Obama and the untold story of American socialism*. New York: Thresholds.

Kuyper, A. (1890). *Enige kameradviezen uit de jaren 1874 en 1875, van Dr. A. Kuyper*. Amsterdam, J. A. Worser.

Kuyper, A. (1917). Anti-Revolutionaire Staatkunde, vol. 2, pp. 460–470. n.p.

Lamb, M. (1997). *The role of the father in child development*. New York: Wiley.

Lamb, S. (1994). Private schools and student attitudes: An Australian perspective. *Journal of Research & Development in Education, 28*(1), 43–54.

Lange, C., Lehr, C., Seppanen, P., & Sinclair, M. (1996). Minnesota charter schools evaluation: Interim report. Minneapolis: University of Minnesota.

Lankford, H., & Wyckoff, J. (2006). The effect of school choice and residential location of the racial segregation of students. In T. Gronberg & D. W. Jansen (Eds.), *Improving school accountability: Check-ups or choice* (pp. 185–234). Amsterdam: Elsevier.

Lauren, D. L. (2009). To choose or not to choose: High school choice and graduation in Chicago. *Educational Evaluation & Policy Analysis, 31*(3), 179–199.

Lee, V. (1985a). Investigating the relationship between social class and academic achievement in public and Catholic schools: The role of the academic. Unpublished doctoral dissertation. Harvard University: Cambridge, MA.

Lee, V. (1985b). *National Assessment of Educational Progress reading proficiency Catholic school results and national averages, 1983–1984, final report*. Washington, DC: National Catholic Association.

Lee, V. (1993). Educational choice: The stratifying effects of selecting schools and courses. *Educational Policy, 7*, 125–148.

Lee, V. E., & Bryk, A. S. (1989). A multilevel model of the social distribution of high school achievement and engagement of middle school students. *Sociology of Education, 62*(3), 172–192.

Lee, V. E., & Smith, J. B. (1995). Effects of high school restructuring and size on early gains, in achievement and engagement. *Sociology of Education, 68*(4), 241–270.

Lee, V. E., & Stewart, C. (1989). *National Assessment of Educational Progress proficiency in Mathematics and Science, 1985–1986: Catholic and public schools compared; final report, 1989*. Washington, DC: National Catholic Association.

Lee, V. E. (1986, April). Multilevel causal models for social class and achievement. Paper presented at the Annual Meeting of the American Educational Research Association in San Francisco.

Lee, V. E., Chen, N., & Smerdon, B. (1996, April). The influence of school climate on gender differences in the achievement and engagement of young adolescents. Paper presented at American Educational Research Association Conference in New York.

Lee, V. E., & Smith, J. B. (1993). Effects of school restructuring on achievement and engagement of middle-grade students. *Sociology of Education*, *66*(3), 164–187.

Leestma, R., & Walberg H. J. (Eds.). (1992). *Japanese education productivity*. Ann Arbor: Michigan University Press, 1992.

LePore, P. C., & Warren, J. R. (1997). A comparison of single-sex and coeducational Catholic secondary schooling: Evidence from the National Educational Longitudinal Study of 1988. *American Educational Research Journal*, *34*(3), 485–511.

Levin, H. M. (2006). The costs of privatization. In P. E. Peterson (Ed.), *Choice and competition in American education* (pp. 23–30). Lanham, MD: Rowan & Littlefield.

Levinson, M., & Levinson, S. (2003). Getting religion: Religion, diversity, and community in the public and private schools. In A. Wolfe (Ed.), *School choice: The moral debate* (pp. 104–125). Princeton, NJ: Princeton University Press.

Lieberman, M. (2000). *The teacher unions: How they sabotage educational reform and why*. San Francisco: Encounter Books.

Lin, J. C. (2005, April). Indian tribe back in yard. *Harvard Crimson*, *11*, 6.

Linsenbach, S. (2003). *The everything homeschooling book*. Aron, MA: Adams Media Corporation.

Lubienski, C., & Lubienski, S. T. (2007). Charter schools, academic achievement, and NCLB. *Journal of School Choice*, *1*(3), 55–62.

Lubienski, S. T., & Lubienski, C. (2006). School sector and academic achievement: A multilevel analysis of NAEP Mathematics data. *American Educational Research Journal*, *43*(4), 651–698.

Lynn, R. (1988). *Educational achievement in Japan*. Armonk, New York: M. E. Sharp, Inc.

Macedo, S., & Wolf, P. J. (2004). Introduction: School choice, civic values, and problems of policy comparison. In P. J. Wolf & S. Macedo (Eds.), *Educating citizens: International perspectives on civic values and school choice* (pp. 1–27). Washington, DC: Brookings Institute Press.

MacMullen, E. N. (1991). *In the cause of true education reform: Henry Barnard & nineteenth-century school reform*. New Haven, CT: Yale University Press.

Mann, H. (1840). *Third annual report*. Dutton & Wentworth.

Mann, H. (1844). *Seventh annual report*. Dutton & Wentworth.

Mann, M. P. (Ed.). (1907). *Life of Horace Mann*. Washington, DC: National Education Association.

Marrou, H. I. (1956). *A history of education in antiquity*. New York: Sheed & Ward.

Marsch, H. W. (1991). Public, Catholic single-sex, and Catholic coeducational high schools: Their effects on achievement, affect, and behaviors. *American Journal of Education, 99*(3), 320–356.

Marsch, H. W., & Grayson, D. (1990). Public/Catholic differences in the High School and Beyond Data: A multigroup structural equation modeling approach to testing mean differences. *Journal of Educational Statistics, 15*(3), 199–233.

Marshall, J. (1967). *John Marshall: Major opinions and other writings*. Indianapolis: Bobbs-Merrill.

Marshall, P., & Manuel, D. (1977). *The light and the glory*. Grand Rapids, MI: Fleming Revell.

Martin, J. (2002). *The education of John Dewey: A biography*. New York: Columbia University Press.

McCallum, J. D. (1939). *Eleazar Wheelock: Founder of Dartmouth College*. Hanover, NH: Dartmouth College Publications.

McCluskey, N. G. (1958). *Public schools and moral education*. New York: Columbia University.

McDonald, A. J., Ross, S. M., Bol, C., & McSparrn-Gallagher, B. (2007). Charter schools as a vehicle for education reform: Implementation and outcomes at three inner-city sites. *Journal of Education for Students Placed at Risk, 12*(3), 271–300.

McEwan, P. J. (2001). The effectiveness of public, Catholic, and non-religious private schools in Chile's voucher system. *Education Economics, 9*(2), 103–128.

McEwen, A., Knipe, D., & Gallagher, T. (1997). The impact of single-sex and coeducational schooling on participation and achievement in science: A 10-year perspective. *Research in Science and Technological Education, 15*(2), 223–233.

McKnight, D. (2003). *Schooling, the Puritan imperative, and the molding of an American national identity*. Mahwah, NJ: Erlbaum.

McLanahan, S., & Sandefur, G. (1994). *Growing up with a single parent: What hurts, what helps*. Cambridge, MA: Harvard University Press.

Meier, D. W. (1992a). Choices: A strategy for educational reform. In P. R. Kane (Ed.), *Independent schools, independent thinkers* (pp. 369–389). San Francisco: Jossey-Bass.

Meier, D. W. (1992b). Myths, lies, and public schools. *Nation*. September 21.

Mentzer, M. S. (1988). Religion and achievement motivation in the United States: A structural analysis. *Sociological Focus, 21*, 307–316.

Messerli, J. (1972). *Horace Mann: A biography*. New York: Knopf.

Meuret, D. (2004). School choice and its regulation in France. In P. J. Wolf & S. Macedo (Eds.), *Educating citizens: International perspectives on civic values and school choice* (pp. 238–267). Washington, DC: Brookings Institute Press.

Micklethwart, J., & Woodridge, A. (2009). *God is back: How the global revival of faith is changing the world.* New York: Penguin.

Miller, H. M. (1999). Without a prayer. *Reading Teacher, 53*(4), 316–317.

Miron, G. (2005). Evaluating the performance of charter schools in Connecticut. Evaluation Center. ERIC Document ED 486072.

Miron, G., Nelson, C., & Risley, J. (2002). Strengthening Pennsylvania's charter school reform: Findings from the statewide evaluation, and discussion of relevant policy issues. Kalamazoo: Evaluation Center of Western Michigan University. ERIC Document ED 480988.

Mocan, H. N., & Tekin, E. (2006). Catholic schools and bad behavior: A propensity score matching analysis. *Contributions to Economic Analysis & Policy, 5*(1), 1–34.

Moe, T. M. (2006). A union by any other name. In P. E. Peterson (Ed.), *Choice and competition in American education* (pp. 123–135). Lanham, MD: Rowan & Littlefield.

Mok, M., & Flynn, M. (1998). Effect of Catholic school culture on students' achievement in the Higher School Certificate Examination: A multi-level path analysis. *Educational Psychology, 18*(4), 409–432.

Monsina, S. V., & Sopher, C. (1997). *The challenge of pluralism: Church and state in five democracies.* Landham, MD: Rowan & Littlefield.

Mora, T., & Escardibul, J. (2008). Schooling effects on undergraduate performance: Evidence from the University of Barcelona. *Higher education: The International Journal of Higher Education & Educational Planning, 56*(5), 519–532.

Morgan, K. O., & Morgan, S. (2008). *State trends: Measuring change across America.* Washington, DC: CQ Press.

Morgan, W. (1983). Learning and student life quality of public and private school youth. *Sociology of Education, 56*(4), 187–202.

Morris, A. B. (1998). So far, so good: Levels of academic achievement in Catholic schools. *Educational Studies, 24*(1), 83–94.

Morris, A. B. (2010). Bridging worlds: Ethnic minority pupils in Catholic schools in England. *Journal of Beliefs & Values, 31*(2), 203–213.

Morris, G. (1994). Local education authorities and the market place. In D. Bridges & T. McLaughlin (Eds.), *Education and the Market Place* (pp. 21–33). London: Falmer.

Mouw, R. (2003). Educational choice and pillarization: Some lessons for Americans from the Dutch experiment in affirmative impartiality. In A. Wolfe (Ed.), *School choice: The moral debate* (pp. 155–172). Princeton, NJ: Princeton University Press.

Moynihan, D. P. (1989). What the Congress can do when the court is wrong. In E. M. Gaffney (Ed.), *Private schools and the public good* (pp. 79–84). Notre Dame, IN: Notre Dame Press.

Munich, D. (2003). Public support for private schools in post-Communist Central Europe: Czech and Hungarian experiences. In D. Plank & G. Sykes (Eds.), *Choosing choice: School choice in international perspective* (pp. vii–xxi). New York: Teachers College Press.

Myers, K. A. (2007). School violence and its effects on academic achievement among eighth graders. *Dissertation Abstracts International, 67*(9-A).

Nagel, S. S. (2002). *Handbook of public policy evaluation.* Thousand Oaks, CA: Sage.

National Education Association. (2010). *Rankings and estimates.* Washington, DC: National Educational Association. http://www.nea.org/assets/docs/010rankings.pdf

National School Boards Association. (2013). Milwaukee Voucher Program. http://www.nsba.org/Advocacy/Key-Issues/SchoolVouchers/Voucher StrategyCenter/State-and-City-Voucher-Programs/MilwaukeeVoucher Program. Retrieved June 26, 2013.

Nationmaster. (2013). http://www.nationmaster.com/graph/eco_gdp_per _cap_in_190-economy-gdp-per-capita-1900. Retrieved August 12, 2013.

Neal, D. A. (1997). The effects of Catholic secondary schooling on educational achievement. *Journal of Labor Economics, 15,* 98–123.

Nechyba, T. L. (2003). Introducing school choice into multicultural public school systems. In C. M. Hoxby (Ed.), *The economics of school Choice* (pp. 145–194). Chicago: University of Chicago Press.

Nelson, F. H., & Van Meter, N. (2003). Student achievement in schools managed by Mosaica Education. Washington, DC: American Federation of Teachers. ED 479914.

Nicotera, A., Mendiburo, M., & Berends, M. (2011). Charter school effects in Indianapolis. In Berends, M. Cannata, M., & Goldring, E. B. (Eds.), *School choice and school improvement* (pp. 35–50). Cambridge, MA: Harvard University Press.

Noell, J. (1982). Public and Catholic schools: A reanalysis of public and private schools. *Sociology of Education, 55*(2/3), 123–132.

Noll, M. A. (2002). *The old religion in a new world.* Grand Rapids, MI: Eerdmanns.

Novak, M. (1993). *The Catholic ethic and the spirit of capitalism.* New York: Free Press.

O'Keefe, J. M. (2003). Catholic schools and vouchers: How the empirical reality should ground the debate? In A. Wolfe (Ed.), *School choice: The moral debate* (pp. 195–218). Princeton, NJ: Princeton University Press.

Olasky, M. N. (1988). *Prodigal press: The anti-Christian bias of the American news media*. Westchester, IL: Crossway.

Olasky, M. (1992). *Tragedy of American compassion*. Wheaton, IL: Crossway.

Pardey, D. (1991). *Marketing for schools*. London: Kogan Page.

Payne, G., & Ford, G. (1977). Religion, class, and educational policy. *Scottish Educational Studies (Edinburgh)*, *9*(2), 83–99.

Perie, M., Vanneman, A., & Goldstein, A. S. (2005). *Student achievement in private schools: Results from NAEP 2000–2005*. Washington, DC: U.S. Department of Education.

Perrone, V. (1990). How did we get here? Testing in the early grades: The games grown-ups play. In C. Kamii (Ed.), *Testing in the early grades* (pp.1–13). Washington, DC: National Association for the Education of Young Children.

Perry, M. J. (2003). What does the establishment clause forbid? Reflections on the constitutionality of school vouchers. In A. Wolfe (Ed.), *School choice: The moral debate* (pp. 231–243). Princeton, NJ: Princeton University Press.

Peterson, P. E., & Hassel, B. C. (1998). *Learning from school choice*. Washington, DC: Brookings Institute.

Peterson, P. E., & Viarengo, M. (2011). Eighth graders and compliance: Social capital and school sector impacts on noncognitive skills of entry adolescents. In M. Berends, M. Cannata, & E. B. Goldring (Eds.), *School choice and school improvement* (pp. 51–75). Cambridge, MA: Harvard University Press.

Peterson, P. E. (2003). *The future of school choice*. Stanford, CA: Hoover Institute.

Peterson, P. E. (2006a). *Choice and competition in American education*. Lanham, MD: Rowan & Littlefield.

Peterson, P. E. (2006b). The use of market incentives in education. In P. E. Peterson (Ed.), *Choice and competition in American education* (pp. 3–12). Lanham, MD: Rowan & Littlefield.

Peterson, P. E. et al. (1996). School choice in Milwaukee. *Public Interest*, *125*, 38–56.

Peterson, P. E., Howell, W. G., Wolfe, P. J., & Campbell, D. E. (2003). School vouchers: Results from randomized experiments. In C. M. Hoxby (Ed.), *The economics of school choice* (pp. 107–144). Chicago: University of Chicago Press.

Phelps, R. P. (2000). Estimating the cost of standardized student testing in the United States. *Journal of Education Finance*, *25*(3), 343–380.

Phi Beta Kappa/Gallup Poll. (2002). *School Choice Poll*. Princeton, NJ: Gallup.

Piehl, N. (2012). *Choosing a college*. Detroit: Greenhaven.

Plank, D., & Sykes, G. (2003). Why school choice? In D. Plank & G. Sykes (Eds.), *Choosing choice: School choice in international perspective* (pp. vii–xxi). New York: Teachers College Press.

Plucker, J., Makel, M. C., & Rapp, K. E. (2007). The impact of charter schools on promoting high levels of mathematics achievement. *Journal of School Choice, 1*(4), 63–76.

Podair, J. E. (2002). *The strike that changed New York.* New Haven, CT: Yale University Press.

Portfeli, E., Wang, C., Audette, R., McColl, A., & Alogozzine, B. (2009). Influence of social and community capital of student achievement in a large urban school district. *Education & Urban Society, 42*(1), 72–95.

Preda, R. (2009). The year 1989 in the history and perception of Romanian society and churches. In H. Von Klauskoschorke (Ed.), *Falling walls: The year 1989/90 as a turning point in the history of world Christianity* (pp. 57–75). Wiesbaden, Germany: Harrassowitz Verlag.

Prince, R. (1960). Values, grades, achievement, and career choice of high school students. *Elementary School Journal, 60*(1), 376–384.

Putnam, R. D. (2000). *Bowling alone: The collapse and revival of American community.* New York: Simon & Schuster.

Raitt, J., & McGinn, B. (1987). *Christian spirituality: High Middle Ages and Reformation.* New York: Crossroad.

Ramler, S. (2001). New Zealand's bold move. *Independent School, 60*(2), 92–98.

Randell, K. (1988). *Luther and the German reformation, 1517–1555.* London: Edward Arnold.

Raudenbush, S., & Bryk, A. S. (1986). A hierarchical model for studying school effects. *Sociology of Education, 59*(1), 1–17.

Ravitch, D. (2000). *The Great School Wars.* Baltimore: Johns Hopkins University Press.

Ravitch, D. (2003). *The language police: How pressure groups restrict what children learn.* New York: Knopf.

Ravitch, D. (2010). *The death and life of the great American school system: How testing and choice are undermining education.* New York: Basic Books.

Regnerus, M. (2000). Shaping school success: Religious socialization outcome in metropolitan public schools. *Journal for the Scientific Study of Religion, 39*(3), 363–370.

Relland, R. R. (1997). Paying twice for education. *American Enterprise, 8*(1), 10–11.

Reuter, L. R. (2004). School choice and civic values in Germany. In P. J. Wolf & S. Macedo (Eds.), *Educating citizens: International perspectives on civic values and school choice* (pp. 157–186). Washington, DC: Brookings Institute Press.

Riley, R. W. (1996). Promoting involvement in learning. *Professional Psychology: Research and Practice, 27*(1), 3–4.

Riordan, C. (1985). Public and Catholic schooling: The effects of gender context policy. *American Journal of Education, 93*(4), 518–540.

Rippeyoung, P. L. E. (2009). Is it too late baby? Pinpointing the emergence of a black-white test gap in infancy. *Sociological Perspectives, 52*(2), 235–258.

Rivero, L. (2008). *The homeschooling option.* New York: Palgrave Macmillan.

Roach, R. (2001). In the academic and think-tank world, pondering achievement-gap remedies take center stage. *Black Issues in Higher Education, 18*(1), 26–27.

Roebelen, E. W. (2008). NAEP gap continuing for charters. *Education Week, 27*(38), 1–14.

Roscigno, V. J. (1998). Race, institutional languages, and the reproduction of educational disadvantage. *Social Forces, 76*, 1033–1061.

Roseburg, B. (1989). How do we balance public school choice? *Education Digest, 55*, 7–11.

Rothstein, S. W. (1994). *Schooling the poor: A social inquiry into the American educational experience.* Westport, CT: Bergin & Garvey.

Rouse, C. E., & Barrow, L. (2009). School vouchers and student achievement: Recent evidence and remaining questions. *Annual Review of Economics, 1*(1), 17–42.

Rowe, M. (1994). *Russian resurrection: Strength in suffering; A history of Russia's Evangelical Church.* London: Harper Collins.

Royster, D. (2010). More than just race: If we're going study culture, let's get it right. *Sociological Forum, 25*(2), 386–390.

Russo, C. J., & Rogus, J. F. (1998). Catholic schools: Proud past, promising future. *School Business Affairs, 64*(6), 13–16.

Ryan, K., & Bohlin, K. E. (1998). *Building character in schools: Practical ways to bring moral instruction to life.* San Francisco: Jossey-Bass.

Salisbury, D., & Tooley, J. (2007). *What America can learn from school choice in other countries.* Washington, DC: Cato Institute.

Sander, W. (1996). Catholic grade schools and academic achievement. *Journal of Human Resources, 31*, 540–548.

Sanders, M. G., & Herting, J. R. (2000). Gender and the effects of school, family, and church support on the achievement of African American adolescents. In M. G. Sanders (Ed.), *Schooling students placed at risk* (pp. 141–161). Mahwah, NJ: Lawrence Erlbaum.

Sass, T. R. (2006). Charter schools and student achievement in Florida. *Education Finance & Policy, 1*(1), 91–122.

Sassenrath, J., Croce, M., & Penaloza, M. (1984). Private and public school students: Longitudinal and achievement differences. *American Educational Research Journal, 21*(3), 557–563.

Scalia, A. (1989). On making it look easy by doing it wrong. In E. M. Gaffney (Ed.), *Private schools and the public good* (pp. 173–185). Notre Dame, IN: Notre Dame Press.

Schiff, P. (2012). *The real crash: America's coming bankruptcy*. New York: St. Martin's.

Schindler, R. B. (2008). Private school diversity in Denmark's national voucher system. *Scandinavian Journal of Educational Research, 52*(4), 331–354.

Schmidt, P. F. (1988). Moral values of adolescents: Public versus Christian schools. *Journal of Psychology and Christianity, 7*(3), 50–54.

Schneider, M., Teske, P., Marshall, M., & Roch, C. (1997). School choice builds community. *Public Interest, 129*, 86–90.

Schneider, W. F. (1965). Comparative achievement of graduates of public and Catholic high schools in their freshman college year. *Journal of Educational Research, 59*(3), 115–121.

Segal, L. G. (2004). *Battling corruption in America's public schools*. Boston: Northeastern University Press.

Shokraii, N. H., Olson, C. L., & Youssef, S. (1997). A comparison of public and private education in the district of Columbia. Washington, DC: Heritage Foundation.

Shrauger, J., & Silverman, R. E. (1971). The relationship of religious background and participation to locus of control. *Journal for the Scientific Study of Religion, 10*, 11–16.

Sizer, T. S. (1984). *Horace's compromise: The dilemma of the American high school*. Boston: Houghton Mifflin.

Skarica, D. (2011). *Money printers and the coming inflation*. Hoboken, NJ: Wiley & Sons.

Slavin, R. E., & Madden, N. A. (2006). Reducing the gap: Success for all and the achievement of African American students. *Journal of Negro Education, 75*(3), 389–400.

Smagorinsky, P. (2000). Reflecting on character through literary themes. *English Journal, 89*(5), 64–69.

Smith, K. B., & Meier, K. J. (1995). *The case against school choice: Politics, markets, and fools*. Armonk, NY: M. E. Sharpe.

Smylie, M. A., & Miretsky, D. (2004). *Developing the teacher workforce*. Chicago: National Society for the Study of Education.

Spring, J. (1997). *The American school, 1642–1996*. New York: Longman.

Starling, G. (2010). *Managing the public sector*. Stamford, CT: Cengage.

State of California, Legislative Analyst's Office. (2006). *Cal facts*. Sacramento: California State Government.

Stein, M. L., Goldring, E. B., & Cravens, X. (2011). Do parents do as they say? In M. Berends, M. Cannata, & E. B. Goldring (Eds.), *School choice and school improvement* (pp. 105–123). Cambridge, MA: Harvard University Press.

Steinfels, P. (2003). *A people adrift: The crisis in the Roman Catholic Church in America*. New York: Simon & Schuster.

Stephens, A. H. (1872). *History of the United States*. New York: Hale & Son.

Stern, S. (2003). *Breaking free: Public school lessons and the imperative of school choice*. San Francisco: Encounter Books.

Stevens, T., Olivarez, A. Jr., & Hamman, D. (2006). The role of cognition, motivation, and emotion in explaining the mathematics achievement gap between Hispanic and white students. *Hispanic Journal of Behavioral Sciences, 28*(2), 161–186.

Stevens, W. D., dela Terre, M., & Johnson, D. (2011). Barriers to access: High school choice, procedures, and outcomes in Chicago. In M. Berends, M. Cannata, E. B. & Goldring, (Eds.), *School choice and school improvement* (pp. 125–145). Cambridge, MA: Harvard University Press.

Stevenson, H. W., & Stigler, J. W. (1992). *The learning gap*. New York: Summit.

Stewart, G. Jr. (1969). *A history of religious education in Connecticut*. New York: Arno Press and the New York Times.

Stolberg, L. M. (2008). *Race, school, and hope: African Americans and school choice after Brown*. New York: Teachers College Press.

Sullivan, L. (2003). How East Harlem hatched a model for public school choice. *Notebook, 11*(1), 1.

Sutton, J. P., & de Diveira, P. C. M. (1995, April). Differences in critical thinking skills among students educated in the public schools, Christian schools, and home schools. Paper presented at the annual meeting of the American Educational Research Association, San Francisco (ERIC Document 390147).

Swift, A. (2003). *How not to be a hypocrite: School choice for the morally perplexed parent*. London: Routledge.

Szasz, M. (1988). *Indian education in the American colonies, 1607–1783*. Albuquerque: University of New Mexico Press.

Tax Foundation. (2013). *Tax rates*. http://taxfoundation.org/

Taylor, R. D., Casten, R., Flickenger, S. M., Roberts, D., & Fulmore, C. D. (1994). Explaining the performance of African American students. *Journal of Research on Adolescence, 4*(1), 21–44.

Tewksbury, S. (1932). *Founding of American colleges and universities before the Civil War*. New York: Teachers College.

Toma, E., & Zimmer, R. (2012). Two decades of charter schools: Expectations, reality, and the future. *Economics of Education Review, 31*(2), 209–212.

Toma, E. F., Zimmer, R., & Jones, J. T. (2006). Beyond achievement: Enrollment consequences of charter schools in Michigan. In T. Gronberg & D. W. Jansen (Eds.), *Improving school accountability: Check-ups or choice* (pp. 241–255). Amsterdam: Elsevier.

Tropman, J. E. (2002). *The Catholic ethic and the spirit of community.* Washington, DC: Georgetown University.

Tyack, D. (1974). *The one best system.* Cambridge, MA: Harvard University Press.

U.S. Department of Education. (1984). *Disorder in our public schools.* Washington, DC: U.S. Department of Education.

U.S. Department of Education. (1992). *National education longitudinal study, 1988: First follow-up. Volume 1: Student data.* Washington DC: Department of Education.

U.S. Department of Education. (1999*). Digest of education statistics.* Washington, DC: Department of Education.

U.S. Department of Education. (2010). *Digest of education statistics, 2009.* Washington, DC: U.S. Department of Education.

U.S. Department of Education. (2011). *Digest of education statistics, 2010.* Washington, DC: U.S. Department of Education.

U.S. Department of Education. (2011). *Fast facts.* Washington, DC: U.S. Department of Education.

U.S. Department of Education. (2012). *Digest of education statistics.* Washington, DC: U.S. Department of Education.

U.S. Department of Education. (2012). *Projections of education statistics to 2021.* Washington, DC: U.S. Department of Education.

U.S. Department of Health and Human Services. (1992). *Statistical abstracts of the United States.* Washington, DC: Department of Health and Human Services.

U.S. Department of Justice. (1993). *Age-Specific Arrest Rate and Race-Specific Arrest Rates for Selected Offenses, 1965–1992.* Washington, DC: U.S. Department of Justice.

U.S. News & World Report. (2013). *U.S. News' best colleges, 2013.* http://colleges.usnews.rankingsandreviews.com/best-colleges

U.S. News & World Report. (2013). *U.S. News' best colleges, 2013.* http://colleges.usnews.rankingsandreviews.com/best-colleges

Van Dunk, E. & Dickman, A. M. (2003). *School choice & the question of accountability: The Milwaukee experiment.* New Haven: Yale University Press.

Viteritti, J. (2003). Defining equity: Politics, markets, and public policy. In A. Wolfe (Ed.), *School choice: The moral debate* (pp. 13–30). Princeton, NJ: Princeton University Press.

Wagner, T. & Vander Ark, T. (2001). *Making the grade: Reinventing America's schools.* New York: Routledge.

Walberg, H. J. (2007). *School choice: The findings*. Washington, DC: Cato Institute.

Walford, G. (1994). *Choice and equity in education*. London: Cassell.

Walford, G. (2003). School choice and educational change in England and Wales. In D. Plank & G. Sykes (Eds.), *Choosing choice: School choice in international perspective* (pp. 68–91). New York: Teachers College Press.

Wallace, B., & Graves, W. (1995). *Poisoned apple: The bell curve crisis and how our schools create mediocrity and failure*. New York: St. Martin's.

Walser, N. (1998). *1998 parent's guide to Cambridge schools*. Cambridge: Huron Village Press.

Washington Post. News Briefs. February 3, 1985, p. A-10.

Weaver, C. N. (1970). A comparison of the achievement of graduates of Catholic high schools measured by ACT scores by grade point averages. *Journal of Mexican American Studies, 1*(2), 97–105.

Wecker, M. (2012). Where the fortune 500 CEOs went to school. *US News & World Report*, May 14. www.usnews.com/education/best-graduate-schools. Retrieved August 18, 2013.

Weir, R. E. (2007). *Class in America: An encyclopedia*. Westport, CT: Greenwood.

Wells, D. K. (2002). *School vouchers and privatization: A reference handbook*. Santa Barbara, CA: ABC-CLIO.

West, A., & Ylonen, A. (2010). Market-oriented school reform in England and Finland: School choice, finance, and governance. *Educational Studies, 36*(1), 1–12.

Westerhoff, J. H. (1982). *McGuffey and his readers: Piety, morality, and education in nineteenth-century America*. Nashville: Abingdon.

Wheelock, E. (1763). *A plain and faithful narrative of the original design, rise, progress and present state of the Indian charity-school at Lebanon, in Connecticut*. Boston: Draper.

White House. (2008). *Preserving a critical national asset*. Washington, DC: White House.

Whitten, C. P. (1986). *Bilingual education policies: An overview*. Washington, DC: U.S. Department of Education.

Williams, J. D. (1983). Do private schools produce higher levels of academic achievement? New evidence for the tuition tax credit debate. In T. James & H. M. Levin (Eds.), *Public dollars for private schools: The case of tuition tax credits* (pp. 223–234). Philadelphia: Temple University.

Williams, T., & Carpenter, P. G. (1990). Private schooling and public achievement. *Australian Journal of Education, 34*(1), 3–24.

Willison, G. F. (1945). *Saints and strangers*. New York: Reynal & Hitchcock.

Willison, G. F. (1966). *Saints and strangers*. London: Longmans.

Willms, D. (1982). Achievement outcomes in public and private schools: A closer look at the High School and Beyond Data. Stanford, CA: Institute for Research on Educational Finance and Governance.

Willms, J. D. (1985). Catholic-school effects on academic achievement: New evidence from the High School and Beyond follow-up. *Sociology of Education*, *58*(2), 98–114.

Wilson, C. M., Douglas, K. S., & Lyon, D. R. (2011). Violence against teachers: Prevalence and consequences. *Journal of Interpersonal Violence*, *26*(12), 2353–2371.

Wilson, M. B. (1994). *Brown v. Board of Education*: A pictorial history of public school segregation. *Update on Law-Related Education*, *18*(2), 32–38.

Wilson, P. (1977). Discrimination against blacks in education: An historical perspective. In W. T. Blackstone & R. D. Heslep (Eds.), *Social justice and preferential treatment* (pp. 161–175). Athens: University of Georgia.

Winn, P. (2011). Gallup: Blacks most religious group in U.S. *CNS News*, July 6. CNS News.com. Retrieved July 29, 2013.

Wirtz, W. (1977). *On further examination*. New York: College Entrance Examination Board.

Witte, J. (1999). The Milwaukee voucher experiment: The good, the bad, and the ugly. *Phi Delta Kappan*, *81*(1), 59–64.

Witte, J. (2000). Selective reading is hardly evidence. *Phi Delta Kappan*, *81*(5), 391.

Witte, J. F., & Thorn, C. (1996). Who chooses voucher and interdistrict choice programs in Milwaukee. *American Journal of Education*, *104*, 186–217.

Witte, J. F., Weimer, D., & Shober, A., & Schlomer, P. (2007). The performance of charter schools in Wisconsin. *Journal of Policy Analysis & Management*, *26*(3), 557–573.

Witte, J. F., Wolf, D., & Dean, J. (2011). School Choice Demonstration Project. Fayetteville, AR: Milwaukee Charter schools study. ED 518594.

Witte, J. F., Wolf, D., Dean, J., & Carlson, D. (2011). Milwaukee independent charter school study: Report on two- and three-year achievement gains. SCDP Milwaukee Foundation. Report 25. Fayetteville: University of Arkansas.

Wolf, P., Gutman, B., & Puma, M. (2009). Evaluation of the DC opportunity scholarship program: Impacts after three years, NCEE 2009-4005. (ERIC Document ED 504783).

Wolf, P. J., Kisada, B., Gutman, B., Puma, M., Rizzo, L., & Fissa, N. (2011). School vouchers in the nation's capitol. In M. Berends, M. Cannata, & E. B. Goldring, E. B. (Eds.), *School choice and school improvement* (pp. 17–33). Cambridge, MA: Harvard University Press.

Wolfe, A. (2003). The irony of school choice: Liberals, conservatives, and the new Politics of race. In A. Wolfe (Ed.), *School choice: The moral debate* (pp. 31–50). Princeton, NJ: Princeton University Press.

Wong, V. (2011). Property taxes reach the breaking point. *Business Week*, March 22. http://www.businessweek.com/lifestyle/content/mar2011/bw20110318_558174.htm.

Woods, P. A., Bagley, C., & Glatter, R. (1998). *School choice and competition: Markets in the public interest?* London: Routledge.

Woodson, C. G., & Wesley, C.H. (1962). *The Negro in our history.* Washington, DC: Associated Publishers.

Woodson, C. G. (1962). *The Negro in our history.* Washington, DC: Associated Publishers.

Woodson, C. G. (1968). *The education of the Negro prior to 1861.* Washington DC: Associated Publishers.

Yeltsin, B. (1992). Reviving people's spirituality. *Los Angeles Times,* June 15.

Young, D., & Fraser, B. J. (1990). Science achievement of girls in single-sex and co-educational schools. *Research in Science & Technological Education, 8*(1), 5–20.

Zehavi, A. (2009). Institutions, actors and choice: Public aid and private school expansion in comparative perspective. Paper presented at the Midwestern Political Science Association. Retrieved from http://tinyurl.com/yjsx9wq.

Zimmer, R., & Budolin, R. (2007). Getting inside the black box: Examining how the operation of charter schools affects performance. *Peabody Journal of Education, 82*(2/3), 231–273.

Zimmer, R., Blanc, S., & Gill, B. (2008). Evaluating the performance of Philadelphia charter schools. Working papers. WR 550-WPF. Washington D.C.: Rand Corporation.

Zylstra, S. E. (2009). Black flight: African American churches leave the inner city for the suburbs. *Christianity Today, 53*(1), 13.

Index

About the Author

William Jeynes is a Senior Fellow at the Witherspoon Institute in Princeton, New Jersey and a Professor of Education at California State University in Long Beach. He has graduate degrees from Harvard University and the University of Chicago. He graduated first in his class from Harvard University and received the Rosenberger Award at the University of Chicago for being named as his cohort's most outstanding student. He has more than 135 academic publications, including 90 articles, 11 books, and 35 book chapters. His articles have appeared in journals by Columbia University, Harvard University (two Harvard journals), the University of Chicago, Cambridge University, Notre Dame University, and other prestigious academic journals. He has also written for the White House and for both the G.W. Bush and Obama administrations. He is a well-known public speaker having spoken in nearly every state in the country and in every inhabited continent. He has spoken for the White House, the US Department of Justice, the US Department of Education, the US Department of Health & Human Services, the National Press Club, UN delegates, members of Congress, the Acting President of South Korea, Harvard University, Cambridge University, Oxford University, Columbia University, Duke University, Notre Dame University, Peking University, and many other well known universities. He has spoken for both the G.W. Bush & Obama administrations and inter-acted with each of these presidents. He has been a consultant for both the US & South Korean governments. His 4-point plan presented to the Acting President of South Korea passed the Korean Parliament and became the core of that nation's 1998 economic stimulus legislation, which helped it emerge from the greatest Asian economic crisis since World War II. As part of the plan, Dr. Jeynes asserted that South Korea should build a high-tech city (which he termed Korea's Brasilia), which continues to be built and is called Songdo. South Korea grew out of the crisis faster than any other Asian nation with a GDP increase of 22% over the period of the next two years.

Dr. Jeynes has been interviewed or quoted by the *Washington Post*, the *Los Angeles Times*, the *New York Times*, the *Wall Street Journal*, the *London Times*, the Associated Press (AP), CBS, ABC, NBC, FOX, Al Jazeera, and many other media outlets. His work has been cited and quoted numerous times by the U.S. Congress, the British Parliament, the EU, and many State Supreme Courts across the United States. Dr. Jeynes has worked with and spoken for the Harvard Family Research Project. He has received recognition as a "Distinguished Scholar" from the California State Senate, the California State Assembly, and his present university. A number of Dr. Jeynes' articles for *Urban Education* and *Education & Urban Society*, according to these journals' websites, are in the top 2-10 of the most cited and read articles published by these journals in their 45-year history. Dr. Jeynes has also gained admission into Who's Who in the World for the last nine consecutive years.